CHILDREN'S SERVICES:

SHAPING UP FOR THE MILLENNIUM

About Children in Scotland

Children in Scotland is the national agency for voluntary, statutory and professional organisations and individuals working with children and their families in Scotland.

It exists to identify and promote the interests of children and their families in Scotland and to ensure that relevant policies, services and other provisions are of the highest possible quality and able to meet the needs of a diverse society. It does this with, through and for its members.

Children in Scotland works in partnership with the National Children's Bureau and Children in Wales.

CHILDREN'S SERVICES:

SHAPING UP FOR THE MILLENNIUM

Supporting children and families in the UK and Scandinavia

Edited by

Bronwen Cohen and Unni Hagen

IN SCOTLAND

CLANN AN ALBA

working for children and their families

EDINBURGH: THE STATIONERY OFFICE

© The Stationery Office Limited 1997

The Stationery Office Limited
South Gyle Crescent, Edinburgh EH12 9EB

Application for reproduction should be made to The Stationery Office Limited
First published 1997

British Library Cataloguing in Publication Data
A catalogue record for this book is available from the British Library

ISBN 0 11 495778 9

CONTENTS

ACKNOWLEDGEMENTS

We are very grateful to the following people for their comments and assistance in relation to various aspects of this book: Kjell Eide, retired General Director, Ministry of Education, Norway; Jon Lauglo, Professor of Sociology, University of Trondheim, Norway; Dr Colin Meyer, Department of Human Resource Management, University of Glasgow; Tom Schuller, Professor of Continuing Education at the University of Edinburgh; Adrian Sinfield, Professor of Social Policy at the University of Edinburgh; Dr Kay Tisdall, Centre for the Study of the Child, University of Glasgow; Peter Moss, Thomas Coram Research Unit; Jackie Igoe, Joan Telfer and Annie Gunner, Children in Scotland.

Finally, we would like to thank our contributors for their patience in coping with the many demands we have made of them.

PREFACE

In recent years there has been an increasing interest in exchanges between the UK and Scandinavian countries on policies and structures relating to children. There are many similarities in the basic principles, as well as in the new trends described by Cohen and Hagen in this book. At the same time, however, national variations also give rise to differences in the solutions that are offered, in the organisation and priorities accorded, in daycare provision, the schools systems, health and social services and so forth. When examined in the light of these differences, the similarities between many of the aims and aspirations highlight the interaction of ideologies with other factors and enable the effects of particular policies to be explored 'experientially'. Comparisons enable us to see how our ideas are influenced by cultural factors and culturally defined views of what is 'right' and 'wrong'. National differences are often invisible as long as we stay inside our own culture and discuss policies with colleagues from the same cultural background. It is enriching to be confronted with alternatives and to try to understand why others choose different solutions. Much can be learned from examining the way social context influences both policy and practical approaches to common problems.

Children's Services: Shaping Up For the Millennium offers a broad approach to these themes and is published at a time of increased co-operation between European countries. Developments within the European Union (EU) influence not only its members but also the 'neighbours' of the Union. Trade and economic questions have, however, featured more prominently in discussions between these nations than social policies in general, and children's policies in particular. Whilst there are considerable differences in child welfare policies between the Nordic countries and southern Europe, the differences between the UK and Nordic countries are less great, and therefore make a good starting point for exploring child welfare policy within Europe.

The focus of this book is Scandinavia, encompassing Denmark, Norway and Sweden. The Scandinavian countries, together with the other Nordic countries of Iceland and Finland, share important parts of their history and have, in an international perspective, considerable similarities in their national policies, developed through close contact and exchanges. There are nevertheless important differences in the organisation of services within the Scandinavian countries, a product of the different demography, economy and culture of each of these countries.

Denmark has a population of 5.2 million and, compared with the other Nordic countries, is densely populated, with 120 inhabitants per square kilometre – half of that of the UK. Denmark is flatter than the other two Scandinavian countries, excellent for farming, and is generally regarded as more cosmopolitan. It is also more closely linked with the rest of Europe than the other two countries. Norway is divided by mountains and fjords. Traditionally, fishing and maritime trade have been important to its economy, although recently North Sea oil has been of great importance. Oslo and its metropolitan area has 17 per cent of the overall population of 4.3 million, but there are over 400 municipalities, half of which have less than 5000 inhabitants and some with only a few hundred. The scattered population, with only 13.2 people per square kilometre, has given rise to a large number of small administrative units, influencing the organisation of services. Sweden has the largest population of the three Scandinavian countries, at 8.7 million, with large administrative units and easier travel than in Norway. Sweden is also more industrialised.

These differences are reflected in trade and economic policies. Denmark joined the European Union in 1972; the other Nordic countries were reluctant to join. In 1994 Finland voted by 57 per cent and Sweden by 53 per cent to join the European Union. Norway, where only 48 per cent voted in support of the Union, did not join. The referenda results reflected differences in the economies and industries of the Nordic countries; discussion in the campaigns also revealed differences in national aspirations. Moral values and ideologies were more evident in the Norwegian debate.

Economic growth in the post-war period and the priority attached to the welfare state has given the Nordic citizens considerable social benefits. The gross domestic product (GDP) in the United Kingdom in 1992 was approximately 70 per cent of that of the Scandinavian countries. Total social security expenditure, encompassing social benefits, assistance to children and families, elderly and disabled people, unemployment and sickness benefit and so forth, make up 32 to 39 per cent of GDP in Scandinavia. In Denmark, 12 per cent of the social security expenditure is used on children and families; in Norway, 13.7 per cent and in Sweden, 14.2 per cent. Sweden has traditionally provided more for children and families, with high standards of services, as well as generous benefits and leave provision. Norway was previously less advantaged than Sweden, but the income from oil has now given more opportunities to assist children and families. Child welfare is given high priority on the political agenda and additional funding has allowed an increase in the quantity and quality of services.

National differences can be difficult to understand without knowledge of the cultural and organisational context of their services. But the differences do generate important questions that enable us to better understand our own systems and options for change. *Children's Services* offers a valuable opportunity to increase our understanding of both the common trends and the important differences in the development of children's services as they 'shape up for the millennium'.

Turid Vogt Grinde, Norwegian Institute of Child Welfare Research, Oslo

Chapter 1

---◆---

INTRODUCTION AND OVERVIEW

BRONWEN COHEN AND UNNI HAGEN

Throughout the UK and Scandinavia, demographic, economic and social changes have contributed to both a growing demand and need for many services for children and young people, and new expectations of the way those services are delivered. All countries have seen substantial revision of their legislation. In many countries the reorganisation of local government and restructuring in other areas – such as health – have had significant implications for children's services. This book examines the changes which are affecting Scandinavian and UK children's services, and some of the policies and structures which are emerging.

A wide range of services provide for the care, protection, education, health and recreation of children and young people and it is with these that this book is concerned. It draws on examples from throughout the UK and Scandinavia (encompassing Denmark, Norway and Sweden), and focuses on three themes which we regard as central to the development of responsive and effective services:

- **collaboration:** structures and methods of working which encourage inter-departmental and inter-agency collaboration and foster understanding and co-operation between different professional groups and families
- **participation:** the response by those planning, providing, using or working in children's services to the growing emphasis on the rights of the child and ways of promoting the involvement of children, young people and their parents or carers in decision-making and policy development
- **accountability:** finding ways in which services can be made more accountable to children, young people and their parents or carers.

In this chapter we outline the trends affecting services, the 'winds of change' which provide the context for the developments illustrated by the contributors. First, we outline reorganisation within local government and recent legislative developments in the UK and Scandinavia. Secondly, we summarise the significant features of 'family change' in creating new needs and expectations of services. Thirdly, we provide an overview of the various approaches to improving collaboration, participation and accountability as illustrated by the chapters in the book, and some of the underlying themes they raise for the development of services into the next century.

1.1 The winds of change: reorganisation and new legislation

All of the countries in the UK and Scandinavia are experiencing changes in the organisation and administrative structure of services, and in legislation relevant to policies and practice within services for children, young people and their families.

UK

Local government reorganisation

Children's services in the UK are the responsibility at government level of departments within the Scottish Office, Welsh Office, Northern Ireland Office and separate Departments of State in England. In Scotland, Wales and England, responsibilities at a local level lie primarily with local authorities, although some other agencies such as Training and Enterprise Councils (Local Enterprise Councils in Scotland) have some responsibilities for employment-related services.

Extensive reorganisation of local government boundaries has recently taken place in Scotland and Wales, and to a lesser extent in England. In Scotland since April 1996 a two-tier structure of 62 regional and district councils has been replaced by 29 all-purpose single-tier councils, with the three existing Island councils continuing to serve the islands. The councils serve populations ranging in size from just under 20,000 in Orkney to just over 600,000 in Glasgow. In Wales 22 unitary authorities have replaced 45 county and district councils. In England, unitary authorities are replacing a number of the existing county councils but, unlike Scotland and Wales, a two-tier system will be retained in a number of areas. Sizes will range from over a million in a number of existing authorities to the smallest new authority serving just over 34,000. Funding is generally provided through block grants to local authorities from central government departments which take account of the different tax base and other criteria.[1]

Reorganisation is leading to new administrative structures and in some areas a growing emphasis on decentralisation. Seven of the new authorities in Scotland and two in Wales have varied the traditional committee structure, developing committee structures which bring together, in varying combinations, education, social work, housing, community and leisure services with a stronger corporate focus (see, for example, the table opposite). In England combined housing and social work departments are now common; one new authority, North Lincolnshire, is developing a combined community services and public protection department, drawing together social services, housing, fire and police.

A number of local authorities began decentralising in the 1980s – the principal aim at that time was generally that of increasing accessibility to services. A decade later local authorities tended to see it as being more about 'responsiveness; tailoring services to local needs; the efficient and fairer allocation of ever scarcer resources and making links at the local level with other organisations (including, in particular, community and voluntary organisations)'.[2] The architect of a pioneering decentralisation scheme within a former Scottish authority – Central Regional Council—has

---

Stirling Council, Scotland: Committee and management responsibilities for children's services

Children's Committee

Housing Social Services Department	*Education Services* (up to age of 18)	*Community Services*
• Children, young people and families with five team managers • Community and Residential Childcare Resources Manager		• Libraries • Community sport • Cultural and youth services for children

Source: Stirling Council

---

described the essence of decentralisation as 'a willingness to share power, influence and decision making difficult to envisage without an accepted understanding and agreement about the need to share power internally within a council and how that sharing of decision making can be extended externally into the wider community.' (*Municipal Journal*, April 1995). Following the recent reorganisation all Scottish local authorities are required to prepare a decentralisation plan; in Wales provision was made for elected members to apply to the Secretary of State for decentralisation.

Reorganisation in Northern Ireland

In Northern Ireland the responsibilities of the 26 district councils have been restricted since 1973 to a limited range of public services, including recreation and leisure, environmental health, maintenance of facilities and public amenities, and a variety of other local administrative and liaison functions. Child welfare services have been delivered through integrated health and social services boards, facilitating closer links between social services and health than elsewhere in the UK. Education services have been delivered through education and library boards. In both cases board members are appointed by the Secretary of State. As noted by Peyton in Chapter 2 (see p. 63), it is a structure which 'has been subject to numerous revisions leading to continual organisational change', and legislation in 1991 and 1994 now allows health and social services boards to delegate responsibility for statutory child care duties to self-governing trusts. By April 1996, 11 health and personal social services trusts had delegated authority to provide statutory child care services. The populations covered by the trusts range in size from 83,000 to just over 300,000.

Impact of the National Health Service and Community Care Act 1990

The reorganisation of local government boundaries is the most recent of the far-reaching changes which have been affecting the organisation and delivery of services in the UK. Amongst the most significant of the developments over recent years has been the evolving concept of the 'purchaser/provider split' – separating the agencies who provide services from those who purchase or 'enable' them, and involving in some instances local authority functions being taken over by non-elected bodies. Within the health services, the National Health Service and Community Care Act 1990 separated out the roles of planning, purchasing and providing of services, with health authorities as the main purchasers of services from self-governing trusts and with the principle of purchasing extending to general practitioners choosing to become fund holders. As described by Waterhouse in Chapter 2 (see p. 47) the aim has been to break down the monopoly of a full public health service, introducing market-style reforms. The community care provisions of the Act encompassed social work services for elderly and disabled people; initial implementation has involved ringfenced government funding. Although it was not directed at children's services, the ideology of purchasing and providing and what has been described as the 'contract culture' is seen as having seeped into children's services.[3] This process has gone furthest in Northern Ireland where the four health and social services boards commission child care services in line with their assessment of need from 11 combined hospital/ community or community trusts. The trusts in turn sub-contract to the voluntary sector for a range of services.

Elsewhere the situation is less clear-cut but in many areas has involved revised expectations of the roles of local authorities as providers, and has changed the nature of the relationship between the local authorities and other providers, substituting, for example, contracts in the place of grants for a growing number of voluntary organisations. The changing nature of this relationship has been reinforced by the separating out of the role of local authorities in inspecting services as distinct from their role as providers, and its extension to other providers. Whilst these changes are seen as having in some cases helped to clarify the purpose of providing or supporting particular services within the growing mixed economy of welfare, they have contributed to an increasingly complex structure, highlighting the need for more effective strategic planning and concerns over the vulnerability of some areas. In Chapter 2 (see p. 60), Sudbury writes of the anxiety of Black voluntary organisations over their 'weak' position within a contract culture, undermining the contribution which their holistic approach has been able to make in meeting the needs of black communities.

Market forces in education

Education has also seen the introduction of market forces. As described by Gillespie (see p. 54), in Scotland this has involved new legislation introducing 'placing requests', allowing parents to request a school outside their local district; (so-called) 'league tables', enabling parents to compare the examination results of individual schools and statistics on issues such as truancy; and 'self-governing status' for individual schools and 'devolved school management', giving schools control over at least 80 per cent of their budget. New education legislation gives parents an entitlement to 'vouchers' to purchase places for their 4-year-old children in public or private services which offer education, defined broadly to include more informal services as well as schools. Other changes relate to the curriculum, including the introduction of a national curriculum, and provisions relating to children with special needs. In England, where the changes have been more extensive, the accountability of schools to local authorities 'has now virtually disappeared' with the new instruments of accountability seen as the publication of test and examination results, accountability to governing bodies and four-yearly inspection by Ofsted.[4]

New child welfare legislation

New child welfare legislation has been progressively introduced across the UK, beginning with the Children Act 1989 in England and Wales and culminating in the Children (Northern Ireland) Order 1995 and the Children (Scotland) Act 1995. The new legislation encompasses a wide range of provisions relating to the promotion of child welfare and aspects of family law affecting children although the legislative content varies—the Children (Scotland) Act for example includes provisions relating to the children's hearing system[5] and adoption law. One of the features common to the legislation across the UK has been a focus on children 'in need'. The legislation strengthens the responsibilities of local authorities and Boards to provide for children 'in need'. However, research in England and Wales has shown that it has also involved the targeting of resources away from universal and preventative services towards children covered by the definition of need. The 1993 report on the operation of the Children Act 1989 in England and Wales noted that 'priority is being given to children

---

Definition of a child 'in need' in the Children (Scotland) Act 1995[a]

A child under the age of 18 is 'in need' because:
- the child is unlikely to achieve or maintain, or to have the opportunity of achieving or maintaining, a reasonable standard of health or development unless services are provided; or
- the child's health or development is likely significantly to be impaired, or further impaired, unless such services are provided; or,
- the child is disabled; or
- the child is adversely affected by the disability of another family member

---

a. The Scottish definition differs from the Children Act 1989 in not further defining 'health' and 'development' and in including children affected adversely by disability of another family member.

Source: Children in Scotland/Scottish Local Government Information Unit, *The Children (Scotland) Act 1995: A Guide*, Edinburgh, 1995.

whose problems are already manifest in contrast to those children whose problems are less critical but may worsen if ignored'. The report cites research which found that whilst family support was being provided, it 'is seen to be at risk of being subordinated to child protection cases and tends to rely on families persisting with their demands'.[6] The focus is also seen as contributing to the tendency for children in need to be placed in segregated services. Further concerns relate to the problems caused by the different definitions of need of the different departments which may be involved. Social work and education departments and health services frequently understand the term in different ways.

The legislation stipulates that services for children with disabilities should be designed to 'minimise the effect of the disability' and to give them the opportunity to lead lives as 'normal as possible'. They have a right to have their need for services assessed – but not necessarily met. The Social Services Inspectorate noted in its report on an inspection of services to disabled children and their families in four local authority social services departments that none had fully met the standards stipulated in the Children Act 1989 and the associated guidance and regulations.[7]

UN Convention on the Rights of the Child

The legislation incorporates some of the principles of the United Nations Convention on the Rights of the Child, ratified by the UK in 1991. The Children Act 1989 and The Children (Northern Ireland) Order include a statement of over-arching principles relating to children's rights, stipulating for example that the child's welfare should be the court's paramount consideration. The Children (Scotland) Act contains no such statement of basic principles relating to children's rights but specifies a number of specific children's rights. These include:

- due regard being given to a child's views, subject to the child's age and maturity;
- the welfare of a child being paramount in determination of any matters affecting them;
- no order being made relating to a child unless it is better for the child than no order at all;
- due regard being given to a child's religious persuasion, racial origin and cultural and linguistic background.

These principles apply to various aspects of the work and decisions of the courts and Scottish children's hearings system as well as directly affecting some local authority duties. For example (subject to some exceptions), local authorities must take the welfare of the child as the paramount consideration in decisions concerning a child 'looked after by' an authority or in decisions about adoption and must give due regard to the child's views. A growing number of authorities and other agencies have extended their commitment beyond the statutory requirements. In Scotland, for example, prior to the new legislation, Lothian, one of the former Regional Councils, established its own Children's Family Charter, described later in this book by its adjudicator. Children's rights, unlike parental rights have not become associated with a market philosophy—perhaps because children, unlike their parents, cannot be expected to pay for services.

Parental responsibilities and rights

New statements of responsibilities as well as rights have been introduced, including the responsibility (as well as the right) to maintain contact if the child is not living with the parent. These have been most clearly defined in the new Children (Scotland) Act 1995.

Parental responsibilities introduced under the Children (Scotland) Act 1995

Parents have responsibilities:

- to safeguard and promote the child's health, development and welfare;
- to provide direction and guidance in a manner appropriate to the stage of development of the child;
- if the child is not living with the parent, to maintain personal relations and direct contact with the child on a regular basis;
- to act as the child's representative.

Source: The Children (Scotland) Act 1995: A Guide, op. cit.

In exercising their responsibilities and rights, and reaching a 'major' decision, parents have to consider not only each others' views, but also 'give due regard' to the views of the child.[8]

Early years services and leave provision

The Children Act 1989 and the Children (Northern Ireland) Order also make changes to the registration and inspection of daycare services which are defined to include less formal services such as play groups as well more formal daycare services provided by childminders (family day carers) and day nurseries. The legislation has involved extending and improving the regulation and monitoring of services providing for children up to the age of 12 in Northern Ireland and the age of 8 elsewhere. (These provisions of the Children Act 1989 also cover Scotland.) The provisions include a requirement for local authorities to review their pre-school education and daycare services for children every three years. As described by Statham in Chapter 8 (p. 213), the review process should involve seeking the views of 'all interested parties and individuals' to encourage the development of services 'planned and delivered in the light of local wishes and expectations'.

The review encourages local authorities to examine the effectiveness of services in meeting the requirements of all families in the community. However the legislation itself only requires them to provide for children defined as 'in need'.

Whilst the legislation also allows local authorities to provide services for children who are not in need, their ability to do so is now financially constrained. As a consequence, the number of places in local authority early years services is now falling, partly due to the conversion of day nurseries offering care into family centres providing for children and families requiring special support. Table 1.1 shows places in pre-school education and daycare services in the United Kingdom. As can be seen from Table 1.2, levels are substantially lower in the UK than in Denmark or Sweden.

Government policy has favoured a 'mixed economy' of public, private and voluntary services and recent initiatives have supported this approach. The most significant of these has been a funding initiative for school age childcare services (out of school services) administered by the training and enterprise companies, and, most recently, the government's vouchers scheme. These initiatives have done little to assist local authorities in meeting the rising levels of demand for services from families not defined as in need. Places in private 'for profit' nurseries have increased—by 337 per cent between 1986 and 1993—but still provide for less than 4 per cent of under-fives; the number of places with privately employed childminders increased in the same period by 124 per cent and account for some 9 per cent of the under-fives population. The number of places in local authority services fell by 15 per cent in this period.[9]

TABLE 1.1 **Places in pre-school education and daycare, UK, 1994.**

		England	Wales	Scotland	Northern Ireland	UK
Day nurseries	Number	22,300	235	5699	22	28,256
(local authority)	% 0–4	0.7	0.1	1.8	0.0	0.7
Day nurseries						
(registered – private and	Number	124,000	5274	10,238	2557	142,069
voluntary)	% 0–4	3.8	2.8	3.2	2.0	3.7
Childminders	Number	357,500	16,654	31,797	14,702	420,653
	% 0–4	11.0	8.8	9.8	11.3	10.8
Playgroups (local authority)	Number	1600	222	168	340	2330
	% 3–4	0.1	0.3	0.1	0.6	0.1
Playgroups (registered –	Number	407,600	25,391	43,167	15,513	491,671
private and voluntary)	% 3–4	31.2	33.3	33.2	29.5	31.4
Nursery education	Number	346,593	27,346	49,760	7969	431,668
(Local authority)	% 3–4	26.5	35.9	38.3	15.2	27.6
Reception class	Number	328,003	27,593	8880	2460	358,056
(local authority)	% 3–4	25.1	36.2	6.8	4.7	23.4

SOURCE: Charlie Owen, Thomas Coram Research Unit, for Children in Scotland.

TABLE 1.2   Comparison of the provision of publicly funded services[a] for young children in the UK, Denmark and Sweden, 1993 and 1994.

Country	Age of compulsory schooling	Provision in publicly funded services as per cent of all children in age group		
		Children 0–3	Children 3–6	Children 6–10
UK (1993)	5[d]	2	60[b]	less than 5 [c]
Denmark (1994)	7[e]	48	82	62[f]
Sweden (1994)	7	33	72	64

NOTES

   a. Publicly funded daycare and education for pre-school children and school age childcare services for school-age children.
   b. Includes children in compulsory schooling from age of five (four in Northern Ireland).
   c. Limited information available.
   d. 4 in Northern Ireland.
   e. Not compulsory.
   f. Includes all 6-year-olds in pre-primary education.

SOURCE: European Network on Childcare and Other Measures to Reconcile Employment and Family Responsibilities, A Review of Services for Young Children, CEC, 1996.

The issue of integrating educational and care aspects of services remains unaddressed at a national level, but from the 1980s a growing number of local authorities have been seeking to do so. In 1987 the former Strathclyde Regional Council established an integrated management structure for all pre-fives services, located within the education department. In Chapter 4 (p. 109), Roy Jobson describes the creation of a children's services division within Manchester City Council.

In Scandinavia, services for young children are considered in the context of other relevant provisions, including leave arrangements. The UK still lacks this wider framework and there have been few developments in leave provision for the parents of young children. Following the agreement of the EU Directive on Maternity Leave, all women in employment now have access to maternity leave, but there is no statutory provision for paternity, parental and family leave; the Government has indicated that it believes that 'a voluntary and flexible approach works best in this area'.[10]

Children's services plans

The Children (Scotland) Act 1995 places a new duty on local authorities to prepare plans for 'relevant' children's services. Children's services plans were first introduced in England and Wales within departmental guidance, and are now becoming mandatory throughout the UK. The plans originated in a recommendation of a Social Services Inspectorate report that residential child care should be located within a wider policy framework, prepared by social services departments with 'other agencies such as education departments, health authorities and the police'. The first plans in England and Wales have tended to be much more limited, as described by Sutton in Chapter 4 (p. 97). A number of reports and studies have criticised the plans on the basis of weaknesses such as providing insufficient information on the extent of need, costs and resources; inadequate monitoring; and insufficient involvement of parents on management and planning groups for services. An Audit Commission Report in 1994 noted the failure of the plans to lay the basis for joint working, and proposed a strategy for addressing this involving defining and assessing the extent of need, deciding cost effective actions and responsibilities of different agencies in meeting the needs, and monitoring and reviewing the process.[11]

Despite the weaknesses which have been identified, children's services plans are now seen as potentially valuable mechanisms for improving collaboration and co-operation. However, Sutton (Chapter 4, p. 97) has questioned the focus on need, noting some of the problems in understanding that this has caused between departments, in particular in providing for children 'in need' within areas such as education and health which offer universal services. Sutton notes that some authorities have attempted to address the needs of whole populations rather than focusing on children defined as in need, and has proposed a concept of 'communities in need'.

> A concept of 'communities in need' might reunite the universal and selective bias of the agencies concerned in the production of children's services plans and might overcome some of the difficulties created by the notion of 'children in need'. Such a concept may also lend itself to the targeting of both universal and selective services through the development of shared or common indices of need across agencies at a strategic level.[12]

Older children and young people

The requirement on local authorities to provide for children in need encompasses young people up to the age of 18, and, for young people who have left the care of local authorities, (or in the new terminology have been 'looked after'), there are further requirements to provide advice, assistance and guidance until they reach the age of 19. However, the evidence suggests that the help offered through these provisions is not covering some groups. For example, a 1993 study found that the majority of social services departments in England did not consider homelessness alone as a sufficient reason to be accepted as 'in need'.[13] It also seems to be the case that, as with provision for young children, a focus on need can obscure the significance of more universal policies. Recent research in Scotland and England of teenagers placed on supervision or looked after in care noted that whilst the study was primarily concerned with the specialist provision offered by the social work services, many of the difficulties faced by a number of the young people were affected by more universal policies such as unemployment and housing.

Whilst some of the teenagers were undoubtedly not easy to manage, it remained true that the mainstream education system had often failed to maintain their motivation or adapt to their abilities and interests. At least half of the teenagers in the sample had been in receipt of specialist educational provision. The older teenagers, with rare exceptions, emerged from school with few worthwhile qualifications to face a generally unfavourable labour market. The availability of housing in the community was of vital concern to many of those aged 16 or over and with no stable social base.[14]

In the UK, the focus on 'need' within child welfare legislation, the continuing marginalisation of non-statutory services such as pre- and school-age childcare, play and youth services, and the failure to adequately consider the impact of social security, employment and housing policies on children, young people and their families has undoubtedly contributed to high levels of child and family poverty and homelessness amongst young people, as described by Waterhouse in Chapter 2 (p. 44). As seen later in this chapter, all of the countries are confronting changes resulting from such factors as 'family change', extending periods of dependency and the impact of unemployment on families as providers and on young people. These are contributing to a need for wide-ranging policies to address issues which are often universal in their impact.

Scandinavia

Reorganisation

All of the Scandinavian countries have a two-tier system of local government. The two tiers, municipalities and county councils, have a high degree of independence and their own tax base; in Sweden and Denmark they set their own tax rate.

Denmark has 275 municipalities—the smallest of which has 3000 inhabitants and over half of which have less than 10,000—and 14 counties. Sweden has 288 municipalities and 244 counties. Here, 42 of the municipalities have a population of over 50,000; a small number have fewer than 4000. Norway has proportionally more municipalities—435—and 19 counties. More than half of the Norwegian municipalities have a population of less than 5000 and only five have a population of over 50,000.

Municipalities *(kommuner)* have generally had the primary responsibility for services such as children's daycare and school-age childcare, education and youth, child welfare and primary health care. County councils have been responsible for more specialised services such as children's residential homes, upper secondary schools and hospitals.

The welfare model developed by all the Scandinavian countries in the post war period involved centrally driven policies, providing a wide range of public services and benefits to meet the needs of all its citizens, including children and young people. The underlying principle was equality of access to services irrespective of social and economic status, individual ability or where families live. The delivery of such services was determined by explicit legislative guidelines accompanied in general by earmarked central funding. Municipalities and county councils followed centrally determined guidelines and policies.

Decentralisation

In all of the Scandinavian countries, the role of the municipalities and county councils has now changed significantly as a result of decentralisation and some other developments. Responsibility for some services has devolved downwards and the relationship between municipalities, county councils and governments has altered. The responsibilities of the municipalities are now more clearly defined although the relationship between county councils and municipalities is in some cases more complex. These changes have involved local government assuming increased financial responsibility for services within a framework of centrally formulated objectives, with municipalities in general being given block grants in place of earmarked funding.[15] Centralised detailed regulation has been progressively replaced by 'framework' legislation.

This process began in Denmark with legislation in 1968 which gave municipalities the right to decide their own tax rate, followed in the 1970s by the move away from earmarked government grants to block grants. Block grants were introduced in 1986 in Norway and in Sweden in the 1990s. The block grant system is much discussed (and frequently criticised) within the Scandinavian countries. Particular discussion points are the adequacy of grant levels in relation to national requirements placed upon local authorities and ways of assisting those with a low tax base. Danish legislation in 1995 sought to simplify the system through, for example, making it more uniform, and making local government income more predictable. In Denmark and Sweden social indicators such as the proportion of lone parents and residents from non-Nordic countries are used to determine the level of central funding. In Norway, where such social indicators are not presently used, the system is under review. The independent government commission reviewing the system, published the first part of its recommendations in January 1996. These include using social indicators to give greater assistance within block grants to smaller and more disadvantaged areas.[16]

As in the UK, block grants were introduced as a means of giving greater local financial accountability and their introduction has been associated with giving municipalities and county councils more freedom in deciding their administrative structures and providing their services. Danish municipalities and county councils were given this freedom in the 1968 Municipal Act. In Sweden the freedom of municipalities and county councils to vary their administrative structures has been progressively extended from the initiation of a 'free *kommune* experiment' in the early 1980s. The 1991 Local Government Act extended this to all authorities, within the context of improving managerial efficiency in service delivery and the contracting out of some services. Amongst other developments, this has led to greater integration of children's services at a municipal level. In Norway, following on from earlier 'free *kommune*' experiments the Local Government Act of 1992 enables municipalities and counties to reorganise their structures and services.

Decentralisation has involved not only greater independence for municipalities and county councils but also devolved decision making within municipalities, in accordance with the principle that decision making should take place at the lowest efficient organisational level. Poulsen describes in Chapter 3 (p. 74) the widening of the decentralisation process which has been taking place in Denmark in the mid-1990s, and Norwegian and Danish examples of what this has involved are described by Toldnes and Blæhr in Chapter 5 (pp. 126, 133). The two municipalities they describe, both small by UK standards, have been further subdivided, with the principle of devolved decision making extending progressively downwards to the services and to include the participation of children, young people and parents in decisions concerning them.

Decentralisation and disability

Decentralisation and community care policies have involved the reorganisation of disability services. In Denmark services were transferred from the state to the municipalities in 1980 and they share responsibility as shown in Table 1.3.

The decentralisation of services has led to an increasing demand for specialised knowledge and professional assistance, and to meet this demand a number of specialised national information centres have been set up for a trial period of three years. In Norway the special residential institutions which used to be run by the government have been closed down, and the children and young adults using them transferred back to their home municipalities. Since 1992 the responsibility for all services for children, young people and adults with special needs has become a shared responsibility between the municipalities and the counties. Thirteen country-wide and seven regional resource centres (led by Boards) have been established to assist the users, schools, pedagogical-psychological services and other municipal and county providers. Legislation in Sweden transferred responsibility for disability services from January 1995 from the counties to the municipalities.

National legislation and policies

Whilst decentralisation has involved greater autonomy for local authorities this has been developed within the context of national legislation and policies. Policy development at a national level has been assisted by some reorganisation of national departmental responsibilities. In all three countries daycare services for children up to the age of six are the responsibility of a single ministry. In Norway, a Ministry of Child and Family Affairs was established in 1991 by the incoming Labour government with a co-ordinating role in relation to national policy development and specific

TABLE 1.3 **Division of local government responsibility for disabled children, youth and adults in Denmark (1995).**

Type of service	Responsible authority	
	Municipality	*County*

Education[a]	• Day-care services
	• Primary and secondary schools
	• Support adult education
	• Out-of-school activities
	• Enabling disabled to use voluntary educational and leisure services
		• Providing compensatory special education, i.e.
		  • teaching
		  • special education
		  • training

Counselling and guidance	• Obliged to offer disabled people counselling and guidance	• Provide services if municipalities lack the required expertise
Other services	• Home-help • Personal support	• Temporary alternative care in care homes • Residential home and home for severely disabled and mentally ill
Employment[b]	• Rehabilitation • Vocational training • Retraining • Subsidised workplaces (50–50 basis) • Day hostels • Day centres	• Disability consultant providing jobs in open employment
Leisure activities	• Sports facilities, e.g. swimming and riding • Activity centres • Cafés • Cultural centres • Clubs for disabled	

NOTES
 a. Municipalities are mainly responsible for educational provision which is within ordinary schooling, with the exception of a limited number of county-run special schools.
 b. No quota schemes.
SOURCE: *Social Policy in Denmark*, Ministry of Social Affairs, Denmark, 1995.

responsibility for a wide range of services including child welfare, daycare services, leave provision, child allowances, the urban youth programme and the Children's Ombudsman. A recent independent commission reporting on the organisation of services for children and young people and the role of the Children's Ombudsman included in its recommendations a proposal that education should also become a direct responsibility of this ministry, which should be renamed the *Oppvekst-og familiedepartementet* (Ministry of 'Growing Up' and Families).[17] In both Sweden and Denmark a separate departmental structure has been retained. In Denmark, an Inter-Ministerial Committee was set up in 1987 to co-ordinate the role of relevant ministries.

Ombudsmen, children's rights and the UN Convention on the Rights of the Child

The development of strategic policies at a national level and national accountability have been supported by the establishment of ombudsmen in a growing number of areas in both Norway and Sweden. The first specialised ombudsmen were appointed for consumers. Equal Opportunities Ombudsmen were appointed in Norway in 1979 and Sweden in 1980. In 1981, Norway established a Children's Ombudsman pre-dating the enactment of the UN Convention which has been ratified by all three counties. This has since been followed by the creation of a similar post in Sweden in 1992 which, as described by Sylwander in Chapter 3 (p. 78), has been assisting the municipalities in implementing the UN Convention. As described by Torgersen and Borgen in Chapter 9 (p. 219), the Ombudsman's duties encompassed recommending changes in legislation, policies and practice to government and local authorities, investigating individual cases, distributing information and making use of the media to highlight issues and promote discussion. In December 1995 an independent commission, appointed by the Ministry of Child and Family Affairs, published its report evaluating the Children's Ombudsman as an institution, as well as reviewing the organisation of services for children and young people. Whilst commending the work of the Ombudsman in supporting the legal rights of some groups of children, it recommended that the Office should become less concerned with individual cases and focus on policies and principles. The report identified a central role for the Ombudsman in leading and co-ordinating a more unified approach to issues relating to children and young people with, as noted earlier, wider responsibilities given to the Ministry of Child and Family Affairs. The Ombudsman's new roles should include that of 'Network Ombudsman' forming close links with the municipalities. Other recommendations included that of the Ombudsman making less use of the media.[18]

Denmark has followed a somewhat different path. The 'lead and co-ordinating' role envisaged by the Norwegian report for the revamped post of Ombudsman has been given to the Inter-Ministerial Committee on Children. As described by Poulsen (Chapter 3, p. 76) there are 16 ministers represented on the Committee, the aim of which is to co-ordinate the policies of the different ministries and develop cross-sectoral initiatives to improve the living conditions of children and young people.

The role of the Norwegian Ombudsman in exploring ways in which children make their views known has been given in Denmark to the *Børnerådet* (National Council on Children's Rights) set up in 1994 for a trial period of three years.

National policies for young children

Over recent decades all of the Scandinavian countries have substantially developed their services for young children, as well as a range of leave entitlements and other provisions designed to assist parents in paid employment and education. As described by Knutsen in Chapter 3 (p. 86), there are significant differences in the systems which

National Council on Children's Rights, Denmark

The Danish *Børnerådet* is an independent agency promoting children's rights. It has a secretariat of three, and seven members representing child health and special needs, child development, education, culture and leisure and children's rights. Its chair and two of its members are appointed by the Ministry of Social Affairs. The Council has 500 children aged 3–16 attached to it, giving its views on questions put forward by the Council. The Council's children's groups comprise seven school classes and one daycare institution with a total of 140 children. In addition there are 29 groups around the country involving children in the same age group forming the Council's Network Groups. The views of the first group are made public through regional newspapers. By November 1995 the group had been responsible for more than 20 articles, radio interviews, and television slots. Children in the Network Group also discuss issues but less often and more informally. In 1995 the Council introduced a free telephone service, *Clear Message*, on which any child or young person may record their views and identify issues for discussion.

The National Council on Children's Rights aims to:
- listen to children
- enable children to contribute to public debate
- initiate new legislation
- collect and disseminate information on children's living conditions
- suggest new research
- put children at the centre of adult discussion

The Council is not involved in individual complaints.

have been developed, but the similarities are also considerable. Arnlaug Leira has commented elsewhere that :

> A basic convergence in the 'daycare philosophies' of Denmark, Norway and Sweden is easily observed, in the ways in which daycare services are conceived and integrated in national welfare policies. The central and local government intervention in early childcare and socialisation was rooted ideologically in the strong egalitarian traditions of the Nordic welfare states. State-sponsored daycare was projected as a benefit for all children, and as an experience that could offer children a chance for more equal opportunities, despite differences in social background.... An expression of a common 'philosophy' underlying public daycare may also be seen in the conceptualisation of 'daycare content', in that all three countries have favoured the development, by professionals, of a public daycare system in which both caring and educational aspects are integrated and attributed equal importance'.[19]

Children start school later in the Scandinavian countries than in the UK although the age is now coming down. In Denmark (where schooling is not compulsory), children normally start school at the age of seven.[20] In Sweden, parents can choose to send their child to school at the age of six, and compulsory schooling begins at seven. In Norway, compulsory schooling begins at seven, but from the school year 1997–8 this will change to six.

All three countries have over recent decades substantially developed their pre-school services which (with the exception of nursery education for 6-year-olds within schools) are integrated within the welfare system. Table 1.4 shows the increase in both pre-school and school-age childcare services over the period 1978–93.

The increase is set to continue as a result of government commitments in both Denmark and Sweden, and similar proposals which are currently under discussion in Norway. In Denmark, a government commitment announced by the Prime Minister in 1993 'guaranteed' all parents a publicly funded place in daycare for children aged 1–5 years by 1996. Whilst waiting lists have reduced there is some doubt that all Danish authorities will be able to meet the target date.[21] In Sweden the Social Services Act 1995 now requires all local authorities 'to provide pre-school and school-age childcare in different forms for children aged 1 to 12 years to the extent that it is needed by parents due to paid employment or studying or because of the needs of the child'. Most municipalities are reported to have already met this requirement.[22] In

TABLE 1.4   Children enrolled in daycare and family daycare aged 0–10 as percentage of all children in specified age group (1978–93).

Country	Daycare institution						Family day care			
	Full-time			Part-time						
	0–10	0–2	3–6	0–2	3–6	7–10	0–10	0–2	3–6	7–10
Denmark										
1978	20	11	28	0	8	9	5	13	4	1
1987	34	19	47	0	9	22	11	27	9	1
1993	43	18	57	0	11	34	11	29	6	0
Norway										
1978	10	3	9	1	14	..	..	..	..	..
1987	20	6	22	1	27	3	..	1	1	..
1993	..	14	37	3	24	..	..	3	2	..
Sweden										
1978	21	10	19	−	29	7	8	9	12	5
1987	33	18	39	−	19	22	15	13	21	13
1993	42	23	49	−	14	32	10	9	14	7

KEY
- − Magnitude zero
- 0 Magnitude less than half of unit employed
- .. Category not applicable

SOURCE: *Nordic Statistical Yearbook*, 1995, Tables 213 and 214.

TABLE 1.5   **Parental leave and benefit in the Scandinavian countries (1995).**

Country	Total leave with benefit	Parental leave (to be shared)	Maternal leave	Paternal leave
Denmark[a] First legislated 1983	• 54 weeks	• 10 weeks with compensation (DK 2556 per week) • +26 weeks care leave to each parent	• 4 weeks before the birth • 14 weeks after the birth DK 2556 per week)	• 2 weeks in con- nection with the birth (paid)
Norway[b] First legislated 1978	• 52 weeks	• 39 weeks (80% paid) or 29 weeks 100% paid) Parents have the right to leave until the child is three years old (unpaid).	• 3 weeks before the birth • 6 weeks after the birth (80% or 100% paid)	• 4 weeks (80% or 100% paid) + • 2 weeks in con- nection with the birth (unpaid)
Sweden[c] First legislated 1974	• 450 days (63.5 weeks)	• 34 weeks (80 % paid) + • 13 weeks (SEK 60 per day)	• 8.5 week before the birth • 4 weeks (90 % paid)	• 4 weeks (90 % paid) + • 2 weeks in con- nection with the birth (paid)

NOTES
   a. First legislated 1983.
   b. First legislated 1978.
   c. First legislated 1974.

SOURCE: NOU 1995:27, *Pappa kom hjem.*, Ministry of Child and Family Affairs, Norway.

addition, from July 1997 municipalities are required to provide places within schools for all 6-year-olds whose parents want a place. Most municipalities have indicated that they will be able to comply with this, but less than half of municipalities have appointed additional staff, raising questions over the quality of provision. The National Board of Health and Welfare has indicated that it will be examining the quality issues in future surveys.[23]

    There have also been substantial developments in the level of school-age childcare services. In Denmark and Sweden these services predominantly take the form of school-based centres, although some operate independently of schools, in some cases taking the form of 'mixed age centres' with younger children as well as children of school age. Denmark and Sweden now provide places in publicly funded services for 62 and 64 per cent respectively of all 6–10 year olds. In Denmark this included all 6-year-olds in pre-primary (nursery) education.[22] In Norway, earmarked grants have been provided since 1991 for the development of services. At December 1995, 85 per cent of municipalities offered school-age childcare services, and 35 per cent of children aged 7 to 10 made use of them.[24]

The Scandinavian approach to meeting the needs of young children has also encompassed a range of leave and other employment entitlements for their parents. In all three countries employed parents now have access between them to some 12–18 months of paid leave with varying degrees of flexibility in the way it can be taken (see Table 1.5). There is also a variety of other entitlements.

This includes provision in Sweden for parents to have up to 120 days of earnings-related paid leave of absence annually for care of a sick child up to the age of 12 (or 21 years in the case of a disabled child). Until January 1996 Swedish parents were also entitled to two 'contact' days of paid leave annually for each child (10 days for parents of a disabled child) to enable them to accompany their child to school, or daycare centre.

National policies for young people

In Denmark, new legislation enacted in 1994 has strengthened the provision of youth services. The Danish Social Assistance Act 1994 relating to 'youth clubs and other social, educational and leisure time activities for children and young people' followed disturbances in Copenhagen, prompting the Danish government to re-examine its services. The legislation is intended to give young people 'a more prominent place in local social affairs' as well as involving them more in the management of services. It requires local authorities to provide opportunities for young people to meet 'on their own ground' and to ensure that young people are able to participate in decision making in their clubs.[25]

In Norway, the Government has responded to increased levels of unemployment and other problems being experienced by young people with a wide-ranging programme, which, as in Denmark, has a strong focus on the participation of young people. The Youth Policy established for the period of 1994–1997 refers to 'ensuring the participation and influence of young people'. This was both predated, as in the example given overleaf from Porsgrunn, and has been followed by further responses by the municipalities.

In its 'Welfare towards 2030' programme the Government outlined a number of measures to address youth labour market issues constituting a 'Youth Guarantee'. These include:

- co-ordinated public assistance
- individual qualification plans
- a requirement for young people receiving benefit to accept job offers, and
- social benefit to be means tested.

In 1994 the Government brought in legislation which guarantees further education for all young people aged 16–19.

Children and young people participating in local democracy: the Porsgrunn Model

The municipality of Porsgrunn established a Municipal Children's Ombudsman in 1991. This combines the role of a general spokesperson for children and young people with providing a meeting place for children and young people. Existing student councils in the schools, which are concerned with not only school matters but wider community issues such as leisure activities, are involved to ensure broad representation. Since 1992 a fund for 'urgent measures' has been made available and children and young people are responsible for allocating the money at the annual Town Hall meeting. The meeting and the fund form part of a wider process known as 'local negotiations' in which children and young people are asked to make specific suggestions for change which are considered for incorporating into the Municipal Development Plan.

At the local elections in 1995, four young people aged 18 and one aged 20 were elected to the municipal council; most of them had been involved in the Student Council and local negotiations.

Source: Lillestøl K, *Porsgrunn modellen*, Ministry of Children and Family Affairs, Norway, 1996.

Child welfare

In Denmark and Sweden there is no specific child welfare legislation; relevant measures form part of more general social legislation, reflecting a greater emphasis in these countries on general rather than targeted services.

In Denmark new children's legislation was enacted in 1993. In Denmark, social services are provided under the 1976 Social Assistance Act as amended by later legislation. Recent provisions (1993) have strengthened requirements in relation to protection and preventive measures and in enabling children, young people and parents to contribute to decisions in relation to children 'looked after' by the municipalities. Municipalities are required to provide counselling and support to parents and carers and young people experiencing problems or living in 'unsatisfactory conditions'.

Norway has a long tradition of child welfare legislation; the first Child Welfare Act was passed in 1896. In 1992 a new Child Welfare Act replaced earlier legislation passed in 1953. The Child Welfare Act of 1953 had introduced preventive measures to reduce the need for children coming into care, as well as extending public responsibilities to include children 'at risk'. Until the 1953 Act all children in public care were removed from their families.

As Grinde describes below, following this earlier legislation the proportion of children receiving preventive measures increased significantly:

> 'In subsequent years the expansion has been in 'open care' while the number of children in residential or foster homes was unchanged from 1970 to 1990. In 1992, 18.9 per 1000 children had some form of child welfare measures but most of them were in 'preventive' assistance to children and families'.[26]

TABLE 1.6 **Child welfare measures in Norway (1950–93) (in per cent).**

Year	Out-of-home measures	Preventive measures
1950	100	0
1955	83	17
1970	56	44
1980	46	54
1992	38	62
1993	29	71

SOURCE: Adapted after Grinde, T. V. (unpublished paper).[36]

The new legislation aims to further improve preventive measures, and diminish the number of children coming into care. The power to take a child away from the family and into public care has been transferred from the municipality to the county. This effectively separates the role of providing care from that of deciding on taking a child into care. It also reflects the problems which decisions of this nature can cause in a small municipality. Municipalities are required to develop preventive measures 'to safeguard against inadequate care and behavioural problems':

> 'The child welfare service has particular responsibility for bringing to light inadequate care, behavioural, social and emotional problems at a sufficiently early stage to avoid lasting problems, and for instituting measures to this end'.[27]

The implementation of the Act was accompanied by a three-year national development plan initiated in 1991. The aim of this was to improve the quality of services, through additional funding for training and innovative approaches to developing, for example, more flexible and 'user friendly' services. Both legislation and development programmes, and local action policies, have sought to create a more pro-active service, involving more effective collaboration between child welfare, health, education, and other children's services, and taking more account of the views of the child or young person. For example, a child under the age of 15 taken into care now has a Child's Representative or advocate to represent the child's views to the County Committee on Child Welfare following discussion with the child.

Education

In all the Scandinavian countries education has been affected, in varying degrees, by the changing relationship between government and local authorities. As a result of decentralisation, teachers in both Denmark and Sweden are now paid by the municipalities rather than the government, and, as noted above, in all the countries, earmarked funding has been replaced by block grants and greater freedom to re-organise structures within the municipalities. In Sweden, an increasing number of municipalities have brought together education, day care, welfare and recreational services within one department. In Norway, changes in education and local government legislation in 1994 have further increased the freedom for municipalities to change the administrative structures of schools, enabling them to take on new roles. Toldnes describes in Chapter 5 (p. 130) the changes in his role as head teacher as a result of reorganisation within the Norwegian City of Trondheim—from the leader of a school to leader of an area, with his responsibilities now encompassing 'all the children in our neighbourhood, not only the pupils of the school where I am head teacher'.

Whilst the new arrangements have given considerable freedom to municipalities, national legislation and policies continue to have a considerable impact. In all the countries national policies have involved extending the period of schooling and education as described by Meisfjord in Chapter 3 (p. 82). In Denmark, legislation has promoted the involvement of parents and children. Parents' councils are now required by law in all services providing education and care, and legislation in 1990 provided for restructuring of the school boards (with parents as a majority), placing a new emphasis on home/school partnership. As described by Ravn in Chapter 9 (p. 236) the Danish Basic School Act 1994 built on this in a way which has significant implications for educational practice. In Sweden new legislation in 1990–91 introduced a range of new provisions including greater parental and student choice between schools and measures to promote increased diversity in schooling. Municipal schools must now in principle compete with the private sector. In 1995 only just over 200 'alternative' schools (in which 85 per cent of the cost of a place is subsidised) were registered with local authorities, providing places for 1 per cent of children. However concern has been expressed about the implications of this policy for the municipalities.[28]

Health

Responsibilities for primary health care have not significantly changed in any of the countries. In Norway and Denmark the responsibility for primary health care remains that of the municipalities; in Sweden, responsibility lies with the county councils. However, municipalities have taken on added responsibilities with the closure of psychiatric institutions and residential special schools. Recent changes in the Swedish health care system include a reduction in central regulation and the introduction on a trial basis in some areas of an internal market in health care through the purchase by county councils of health and medical services from different primary care units— public and private as well as hospitals.

Scandinavian welfare model: developments and trends

Decentralisation has been a major theme in the reorganisation of services in Scandinavian countries over recent decades, and has brought significant changes in the roles of local authorities (municipalities and county councils) with increasing attention paid to developing collaborative structures. The principle of devolved decision making which underpins decentralisation policies has extended downwards into the services and has focused attention on increased participation by children and parents.

Over recent years there has been some concern over the prospects for the Scandinavian welfare model and whether the levels of provision can be sustained. Decentralisation has contributed to greater awareness of local tax expenditure. The extending responsibilities of municipalities, combined with the change to block grants, has meant that, as in the UK, service areas are now competing for resources within municipalities. The distributive effects of daycare services, in which, research has suggested, middle-class children are over-represented, has been the subject of some debate.[29] The cost effectiveness of services has been under examination and in Sweden, 1991 legislation has led to the contracting-out of public services by some authorities and the introduction of the concept of internal competition, as described by Andersson in Chapter 9 (p. 226).

Despite this, the basic model remains and in some areas continues to develop, with the governments themselves setting targets and policies for local authorities to meet in the areas of services for young children and young people.

1.2   The winds of change: new needs and expectations

In both Scandinavia and the UK restructuring has taken place against a backdrop of what has come to be known as 'family change', economic trends and restructuring including increased unemployment, a growing emphasis on the rights of children and parents, and more generally consumers and users, and wider anti-discrimination movements relating to sex, race, disability and sexual orientation.

Impact of family change

'Family change', comprising a range of demographic, economic and social changes, affecting the size and structure of families and the roles within them, has had major implications for children's services. Figure 1.1 illustrates some of these changes.

Reduced fertility rates have meant that children are now a diminishing proportion of the population competing for resources with a growing number of older people requiring care. At the same time the decline in the child population which, subject to community age profile, can result from this, can increase the cost per child of providing a service—a factor of particular significance for rural and scattered populations.

Smaller families, with less access to sharing of care within the extended family, and changing family structures with high rates of divorce and separation have brought a greater need for family support services and contributed to the dramatic increase in maternal employment which has posed a major challenge for the provision and structuring of early years services in all of the countries concerned—a challenge which has been met with noticeably more success in Scandinavia than the UK.

FIGURE 1.1   'Family Change' in the UK and Scandinavia

Fewer children

UK
In 1971, the total period fertility rate dropped below replacement level for the first time since records began in and has remained below it ever since. The average age at which women have their first child has risen from 24 in 1971 to 27.8 in 1992 and the average number of children per woman has dropped from 2.9 children in 1964 to 1.8.[a]

Scandinavia
In Scandinavia, total fertility rates have increased in all the countries over the last decade but remain below replacement level. In Norway the total fertility rate dropped from 2.9 children per woman in 1964 to 1.66 children in 1983 (the lowest ever registered) and in 1993 was 1.8. The average age at which Norwegian women have their first child increased from 23.5 in 1970 to 26 in 1993. In Denmark and Sweden total fertility rates in 1993 were 1.7 and 1.9 respectively; the average age at which women have their first child is 26.8 and 27.8.[b]

Smaller families

UK
Households contain fewer children, and also fewer adults with grandparents and other relatives less likely to be living in the same household. The proportion of large families (which as defined by the General Household Survey may include adults other than parents) has declined from 12.5 per cent in 1971 to 6 per cent in 1993.[c]

Scandinavia
Scandinavian countries have experienced a similar trend. In Norway the proportion of large households (five persons or more) declined from 17 per cent in 1970 to 8 per cent in 1990. In Norway over the same period the proportion declined from 10 per cent to 5 per cent. In Denmark the proportion of large households with six persons or more declined from 10 per cent in 1970 to 2 per cent in 1985.[d]

Rising divorce rates

UK
There has been a sixfold increase in the annual divorce rate in the UK since 1961. If present trends continue it is estimated that one in four children will experience the divorce of their parents before they reach the age of 16. The divorce rate in 1992 was 3.0 per 1000 of the population.[e]

Scandinavia
Divorce rates started to rise later in Norway than elsewhere in Scandinavia but it is estimated that every third child born in Norway in 1984 will experience the divorce of their parents before the age of 16—twice as many as those born in 1972. These figures do not include children experiencing the separation of cohabiting parents who are two or three times more likely to experience the break up of their parents' relationship.[f] In Denmark (where the divorce rate has now started to fall) 29 per cent of children born in 1984 and 30 per cent of those born in the 1990s will experience the divorce of their parents before the age of 16. In Sweden the divorce rate is at the same level as Denmark—2.5 per 1000 population in 1993.

Changing family structures

UK
One in 5 families (4 in 10 of black families) are now headed by a lone parent compared with 1 in 12 in 1971. The proportion of families headed by single mothers who have never married has grown from 1 per cent to 7 per cent and, in 1992, 31 per cent of children were born to unmarried mothers compared with 21 per cent a decade earlier. Only 15 per cent of births to teenage women took place within marriage in 1992 compared with 75 per cent in 1971. Over 1 million British children are estimated to be living in stepfamilies including some 800,000 stepchildren and another 300,000 children born to both parents.[g]

Scandinavia
An increasing number of children are born to cohabiting couples. In Norway 46 per cent of babies were born to unmarried mothers in 1994 compared with 26 per cent in 1985. Only 1 in 10 of babies were born to single mothers who were not cohabiting, a proportion which has remained fairly stable over the last decade. In Sweden, half (and in Denmark 47 per cent) of children born in 1993 were born to unmarried mothers. In Sweden and Denmark respectively 19 per cent and 20 per cent of families are headed by a lone parent.[h]

Changing patterns of parental employment

UK
In the UK the proportion of families with dependent children where both parents work has increased from 43 per cent in 1973 to 60 per cent in 1993. Over the last decade the greatest increase has been among women with children under five (from 37 per cent in 1984 to 52 per cent in 1993–4), and, within this group, of women with children under three, 44 per cent of whom were in paid employment in 1993 compared with only 38 per cent two years earlier. The employment rates of lone mothers have run counter to this trend—dropping from 49 per cent in 1979 to 41 per cent in 1992. However, of those lone mothers who are in employment a higher proportion work longer hours than their married counterparts. UK women with a child under 10 work on average 24 hours a week—the second shortest number of hours in the EU. But their hours are getting longer—the percentage of women with a child under ten employed in a part-time job has decreased from 74 per cent in 1985 to 66 per cent in 1993 and UK fathers have the longest working hours in the EU, with a third of fathers working 50 hours a week or more.[i]

Scandinavia
Maternal employment participation rates are highest in Scandinavia where most children now have parents who are both economically active. In Denmark 70 per cent of mothers with a youngest child aged 0–3, and 78 per cent of mothers with a youngest child aged 3–10 years, are in paid employment. In Norway almost three out of four Norwegian mothers with a child under the age of 16 were in paid employment in outside the home in 1994 compared with two out of four in 1976. The majority of mothers with a child under the age of 7 work full-time; part-time work is more common among women with two or more children amongst whom 63 per cent worked part time in 1991. Whilst the weekly working hours of Norwegian men have reduced overall over the last decade; fathers now work slightly longer hours. In Norway the average weekly hours for fathers with a child under the age of 7 in 1991 was 35.7 hours a week. Compared with 35 hours per week worked on average by fathers of under sevens in 1981. The trend is now towards a reduction in the working hours of fathers.[j]

SOURCES
a, b. (Family Policy Studies Centre, *Families in Britain*, 1995; D. Utting *Family and Parenthood* Joseph Rowntree Foundation 1995) (Statistisk sentralbyrå. *Sosialt utsyn*, Oslo – Konsvinger 1993 p. 30 and Figure 5) (Ombudet for barn og unge, *Under 18 - fakta om barn og unge i Norge*. Oslo 1995 p.7) (Nordic Statistical Yearbook 1995: 1 Table 33) (Eurosocial/36/15 1993 Table 1 p. 12).
c, d. (General Household Survey 1971 and 1993) (Statistisk sentralbyrå. *Sosialt utsyn*. Oslo-Kongsvinger 1993 p. 294 and Table 1) (The Swedish Institute *Factsheets on Sweden*, December 1993) (Euro Social 36/3 1990, p. 14 Figure 2).
e, f. (Family Policy Studies Centre in Britain, 1995) (Family Policy Studies Centre, *Social Trends* 25 1995) (Jensen and Moen, Enebarn, delebarn, stebarn? Report No.14 NIBR 1994) (Ombudet for barn og unge, Under 18 - fakta om barn og unge i Norge Oslo 1995).
g, h. (Social Trends 25, Table 2.1) (Utting *Family and Parenthood*, Family Policy Studies Centre) (Statistiska Centralbyrån. Statistisk Årsbok 1995). Nordic Statistical Yearbook (1995: Table 28) (European Network on Childcare).
   i. (Family Policy Studies Centre *Families in Britain*, 1995; European Commission Network on Childcare and Other Measures to Reconcile Employment and Family Responsibilities, *A review of Services for Young Children in the European Union* 1995, CEC) (Ombudet for barn og unge. *Under-18 fakta om barn og unge i Norge* Oslo. 1995 p. 12) (Statistisk sentralbyrå. *Sosialt utsyn*. Oslo-Kongsvinger 1993 pp. 172–3 and 186) (Kitterød, R. H. and Roalsø R.M. 'Arbeidstid og arbeidstidsmønster blant foreldre' *Samfunnsspeilt* 1/96 Oslo pp. 12–23)

Impact of unemployment

On families

Unemployment has had, and continues to have, a major impact upon families, disproportionately affecting some families, and redrawing the boundaries of dependency for many young people.

In the UK the number of two-adult households of working age with no work increased from 4 per cent in 1975 to 11 per cent in 1993 and periods of unemployment have lengthened. Mothers with unemployed partners are far less likely to be in employment than those with employed partners. In 1993–4, among mothers with employed partners, 68 per cent were also in employment compared with only 24 per cent of those with an unemployed partner. In 1991–2 over two thirds (2.8 million) of the 4.1 million children living in poverty (in households below half average income) were in families where no-one had a full-time job.[30]

Within Scandinavia, Denmark has seen the greatest fluctuations in rates of unemployment over the last two decades, and currently has the highest level of unemployment with 10.7 per cent of the working population unemployed compared with 8.1 in Sweden and 6.0 in Norway. In Norway it is estimated that at least 1 in 10 children have one or both parents unemployed. In 1991 1 in 15 children had a parent who had been in long-term unemployment.[31]

On young people

Unemployment has disproportionately affected young people. In Scotland the rate of unemployment amongst 16 and 17 year olds rose by 25 per cent between 1991 and 1993 and over a quarter of unemployed people are aged between 16 and 25. Some groups are particularly affected—in 1989, 22 per cent of the disabled population in Scotland were unemployed and in the UK as a whole 18.3 per cent of the black and minority ethnic population were unemployed compared with 8.8 per cent of the white population.[32] Scandinavian teenagers are now also far less likely to be in employment. In 1992 less than 10 per cent of Norwegian young people aged 15 to 19 had employment as their main activity compared with 80 per cent in 1950; in 1993 18.2 per cent were unemployed. The main reasons for this have been the rise in the school leaving age and increased participation in further and higher education but, as in the UK, unemployment is now also affecting many young people. In 1993 unemployment amongst the age group 15/16 to 19 ranged from 9.1 per cent in Denmark to 19.2 per cent in Sweden (where it has more than tripled since 1991).[33] Youth unemployment in both Denmark and Norway has now started to decrease significantly as a result of government measures.

Extending boundaries of dependency

Economic uncertainty has further extended the period of dependency of many young people. As Ola Stafseng points out in Chapter 3 (p. 67) young people lack the economic

TABLE 1.7   16–18 year olds in education and training, UK, Sweden and Denmark, 1990.
(Percentages)

Country	Minimum leaving age (years)	16 years			16-18 years		
		Full-time	Part-time	Total	Full-time	Part-time	Total
Denmark[a]	16	92	0	92	79	0	79
Sweden[a]	16	83	0	83	73	0	73
UK[b]	16	57	37	94	40	31	71

NOTES
a. All regular formal education now classified as full-time.
b. Includes estimates for public sector evening study and for private sector further and higher education.
SOURCE: Social Trends 24.

advantages of some previous post-war cohorts upon entering adulthood and can find it difficult 'to move on from adolescence', a trend which has had considerable implications for youth policy.

All of the countries have seen a substantial increase in the proportion of young people within education and training, although as seen in Table 1.7 the levels of full-time participation of 16–18 year olds are substantially higher in Scandinavia than in the UK.

Impact of rights movements

The last few decades have also seen an increase in needs and expectations associated with the 'rights' movement—the rights of individuals as consumers or (a somewhat different concept) users; the rights of children and parents; and rights associated with anti-discrimination movements relating to sex, race, disability and sexual preference.

Consumers and users

In the UK, the influence of consumerism has contributed to many of the changes outlined above, and as noted by Sutton elsewhere 'there is no doubt that the concept of consumerism has taken hold in the wider public sector and is gradually moving the status of service users from client to customer and introducing a competitive element into service provision'.[34] Ogden and Backe-Hansen note in Chapter 5 (p. 117) the greater significance accorded to user or client perspectives in Scandinavia over recent decades which has raised questions over 'whether the users or the professionals are best served by today's models of organisation and service delivery'.

Children's rights

The children's rights movement shares an association with user rights, but has also been propelled forward by the United Nations Convention on the Rights of the Child which has provided a vehicle for influencing legislation and practice. In the UK, the influence of the Convention can be seen within children's legislation, and increasingly within the policy and practice of local authorities, with some key principles of the Convention incorporated into legislation which directly affects the duties of local authorities.

In Norway the establishment of the Children's Ombudsman's post in 1981 predated the Convention and, as described earlier, the Convention has had, and continues to have, a significant impact throughout Scandinavia, contributing to the creation of an Ombudsman post in Sweden in 1992 and the establishment of the National Children's Council in Denmark.

Parental rights

Parental rights have formed a particular strand within a wider emphasis on consumer and user rights and have contributed to the establishment of parent-led organisations and some services, and legislative provision for parental rights. Within education in the UK, Gillespie notes an association of parental rights and parental choice with a market philosophy. 'The rhetoric has been about involving parents in their children's education, but the policy has been about turning parents into consumers'. (See Chapter 2, p. 54.)

Sex equality movement

Sex equality legislation and aspirations have focused attention in all countries (in varying degrees) on the daycare requirements associated with parental employment, on the structural issues this has posed for services, on wider reconciliation strategies and on gender issues within services. Within the EU an extensive programme has developed over the last 15 years on measures promoting the reconciliation of work and family life and the sharing of family responsibilities between women and men. Of the two countries examined here which are the longer standing members of the Union, the programme has been accorded more importance by Denmark, although its potential for improving provision is greater in the UK. Denmark, in common with other Nordic countries, has to some degree provided some of the inspiration behind the programme. With the advent of Sweden and Finland, the European programme is expected to be further influenced by the Nordic provisions.

Race discrimination legislation

In the UK racial conflict and race equality legislation, and wider recognition of issues relating to ethnicity are now, in varying degrees, informing policy development and practice within services. Race discrimination legislation enacted in England, Wales and Scotland in 1976 is to be extended to Northern Ireland where legislation presently relates to religion and politics. Recent children's legislation includes provisions for taking account of a child's religious persuasion, racial origin and cultural background in a number of areas, including adoption and accommodation for children who are 'looked after'.

In Sweden, legislation introduced in 1986 with the office of Ombudsman against Ethnic Discrimination, was replaced in 1994 by the Act to Counteract Ethnic

Discrimination. Norway has no separate race discrimination legislation but there are a number of provisions in the penal code, and rights to develop the language, culture and life style of the Sami people (an indigenous nomadic group) have been incorporated in the Norwegian Constitution, a separate Sami Act and other relevant legislation.

Disability discrimination legislation

Disability is beginning to give rise to similar legislation. In the UK, the Disability Discrimination Act 1995 covers some aspects of discrimination in relation to employment, access to goods, facilities and services and premises and a number of limited provisions relating to education and public transport. In Sweden new legislation in 1994 gives entitlement to a range of support and services including personal assistance, home care and respite services and promotes an 'inclusive ' approach to provision for children, young people and adults. In the same year Sweden also established the Office of the Disability Ombudsman. In 1993, the Danish Parliament decided against special legislation for the disabled but established the Equal Opportunities Centre for Disabled People, which works across the different sectors and government departments. A National Handicap Council established in 1980 brings together representatives of organisations of people with disabilities, local authorities and government departments. In all the countries a developing focus on integration/ inclusion has had considerable implications for services.

Revision of the European Treaties and non-discrimination legislation

At the moment sex discrimination is the only one of these areas reflected within policy development at a European level. The effect of policy at an EU level upon children's services will further increase if the European treaties, presently being reviewed at an inter-governmental conference (1996), are revised to include more direct reference to children and families, as canvassed by a large number of children's organisations. Proposals made in December 1995 by the Reflection Group of the Council of Ministers to extend the principle of non-discrimination to cover not only sex but also race, disability, age (which would encompass children as well as the opposite end of the age spectrum) and sexual preference have been widely supported by many organisations. Many children's and family organisations would like to see this approach extended to incorporate a 'family policy' dimension and the adoption of relevant international conventions such as the United Nations Convention on the Rights of the Child.[35]

1.3   Children's services: responding to change

In Scandinavia and the UK the challenge for policymakers and service providers is considerable. Family change, the effects of unemployment and longer term restructuring have brought new requirements for services both in the early years and for older children and young adults. All families are requiring more support. At the same time, some families, some children and some young people are requiring even more support. All countries have seen an increase in child welfare interventions although in the Scandinavian countries these are more likely to be of a preventive nature.

The chapters in this book explore themes which are important in all the countries. However, they also demonstrate some of the important differences between them. Scandinavians often point out that the concept of the Scandinavian welfare state can sometimes obscure significant differences between their countries. For example, there are significant differences in historical developments and trends within early years services in Scandinavia, examined here in Chapter 3 (p. 86) by Knutsen. Grinde has described elsewhere the differing importance attached in Scandinavian countries to general and targeted services, with the particularly strong emphasis in Denmark on improving the general living conditions of all children while in Norway somewhat more attention is given to supplementary services for children 'at risk'.[36]

Similarly it is also easy to overlook differences within the UK. Examples of this include the totally different systems of education and juvenile justice in Scotland, the distinctive administrative structure for children's services in Northern Ireland and the implications of the Welsh language—the subject of recent legislation in the form of the Welsh Language Act—for services in Wales.

Undoubtedly the greatest differences lie between the Scandinavian countries and the UK. The Scandinavian welfare model, established in the same period as the UK has now developed further and been more effectively sustained. Funded at a considerably higher level, it has been able to take on new service areas. In Scandinavia, pre-school and school-age childcare services have become major public service areas and services for older children and young adults are increasingly becoming so. By contrast, the welfare system in the UK has failed to develop in the same way. An increasing 'needs' focus in national legislation and resourcing have constrained local authorities from responding effectively to new requirements. Pre-school and school-age childcare services remain non-statutory and poorly supported areas of provision. A policy of encouraging private purchase of these services has not ensured their availability and has contributed to high levels of poverty, most notably amongst one-parent families. Youth services remain similarly poorly supported. In Denmark, as described earlier, concerns relating to youth prompted the government to examine how social institutions might be failing them—leading to new legislation in 1994 requiring municipalities to provide appropriate services involving young people in their management. As has been noted elsewhere, similar UK concerns have instead given rise to 'moral panic … (which) has focused on the increased level of juvenile crime and problematic young people'.[37]

Despite very different starting points and structures the three themes of collaboration, participation and accountability which are examined in this book are key issues in all the countries and central to the developing shape of their services.

Collaboration

Collaboration is a major issue for all children's services, and ways of promoting collaboration preoccupy policymakers and practitioners in all of the countries concerned. The issue encompasses inter-professional, inter-service and inter-sectoral collaboration as well as the relationship between different levels of government, services and children and families themselves.

In Chapter 4 (pp. 93–115), Paul Sutton describes the 'sense' in the UK that, despite wide ranging child care legislation and far-reaching reforms in education and health, services 'are more fragmented than ever'. He examines the use that has been made of children's services plans in England and Wales in promoting collaboration, finding it most successful in traditional areas of cross-sectoral co-operation such as children with disabilities, and weakest in the provision of family support services. In their contribution, Williams and co-workers describe an initiative undertaken in Wales to provide a common framework for promoting health and social gain for children living in Wales. Roy Jobson outlines Manchester City Council's progress towards an integrated children's services division, focused today on early years services but seen as laying the groundwork for 'the creation of a new service for children and young people'.

Ogden and Backe-Hansen (Chapter 5, pp. 117–125) examine the way in which increasing professional specialisation in Scandinavia (as in the UK), has produced a variety of services and ask whether users or professionals 'are best served by today's models of organisation and service delivery'. They review some of the approaches which are being tried. These include examples of vertical and horizontal collaboration, the latter including the restructuring which has taken place in the Saupstad district of Trondheim in Norway, described by Per Egil Toldnes in Chapter 5, (pp. 126–129). Toldnes notes that reorganisation and administrative changes are insufficient by themselves; effective collaboration 'requires changes in working methods for schools and kindergartens as well as social services and leisure activities, and it applies to parents as well as professionals'. Blæhr (pp. 130–138) describes reorganisation in the Danish municipality of Sæby and the use that was made there of the Danish government's pool policy for children and young people at risk.

Participation

Ogden and Backe-Hansen note the extent to which the growing focus on user perspectives has highlighted collaboration issues and requires organisational solutions to take account of their perspectives. In the UK, Gerison Lansdown (Chapter 6, p. 141) takes as a starting point the process by which the concepts of user participation and individual choice, together with the philosophy of the market have begun to enter the language of welfare, questioning their relevance to children. Lansdown examines ways in which choice can be made a meaningful concept for children, through involving them 'in decisions which affect their lives'. Deirdre Watson (pp. 150–155) considers ways in which children's participation can be made more effective within the children's hearings system in Scotland, and Mary John and Penny Townsend (pp. 156–166) describe an initiative in Devon to involve young people in decision making through the establishment of a youth council, and look at a number of examples of what this involves.

Carole Moore (p. 167) examines provision for 'a Named Person' to support parents of children with special educational needs, enabling them to contribute to assessments of their children. She suggests that, while the system offers considerable potential, the time and training implications have been insufficiently recognised, particularly in Scotland.

As described in a number of the contributions, parental involvement in early years services is supported by legislation in all Scandinavian countries. Jessen (Chapter 7, pp. 169–173) examines the role of the Association of Danish daycare institutions in facilitating parental involvement in daycare in the Danish municipality of Aarbenraa, and Mordal (p. 174) describes the findings of a survey examining how this works in practice in Norway.

Skeidsvoll (p. 179) considers parental participation from the perspective of her own experience as an articulate professional as well as a mother of a child with special needs. She emphasises that participation for her takes place on many different levels: participation in her child's treatment and exercise (in conjunction with doctors and others); participation in parent organisations and groups deriving strength and knowledge from other parents; making sure a child obtains what he or she is entitled to; taking part in developing a society for everyone. She sees these as all interlinked and some more prominent than others at different stages of her and her child's life. Nielsen (p. 184) considers parental participation from the perspective of a parent whose child was taken into care for 10 years and describes the role of the National Parental Association for Child and Youth Support in Denmark in helping parents of children and young people at risk.

Accountability

Growing interest in promoting the participation of children and parents in services is reflected in changing perceptions and structures of accountability. In the UK, Bilton (Chapter 8, p. 191) describes the way in which traditional lines of accountability—to line managers and elected representatives—are having now to consider service users and representative organisations within the local community, and the issues posed for accountability by the two themes of collaboration and participation. Collaboration is essential, and now required within a number of aspects of legislation, but he points out that there are few effective mechanisms for enforcing co-operation and therefore no apparatus for accountability to ensure it. Similarly, legislation now provides for some participation by children and parents in decision making but, as Bilton notes, whilst 'these arrangements for participation can clearly be helpful in providing opportunities for accountability to children and families ... they operate very much on the agency's terms and in accordance with its policies and in response to government guidance'.

Children's Rights Officers are one of the means which Bilton identifies as being important in ensuring accountability and his review of some of the mechanisms which can be used to increase accountability to service users suggests that 'in view of the low economic and political status of children, accountability systems based on their legal rights may serve them best'.

Alan Finlayson (p. 200) describes the Children's Family Charter (of which he was the Adjudicator) developed by the former Lothian Regional Council, and offering a rights framework at a local authority level. Incorporated within the Charter is the right of adjudication for complaints over entitlements. Cathy Jamieson (p. 206) describes the role of a representative organisation of young people with experience of public care in Scotland in promoting accountability in public care services.

June Statham (p. 211) describes the effectiveness of early years reviews as a mechanism for examining whether services meet the community's needs, and for future planning. Her research shows the need for reviews to be 'clearly linked into the decision making structure of the local authority and part of an ongoing process of working with local childcare groups'. A review of recommendations needs to be incorporated into children's services plans and requires 'the commitment and backing of senior officers and elected members'. Statham argues that, whilst local accountability is important, 'a balance needs to be struck between local accountability with the flexibility to respond to local circumstances and the need for a clear framework of agreed policies and principles for an early years service'.

Within the Scandinavian countries, Torgersen and Borgen (Chapter 9, p. 219) describe the role of the Norwegian Ombudsman for Children in investigating individual cases and identifying new policy and legislative requirements, a role in which considerable efforts have gone into finding ways in which children and young people can give their views. As described earlier in this introduction, the role has now been revised following a review. Andersson (p. 226) describes the restructuring of the public subsidy system for pre-school services in one district of Stockholm, arguing that the increased competition it has involved between services in the public and private sectors has made services more accountable to parents through offering them more choice. Hovdenak (p. 232) examines issues of accountability in the context of her study in a school in the northernmost county of Norway. Hovdenak found that pupils and their parents felt that what they were taught in school insufficiently reflected their own experience; the findings led to the introduction of local studies within the curriculum. Birte Ravn (p. 236) examines new evaluation procedures in Danish schools and their implications for accountability and describes a particular model offering 'mutual accountability' for teachers, parents and children.

Looking forward

The chapters in this book illustrate some of the issues which are being explored and the means by which services can and are being reshaped, in many cases providing a vehicle for wider changes than those on which they directly focus. The themes of collaboration, participation and acountability will, we believe, prove to be key influences on policies and practice for children's services well into the next century. Improving collaboration between sectors, services, different professional groups and families; enabling participation by children, young people and parents/carers in decision making and policy development; making services more accountable to children and families; these require major changes not only in the organisation, management and resourcing of services but also in the attitudes, values, and concept and language of services.

The concept and language of services (tjenester)

Linguistic argument often accompanies change, and can illuminate some of the principles and processes of change. In Scandinavia there is discussion of the term 'services', which, it is argued, implies a passive relationship in which children receive but do not assist in determining the care or learning experience.[38] The term 'services' is unlikely to be easily replaced, but the discussion does draw attention to some of the new thinking about them. New phraseology can signal a new approach—as noted earlier, in the UK children 'in care' are now described as 'looked after', signalling a less stigmatising approach. Language can certainly devalue, as even a cursory examination of the language of disability demonstrates.

The language used for services sometimes reflects past or present structural confusion over functions and roles. An obvious example in this respect is that of the confused and/or inappropriate terminology in relation to services providing care, education and play for young children, described in Scandinavia in relation to only one of its functions—care—and with a plethora of terms in use in the UK, reflecting its fragmented structure and marginalised status. The compartmentalisation of professionals and services is sometimes reflected in the language. In the UK, the concept of children 'in need' is often understood in different ways by different agencies. Similarly, the language used in services can be inaccessible to children and families, rendering irrelevant provisions which promote their participation in services.

Child and family centred/focused structures

New perspectives on services offered by children and families can require rethinking of boundaries and structures. As Ogden and Backe-Hansen point out in Chapter 5, (p. 117) traditional structures reflect historical, legal and professional concerns; child and family centred structures must be directed towards promoting collaboration and participation. Services are experiencing shifting boundaries; horizontally, between services themselves, between services and those that use them, between services and other relevant provisions such as leave for parents; vertically, between services and different tiers of local and national government. Education, for example, is no longer (if it ever was) just the business of schools; equally schools are no longer just about education—in the Saupstad district of Trondheim they are no longer just schools but 'growing up centres' with head teachers responsible not just for their own pupils but 'all the children in our neighbourhood'.

The responsibilities of schools have not only extended outwards but also downwards, with children starting school at an earlier age, and upwards, with many staying on longer. In Scandinavia where children have started at age 7, the trend is now to lower the starting age. In the UK the earlier starting age for children of 5 (now 4 in Northern Ireland) is beginning to prompt some discussion of whether the age of compulsory schooling should be raised, enabling services for young children to be perceived and developed less as 'pre-school' and more as important services in their own right, meeting a range of needs for children and their families. A 1994 report proposed raising the age to six and this proposal has been echoed in subsequent publications.[39]

A new balance is being sought between child protection and prevention—a search felt to be particularly urgent in the UK where the focus on 'need' has involved the targeting of resources away from universal and preventive services. Within child protection, the roles and boundaries of professionals and the relationship between families and the state are issues discussed in all countries, influencing structures and procedures.

The strong emphasis which has developed over recent years on the rights of children, focused by the United Nations Convention on the Rights of the Child, has contributed to a re-examination of management structures and policies at national and local levels, with a view to improving co-ordination and collaboration and protecting the interests of children. In Scandinavia there has been extensive examination of national and government structures. In Denmark the approach has been that of co-ordination through an Inter-Ministerial Committee on Children. In Norway, where there has been a Children's Ombudsman since 1981, a recent report identifies a central role for the Ombudsman in leading and co-ordinating a more unified approach to issues relating to children and young people, with wider responsibilities being given to the current Ministry of Child and Family Affairs. In the UK there have been no national developments, but much discussion and specific proposals from non-governmental organisations on establishing a children's rights commissioner. It has also been suggested that such commissioners could also be appointed at a local level, a concept which builds on some local initiatives such as the Lothian Children's Family Charter and Ombudsman, and one which has some resonance in the proposals of the Norwegian review of the Norwegian Children's Ombudsman.[40]

Local authorities are developing new management structures for children's services. In some cases these bring together separate departmental responsibilities for different aspects of children's services; in others, improved co-ordination through a more corporate approach. The benefits of an integrative approach are virtually unquestionable in relation to early years services, and have considerable advantages in developing child-focused structures. However, they can involve a loss of distinctiveness of professional input and do require major investment in training and support.

Training

Training has always been recognised as important in determining the quality of services; new structures and approaches also have implications for both initial and related training. Collaboration can require examination of separate training structures; participation can require development of new areas of training. For example, Moore (Chapter 6, p. 167) notes the inadequate recognition given to training issues around the 'Named Person' provision in Scotland for enabling parents of children with special educational needs to contribute to assessment. In many areas, insufficient attention has been given to the training implications of adopting policies such as that of promoting equality of opportunity.

Strategic planning

Today's services have to be outward looking and much attention now focuses on their relationships: relationships within services with those that use them and the wider community, between services themselves and between services and government at local, regional and national levels. Planning is seen as critical in creating the appropriate conditions for these relationships to operate effectively. If planning is to produce services which are child and family focused, directed towards meeting the needs of the whole child and supporting families in bringing up children it is important that the planning process involves them. In the UK children's services plans are seen at a local level as a possible route for developing such an approach, but currently fall far short of expectations.

Planning at a local level is assisted by coherent national policies, locating policies for particular service areas within a wider framework which may be required of, for example, benefits, taxation, leave provision, employment policies, and so forth. In the UK the absence of such policies in relation to young people and services for young children have posed considerable problems for those seeking to meet the needs of these groups at a local level.

Funding and the inter-generational social contract

Demographic trends, which in all countries mean that children are a diminishing proportion of the population, raise concerns over their ability to command adequate resources. In Scandinavia decentralisation and the shift to block grants has involved service areas having to compete at a local level with other services, some of which may attract greater electoral support. There are also fears that such government commitments as the Swedish guarantee to provide daycare 'for all parents employed or studying or because of the needs of the child ' may only be met by the municipalities through sacrificing some aspects of quality. In the UK tight government constraints on local authorities in recent years have affected many children's services and left non-statutory areas particularly vulnerable. These include important preventive services for young children and adolescents, and service areas such as daycare, which unlike those in Scandinavia have failed to develop into substantial areas of public provision. In all countries there is discussion on how to ensure that central funding adequately recognises social and economic disparities between authorities and that funding mechanisms diminish rather than exacerbate inequalities.

Block grants are important mechanisms for providing local accountability, but do not enable authorities to fulfil government commitments when inadequately funded or to develop provision in a national policy vacuum. In Norway, an independent Government commission is currently examining the possibility of earmarked funding for the further development of full daycare services by the year 2000. Such funding can be a means of developing particular areas of services and of protecting services to those groups less visible in the political process. A Canadian sociologist has argued for a new commitment of civic responsibility to improve the life chances of children and young people through strengthening 'those agencies of the welfare state that will link sustainable communities, families, children and youth in ways that will reduce the risks of inequality of income, health and education to which market society remains wedded'—a new inter-generational social contract.[41] The fulfilment of such a contract is a responsibility at a national and a local level. For those countries within the EU it is also a responsibility at that level.

The selection of contributions in this book is not intended to offer a blueprint for change but rather to shed some light on this process and on the approaches which are being taken in the countries concerned. A variety of groups, comprising parents, children and young people, providers, professionals, policymakers, interest groups and researchers, are stakeholders in this process. A selection of these groups from Scotland, England, Wales and Northern Ireland within the UK, and the Scandinavian countries of Norway, Denmark and Sweden, have been invited to contribute to this book. Their contributions illustrate some of the changes and structures which are influencing the development of children's services into the next century. Part I presents some perspectives on these changes. Parts II, III and IV, the main body of the book, provide a wide range of case studies, relating to the responses which are emerging in the different countries, focusing on what we have described as the key themes of collaboration, participation and accountability.

Notes and References

1. In Scotland funding relates to the size of the client group for the particular service (accounting for 97 per cent of grant) and additional socio-economic factors relating to the client group within the area. In England and Wales funding may take account of a wider range of indicators including, for example, research. Some funding also takes the form of specific grants.
2. Gaster, L. and O'Toole, M., *Local government decentralisation: an idea whose time has come?* SAUS Working Paper 125 (Bristol, 1995).
3. Sutton, P. *Crossing the boundaries: a discussion of children's services plans.* (London: National Children's Bureau,1995).
4. Jones, A. and Bilton, K., *The future shape of children's services* (London: National Children's Bureau, 1994).

5. Within the UK, the hearing system exists only in Scotland. It was established under the Social Work (Scotland) Act 1968 and took over from the courts most of the responsibility for dealing with children under the age of 16 who commit offences or who are in need of care or protection.

6. Secretaries of State for Health and for Wales (1994). *Children Act Report 1993* presented to Parliament on the Children Act 1989, Cm. 2584 (London: HMSO).

7. Social Services Inspectorate *Services to Disabled Children and their Families,* a report of the national inspection of services to disabled children and their families in England and Wales, January 1994.

8. Children in Scotland, *Children (Scotland) Act 1995: Information Pack,* (Edinburgh, 1996).

9. European Commission Network for Childcare and Other Measures to Reconcile Employment and Family Responsibilities. *A Review of Services for Young Children in the European Union 1995* (CEC, forthcoming).

10. Department of Health *Response to Questionnaire on Implementation of the Council Recommendation on Childcare,* (London: HMSO, 1995).

11. Social Services Inspectorate. *Report on the National Survey of Children's Services Plans* Birmingham: Social Services Inspectorate. Secretaries of State for Health and Wales (1994). *Children Act Report 1993* Presented to Parliament on the Children Act 1989 Cm. 2584 (London: HMSO); *Children's Services Plans* in *Children (Scotland) Act 1995 Information Pack Factsheet* (Children in Scotland, Edinburgh 1996); Audit Commission *Seen But Not Heard: Co-ordinating Community Child Health and Social Services for Children in Need* (London: HMSO, 1994).

12. Sutton, P., *Crossing the Boundaries: A Discussion of Children's Services Plans,* (London: National Children's Bureau, 1995).

13. McCluskey, J., *Reassessing Priorities: The Children Act 1989 – A New Agenda for Homeless Young People?* (London: CHAR Housing Campaign for Single People, 1993).

14. Triseliotis, J., Borland, M., Hill, M. and Lambert, L., *Teenagers and the Social Work Services.* (London: HMSO, 1995).

15. Earmarked funding is still used for implementing national policies for developing some service areas such as daycare.

16. NOU 1996:1 *Et enklere og mer rettferdig inntektssystem for kommuner og fylkeskommuner.* (Oslo: Kommunal- og arbeidsdepartementet, 1996).

17. NOU 1995:26. *Barneombud og barndom i Norge.* (Oslo: Barne- og familiedepartementet, 1995).

18. NOU 1995:26, *op. cit.*

19. Leira, A., *Welfare States and Working Mothers. The Scandinavian Experience,* (Cambridge: Cambridge University Press, 1992, pp. 48–9).

20. In Denmark, nine years of basic education, but not schooling are compulsory; it is left to parents to decide in what way their children are educated.

21. European Commission Network for Childcare and Other Measures to Reconcile Employment and Family Responsibilities, *A review of Services for Young Children.* 1996. Det Tværministerielle Børneudvalg, *Statistik om Børn;* Denmark (København: Socialministeriet) December 1995.

22. European Commission Network for Childcare and Other Measures to Reconcile Employment and Family Responsibilities, *A Review of Services for Young Children,* 1996. Kommunernes Landsforening, *Pres på den kommunale dagpasning,* København 1995.

23. Socialstyrelsen. *Meddelandeblad No.22/95* (Stockholm: Barn- och Familjeenheten) Nov. 1995.

24. Ministry of Church, Education and Research, Norway—unpublished data.

25. Nielsen, Carsten S., 'Troubled Teenagers. Young people in difficulties from a Copenhagen perspective' in Children in Scotland *Child Welfare Reviewing the Framework,* ed. K. Tisdall, Edinburgh: HMSO, 1996.

26. Grinde, T. V., 'Developmental Trends in Child Welfare: UK and Nordic Views and Priorities' in Children In Scotland *Child Welfare: Reviewing the Framework,* Edinburgh: HMSO, 1996.

27. *Child Welfare Act 1992* Chapter 3.
28. Statskontoret. *Valfrihet inom skolan- konsekvenser for kostnader, resultat och segresjon* (Stockholm: DS, 1994).
29. Leira, A., *Welfare States and Working Mothers. The Scandinavian Experience* (Cambridge: Cambridge University Press, 1996).
30. Family Policy Studies Centre *Families in Britain* FPSC: London, 1995; Utting, D., *Family and Parenthood* (Joseph Rowntree Foundation, 1995).
31. Ombudet for barn og unge. *Under 18 – fakta om barn og unge i Norge* (Oslo: Barneombudet/ Statistisk sentralbyrå, 1995). There are difficulties in comparing unemployment data due to data collection differences and variations in social welfare measures.
32. Children in Scotland, *Scotland's Families Today,* (Edinburgh: HMSO, 1995).
33. Nordic Council of Ministers. Nordic Statistical Yearbook, Nord 1995:1 (Stockholm: NCM, 1995).
34. Sutton, P., *Crossing The Boundaries, A Discussion of Children's Services Plans* (London: National Children's Bureau,1995).
35. *Revising the European Treaties: Including a Dimension for Children and Families Factsheet,* Confederation of Family Organisations in the European Union and European Forum for Child Welfare, 1995.
36. Grinde, T. V., 'General versus specialist services: some principles for addressing the needs of vulnerable families with young children', Unpublished paper, Institute of Education University of London, 1995.
37. Tisdall, K., *Child Welfare: Reviewing the Framework,* Edinburgh: HMSO 1996.
38. For some of the Scandinavian discussion see Qvortrup, *J Børn halv pris. Nordisk barndom i samfundsperspektiv.* (Sydjysk Universitetsforlag 1994); Dahlberg, G. 'Home for the people – folkhemmet' (forthcoming).
39. *Start Right,* (London: Royal Society of Arts, 1994); Moss, P. and Penn, H., *Transforming Nursery Education,* (London: Paul Chapman, 1996).
40. Rosenbaum, M. and Newell, P., *Taking Children Seriously: A Proposal for a Children's Rights Commissioner* (Calouste Gulbenkian Foundation 1991); Jones, A. and Bilton, K., *The Future Shape of Children's Services* (London: National Children's Bureau, 1994).
41. O'Neill, J., *The Missing Child in Liberal Theory: Towards a Covenant Theory of Family Community Welfare and the Civic State* (Toronto: University of Toronto Press, 1994).

PART I
PERSPECTIVES ON CHANGE

Chapter 2

◆

PERSPECTIVES ON CHANGE: UK

2.1 TRENDS AND DEVELOPMENTS IN CHILDREN'S SERVICES

OVERVIEW

Lorraine Waterhouse
Professor of Social Work, University of Edinburgh

The landscape of children's services in the UK is changing rapidly. The Children Act 1989 in England and Wales introduced major legislative reform. Scotland and Northern Ireland have recently adopted new children's legislation. Further changes are anticipated in the organisation of children's services as a consequence of local government reform in Scotland from April 1996. Recent UK studies find an alarming growth in child poverty. In this chapter the consequences of these changes for children's services in the UK are discussed. The importance of parents, professionals and politicians working together to secure material and social support for children growing up in the UK today is argued.

Time is of the essence. A better future for children depends on comprehensive and co-ordinated services in education, health and social work. Yet a continuing failure to develop early years services, the possible fragmentation of planning and service development which may result from local government reorganisation, and the political and economic drive towards more selective targeting of services for only some children, pose a major challenge to fulfilling this need.

The status of children

Children are a nation's future. Their welfare and well-being are the responsibility of adults, especially parents whose purpose in bringing up children is to protect, nurture and encourage their personal and moral development. Yet it is not just children who reap the benefits of parental love and labour but the whole of society who come to share the skills and vision of future generations. All parents are entitled to expect the support of the state and their local communities in meeting their children's needs and fulfilling their parental duties.

Children matter as people in their own right. All children and young people deserve to expect a reasonable standard of health and development. They have needs and rights: needs of care and protection; rights of being treated humanely and with due consideration of their wishes.

For children and their families to flourish with hope, good, comprehensive and co-ordinated services are the key. Health, education and social services must remain central services for any responsive government. Recognition of children with special needs must increasingly be incorporated so that all children have a chance to develop their full potential. Income support, housing, recreation and the arts must be seen to have an important place in helping children to thrive with confidence.

Children and families in the UK

The Joseph Rowntree Foundation (1995)[1] in their recent inquiry into the distribution of income and wealth in the UK found that children comprise 30 per cent of the poorest tenth of the population. Single parents and their children who make up 6 per cent of the population are significantly over-represented in the poorest fifth. Not surprisingly, 70 per cent of the gross incomes of families in the poorest two-tenths of households come from social security benefits.

The proportion of children living in relative poverty in the UK has increased threefold since 1980 and almost a third of children come from homes below the EC poverty line – households with less than half the national average income.[2] Absolute poverty further blights the life chances of children. It is estimated there are 33,000 children affected by homelessness in Scotland.[3] The rise in homelessness and the privations this brings pose serious threats to the health and development of children and young people.

The UK has no official poverty line. Between 1979 and 1989 the number of citizens living on the safety net was up by two-thirds and by one-third for those living below the level which income support is intended to guarantee. Income inequality has been rising more rapidly in the UK than other western countries with the exception of New Zealand. In Scotland, marked disparities exist between the east and west with the latter having less disposable income per head and more households depending on income support.

The proportion of children living in relative poverty in the UK has increased threefold since 1980 and almost a third of children come from homes below the EC poverty line, households with less than half the national average income.

In Scotland children account for 20 per cent of the population. 3 per cent have disabilities, and of these two-thirds will experience chronic problems.[3] 1 per cent come from black and other minority ethnic groups. 1 in 6 children live in lone parent households. Only one-third of children aged 3 and 4 are in nursery education; and childminding is available for only 6 per cent of the population. Up to 10 per cent of young people and children have persistent psychological difficulties. Accidents in the home are the most common cause of death in young children. 38 per cent of Scottish children live below the EC relative poverty line. 5000 young people sleep rough every night in Scotland. One-fifth of the Scottish prison population is under 21 years of age.

Between 1981–1991 mortality rates for adults in prime parenting years widened.[2] Standardised mortality ratios for Greater Glasgow Health Board 1991–2 show a steady rise in death rates since 1985.[2] Glasgow is the most materially deprived area of Scotland and this rise in mortality rates appears to coincide with the growing disparities in income differences nationally.

The Rowntree Inquiry (1995)[1] and Wilkinson (1994)[2] highlight the range of social problems associated with areas of low income and poverty. Problems in the poorest areas are found to have increased with high rates of family break-up, high levels of crime and vandalism, youth unemployment and growing numbers of children registered with local authorities as at risk of abuse. The steady decline of public sector provision in favour of home ownership and the private rented sector is resulting in poorer standards of housing for families unable to compete in the new market economy. Ironically, the general rise in car ownership leaves the poorest families exposed to all the risks of pollution and road traffic accidents (still one of the highest causes of child mortality in the UK) without the benefits of good public transport, especially in rural areas. The impact of poor parenting is also attracting wider recognition (Rutter and Quinton)[4] as a significant factor in the safety, health and development of children.

Wilkinson[2] points to the worrying effects which widening differences in income distribution are having on the welfare and well-being of children and young people. Widening of income differences since 1985 appears to be matched by a marked slowing of the decline in national death rates for infants and children and an apparent decline in reading standards over the same period which are not adequately explained by differences in teaching methods.

Against this background of widening social and economic disparities children's services have a key role to play in mediating the consequences of growing inequality for children and families. Children's services face the challenge of providing universal and additional help for a wide range of children from infants to young people with differing material and social needs. Family life is changing and continuity of parenting for children can no longer be assumed. The development of children's services to match changing circumstances and yet to recognise the continuing needs of children for a sense of security, of belonging and of their own importance to others requires a responsive and flexible approach. The force of legislative and organisational change is being felt in education, health and social work services. How are these three agencies with a major stake in child health and welfare responding?

Education

Education policy has seen significant changes (Education Reform Act, 1988) with the introduction of the national curriculum, parental choice leading to open enrolment, the publication of exam results and local management of schools with an increased role for parents in school governance. There has been a drive by central government to free schools from local authority control, to encourage schools to compete for pupils and to shift responsibility and accountability to local communities. Scottish schools unlike some of their English counterparts have not pursued grant-maintained status and have chosen to remain within the local authority.

The implications of these changes for children is concerning. The pressure of competition may lead to an emphasis on academic achievement and enhancement of the reputation of the school to the detriment of children with troubling and troublesome behaviour who are more likely to be excluded.[5] Rutter and Quinton[4] have shown the importance of education in mediating adverse outcomes in adulthood, especially for children who come from families where poor relationships feature. Similarly, there is some evidence[6] to suggest that children with special needs are being singled out and are prone to segregation.

Part III of the 1993 Education Act places a qualified duty on social work services and health authorities to assist education in their response to children with special needs. When educational needs of children fail to be met, the likelihood of difficulties in childhood development increases (Rutter and Quinton[4]). This poses a jeopardy not only for children but for the agencies of health and social work who look to education for their critical contribution in overcoming social adversity in childhood.

Pre-school education is discretionary despite widespread recognition of its importance to future outcomes for children[7] and significant growth in demand arising from such factors as increasing women's employment and the wish to provide stimulating environments for children in the early years. The most systematic study[7] of long-term benefits for children of high quality pre-school education concludes that cognitive and social development is enhanced. Traditionally provided by the statutory and voluntary sectors, there has recently been a rapid growth in private nurseries and daycare centres, available at cost to those families who can afford them. The UK still compares unfavourably with other European and Scandinavian countries, the majority of whom provide high levels of pre-school services.[8,9]

A variety of services including childminders, playgroups, family centres, day nurseries and nursery schools is available. Jones and Bilton[10] stress that despite this apparent variety, choice is largely restricted to those who can afford to pay. Children from poor families in the UK are most likely to be placed in local authority nurseries which sets them apart from other children.

Health

The National Health Service has seen sweeping managerial change these past 20 years. There is a new emphasis on consumer need and preference (NHS and Community Care Act 1990). The three major tasks of planning, purchasing and providing health services are no longer solely handled by health authorities; instead authorities are encouraged to mix the buying-in of services at competitive tender with some direct service provision and to draw on private and voluntary contributions. A split between the commissioning of services and their provision was recently adopted to increase competition in the pursuit of apparently more effective and cost efficient services. Trust status for hospitals has been introduced to break down the monopoly of a full public health service and fundholding general practices have been developed seemingly to encourage the most cost effective match between health services and patient need.

Universal health services include, for example, health checks to monitor children's maturation, programmes of immunisation, dental checks and medical and nursing care at times of illness. The Audit Commission Report[11] in England and Wales identifies that most commissioning health authorities have yet to assess the full needs of children in their areas for community child health services. While immunisation programmes have largely been successful, child health surveillance where extra need is identified has yet to change significantly.

Social work

Social work services, selective to those families and children most in need, sit uneasily against health and education with their universalist concerns. It is less than 30 years since the newly created Departments of Social Work were introduced in Scotland under the Social Work (Scotland) Act 1968 and their counterparts Social Services in England and Wales (1971). Social services came of age during a political era of economic restraint without the benefit of professional traditions already well established.

Where children are concerned social work has been highly concentrated on children in need, those facing cumulative social adversity, on children in public care and on children in need of care and protection on offending and non-offending grounds (Jones and Bilton 1994).[10] This may contribute to the stigma which families who are in receipt of social work child care services are reported to experience (Farmer 1993).[12]

Social work and social services departments throughout the UK hold a central position in the working of child care law with a duty to provide for children who are in need of compulsory measures of care or control and to promote welfare. Children may be looked after away from home in foster care or residential care if their families are unable to look after them either briefly or long term.

There is a notable increase in the use of fostering, especially for young children, and a decline in the use of residential care.[11,13] This shift in policy reflects a growing preference for families rather than institutions as the best solution for children living away from home. Residential care is still seen as the preferred option for some young people, especially those whose behaviour is dangerous to the community or themselves. There is also a move towards specialist children and families teams in social work services. This new pattern of specialism may promote more working together with other disciplines and may lead to a clearer articulation of policies and planning requirements for children and families.

Social work, like education and health, has recently experienced radical change with the implementation of the Children Act (1989) in England and Wales, and the NHS and Community Care Act (1990) which separates the commissioning of services from their provision.

The Children Act 1989 in England and Wales requires local authorities to provide for children deemed in need. The Act defines children in need as those whose health or development is at risk; and those with disabilities.[14] It also stresses the importance of parental responsibility as a lifelong commitment to children.

The Act, while stressing need as the primary concept behind children's services, highlights the interrelationship between needs, rights and responsibility. Need and demand are, however, very different concepts on which to plan children's services. Need may be politically determined by altering the threshold at which want ends and need begins. It is open to a sectarian rather than bipartisan interpretation and is likely to be determined by audit and resources. Demand may more accurately reflect the wishes of consumers but is also likely to be associated with rising public expectations for improved services. It is not surprising, then, as costs for the care of dependants escalate and continue to shift from the state to individual citizens, that need rather than demand takes centre stage in policy making.

Further change is seen in the Children (Scotland) Act 1995 and local government reform (Local Government etc. (Scotland) Act 1994) which will introduce smaller unitary authorities. The Children (Scotland) Act 1995 brings together private, public and adoption law. New requirements are placed on Scottish local authorities to assess the social care needs of children with disabilities; to promote welfare and to provide assistance for children under 18 years; to assess children who may be at risk of abuse. One central assumption underlying the philosophy of the Act is that parents' responsibilities towards a child are not dependent on their relationship to each other and that parents and professionals need to work in partnership with each other. Yet the Act has missed the opportunity to co-ordinate the full range of children's legislation and to require planning for children's services to be co-ordinated between health, education and social work.

Local government reorganisation

Extensive reorganisation has recently taken place of the local government boundaries in Scotland and Wales and is, to a lesser extent, taking place in England. In Scotland, from 1 April, 1996 the existing two tier structure of local government of 62 regional and district councils has been replaced by 29 all purpose single-tier councils (with the three existing Island councils continuing to serve the islands). These changes, which include a requirement for Scottish authorities to prepare a decentralisation scheme, are leading some authorities to re-examine their traditional structures with new links forming between housing and social work/services .

Reorganisation has raised serious concerns over the ability of smaller authorities to deliver a full range of services and to collaborate effectively with child health services. Health services in Scotland will have to link with three times as many local authorities. These new authorities have to develop not only inter-authority co-ordination but also inter-sectoral co-ordination between health, education, housing and social work services. Concerned to match services to local requirements, local authorities may lose sight of progressive developments in other authorities, leading to increased regional variation in the range and quality of children's services nationally.

Better collaboration between social work and housing, however, will hopefully be found in the new unitary authorities where old divisions between district and local government no longer exist. New administrative structures are likely to emerge with a growing emphasis on decentralisation.

Chief Social Work Officers have been appointed to the new authorities and many are concerned to find a better balance in social work services for children between the protection of children's safety and the prevention of difficulties which hinder personal growth and development. This growing concern with the contribution of social work services to prevention should pave the way for better collaboration not only with housing but also with health and education.

Discussion

Children in need and their families run the risk of falling between the priorities of mainstream schools and the highly selective provision of social work and social services departments.[2] The Audit Commission Report (1994)[11] points to the importance of health, education and social work defining together what they mean by 'needs' and

> Principles which promote child welfare are needed as the way forward if the changes taking place in the philosophies and organisational structures of education, health and social work are to be used positively and collectively to preserve what is good in children's services and to make good what is wanting. These principles include equality of opportunity for all children; inclusion rather than exclusion from public life; normalisation to make the circumstances of all children as near to ordinary living as possible; best interests of children taking precedence; freedom from harm; partnership with parents and children from all communities; and social justice in the policies and practices which affect children's health and development.

developing together a joint strategy for children's services. Encouragement is given to the three agencies to take a more equal share in the responsibility to provide for children in need. Children's services plans, documents to be produced by social work/ services departments detailing plans for children's services to take account of links between health, education and social work, are seen as the way forward in the UK. They have already been implemented in England and Wales and appear in primary legislation in Scotland for the first time. Sutton (Chapter 4, p. 93) notes a lack of analytical tools in any of the three agencies to jointly identify the parameters of need or priorities for children's services.

In social work/social services the Audit Commission (1994)[11] calls for a re-balancing towards a greater emphasis on family support services drawn from a wider range of options in the community provided by voluntary bodies, health and education professionals. Health is asked, especially through GPs, to take a full and active participation in responding to health matters for children in need. Education is expected to accept joint ownership of the problem of disrupted education for children looked after by social work and social services. Family centres are proposed as a suitable focus for developing joint ventures between health, social work and education. These could act as an integrated base for child health clinics, peer support groups, nursery classes and other pre-school provision, and advice centres on housing and social security benefits. This recommendation is timely when many of the preventive and early intervention strategies such as Homestart, playgroups and youth work are under threat. At present, there is no infrastructure to ensure inter-agency and inter-disciplinary collaboration in setting the aims, philosophy and principles for children services in the UK.

Collaboration across health, education and social work has been significantly promoted and advanced in child protection[15] but has failed so far to generalise to children in need. Perhaps the principles to guide a system of integrated children's services have been less clearly articulated than those which have, for example, informed policy and practice for people with learning difficulties. Here an emphasis on normalisation and ordinary living has set the benchmark for services and has caused health, education and social services to find innovative and co-ordinated solutions in the community and to a lesser extent in residential care.[10]

The purchaser and provider split, the hallmark of community care legislation, is not formally directed at children's services, although it will be hard for local authorities to resist applying the same management to different service recipients whether they be young or old. This split, if pursued further than already is the case, will serve only to heighten the fragmentation of children's services, diluting responsibility and accountability rather than strengthening links between health, education and social work. Indications from England where the purchaser and provider split has gone further, with an associated growth in private children's services, confirm that accountability for children's services is becoming increasingly complex. This runs the risk that profit margins may prove a leading factor in determining the shape of children's services to come. Some families most in need of good quality children's services have few means, either material or political, by which to prevail on behalf of their children. Will families and children increasingly find themselves on the receiving end of a two-tier system?

The increased emphasis on the importance of consumer opinion found in community care legislation needs to be set against balancing the interests of parents, children and the wider community and recognising children and adults may have conflicting and competing claims. Children are economically and physically dependent on adults whose good faith they deserve but cannot command. Rarely do they attract political priority[10] as the conditions in which some children grow up described at the outset of this chapter confirm. If consumer opinion is to count, then children need a voice. Taking their wishes into account needs to be honoured in spirit as well as law.

The health and development of children may become an ever increasing artefact of locality unless the opportunity which confronts the new authorities is faced head on to develop a corporate approach to planning and auditing services for children and families.[10] Children's services need to be seen in the round, with policies and practices that are guided by principles which seek to ensure that a proper balance is struck, on the one hand between facing up to the reality that some children are in need of additional help if the social and material adversities they experience are to be mediated, and on the other overcoming the potentially stigmatising impact which a growing reliance on selective rather than universal services for children brings.

Principles which promote child welfare are needed as the way forward if the changes taking place in the philosophies and organisational structures of education, health and social work are to be used positively and collectively to preserve what is good in children's services and to make good what is wanting. These principles include equality of opportunity for all children; inclusion rather than exclusion from public life; normalisation to make the circumstances of all children as near to ordinary living as possible; best interests of children taking precedence; freedom from harm; partnership with parents and children from all communities; and social justice in the policies and practices which affect children's health and development.

Conclusion

Government and parents have a major role to play in ensuring the material and social support of children growing up in the UK today and in the future. Legislative changes

> The personal social services need to fight against the political and economic tide which pushes them to become services of last resort for children and families and instead to take a lead role in working together with other agencies to promote children and family services based on principles which social work upholds.

may bring a new emphasis on the continuity of parental responsibility for the upbringing of children in good times and in bad, yet governments need to face up to their responsibilities and to do their part by providing good quality services for all children. Education, health and social work services have undergone major reforms over the last decade. These have resulted in an increased role for private and voluntary agencies in children's services and a greater emphasis on cost efficiency. There has been a widespread drive to free schools from local authority control and to separate the purchasing of services from their provision in health and social work/social services. Concern remains whether these changes and cost cutting will lead to further fragmentation in children's services, failure to develop much needed early years services and loss of critical support services for families, already too thin on the ground. Local government reorganisation follows swiftly on the heels of these already considerable changes. How these new authorities will find a balance between local concerns and developments and inter-authority collaboration and co-ordination remains to be seen.

Of primary importance is the need to create comprehensive and family-centred services for the broad range of children in need of additional help. This selective principle is, however, only likely to work against a baseline of universal provision for young children with an emphasis on early years services in health and education. The personal social services need to fight against the political and economic tide which pushes them to become services of last resort for children and families and instead to take a lead role in working together with other agencies to promote children and family services based on principles which social work upholds. Children and their families need non-stigmatising and positive services. Child poverty and unfair shares for some children need to be combated. This is more likely to be achieved if parents and professionals work together in pursuit of putting children's welfare first.

References
1. Hills, J., *Inquiry into Income and Wealth* (York: Joseph Rowntree Foundation, 1995).
2. Wilkinson, R. G., *Unfair Shares: The Effects of Widening Income Differences on the Welfare of Young Children* (Essex: Barnardo's,1994).
3. Children in Scotland, *Scotland's Families Today* (Edinburgh: HMSO, 1995).
4. Rutter, M. and Quinton, D., *Parenting Breakdown: the making and breaking of intergenerational links* (Aldershot: Avebury, 1988).
5. Department for Education, 'A new deal for "Out of School" pupils' in *DFE News*, 126 1993.
6. Audit Commission/HMI, *Getting in on the Act: Provision for Pupils with Special Educational Needs: The National Picture* (London: HMSO, 1992).
7. Berrenta-Clement, J. R., Schweinart, L. J., Barnett, W. C., Epstein, A. S. and Weikart, D. P., *Changed Lives: The Effects of the Perry Pre-school Programme in Youths Through Age 19* (Ypsilanti: High Scope, 1984).
8. Cohen, B. and Fraser, N., *Childcare in a Modern Welfare System: Towards a New National Policy* (London: Institute for Public Policy Research, 1991).
9. CEC Women in Europe, *Childcare in Europe* (Brussels: CEC, 1990).
10. Jones, A. and Bilton, K., *The Future Shape of Children's Services* (London: The National Children's Bureau, 1994).

11. Audit Commission, *Seen But Not Heard: Co-ordinating Community Child Health and Social Services for Children in Need* (London: HMSO, 1994).

12. Farmer, E., 'The impact of child protection interventions: the experiences of parents and children', in *Child Abuse and Child Abusers: Protection and Prevention* Waterhouse (ed.) (London and Philadelphia: Jessica Kinsley Publishers, 1993).

13. Waterhouse, L., 'In defense of residential care', *Maladjustment and Therapeutic Education, Special Edition: Residential Care,* Wolff, S. (guest editor) (1987) vol. 5, no. 2, pp. 39–54.

14. Eekelarr, J. and Dingwall, R., *The Reform of Child Care Law: A Practical Guide to the Children Act 1989* (London: Tavistock/Routledge, 1990).

15. Hallett, C. 'Child protection in Europe: convergence or divergence?', *Adoption and Fostering,* (1993) vol. 17, no. 4., pp. 27–32.

2.2 CHANGES IN SCOTTISH EDUCATION
A PARENT'S PERSPECTIVE
Judith Gillespie
Convener, Scottish Parent Teacher Council

In looking at change in Scottish education over the last 10 years or so, it is possible to identify a number of distinct types of change emanating from separate sources and designed to serve different needs. These changes have been variously successful. Those which are most sympathetic to the needs and wishes of the people actively involved in education have worked best, whilst those which have been imposed for non-educational reasons have worked less well and are potentially the most damaging.

The rhetoric has been about involving parents in their children's education, but the policy has been about turning parents into consumers.

It is not surprising that the government, as the main source of funding for education, has been an important player in the process of change. It has focused on organisational changes arising from a policy decision to introduce market forces into education. These changes include the 'placing request' legislation[1], the introduction of school boards,[2] 'league tables',[3] the option of self-governing status,[4] devolved school management[5] and local government reorganisation.[6] The rhetoric has been about involving parents in their children's education but the policy has been about turning parents into consumers. It was envisaged that parents would use information provided by the 'league tables' to judge between good and bad schools, thereby essentially policing the system. However, parents on the whole have rejected the market model of education and have used their power as 'consumers' to inhibit the government's 'marketisation' programme.

'Placing request' legislation

From the parents' perspective probably the most popular of these changes is the 'placing request' legislation. Parents have a right to send their child to their local 'district' school but, under this legislation, can request a place at a non-district school. Such a request must be granted if there is space. The policy is sold as 'the parents' right to choose a school' but it should more properly be presented as their right to express a choice because, until there are elastic-sided schools with elastic-sided classrooms, then not all placing requests can be granted, particularly not to popular or magnet schools. This is a case where the rhetoric over-sells reality. In terms of satisfying the government's requirement that parents police the system by acting as consumers, then it has also failed, as parents have tended to choose schools on social grounds rather than strict educational grounds. Middle-class schools in the proverbial leafy green suburbs have become magnet schools more because of their natural client group than because of their superior educational provision.

School boards

In looking at the other strands of government-inspired change, parents have taken the rhetoric about parental involvement and used it for their own ends, rather than to deliver the market. So, school boards, which were born into a barrage of parental criticism, have been turned into support systems for schools by parents who were quite deliberate in their actions and knew exactly what they were doing. Self-governing status has been rejected as 'unfair' except in those few cases where parents have used it to protect their school. One of the most striking examples of parents hi-jacking government legislation was a Parents Action Group in the southside of Glasgow who used a loop-hole in the self-government schools legislation to prevent a school closure.[7] The parents had no intention of their school becoming self-governing. It was a clear case of parents using the government's rhetoric for their own ends.

Curriculum

The second level of change largely emanated from professional educationists and was intended to satisfy two needs—those of the increasing numbers of pupils staying on at school and those of employers. Comprehensive education and the raising of the school leaving age meant that more and more youngsters were staying on first to 16 and then beyond 16, so there was a need to provide them with worthwhile courses. This led first to Standard Grade and now the emergent Higher Still proposals, both of which are designed to give youngsters of all abilities worthwhile and appropriate courses which result in valued certification. Meanwhile, employers have asked those that draw up the curriculum to consider their requirements for a skilled workforce, so course content has been modified to satisfy work based requirements for more oral skills and more awareness of information technology (IT). The 5–14 programme was both a tidying up of the primary curriculum, a building on best practice, and a way to make the primary school mesh better with Standard Grade provision.

National testing

Parents have been rather outside these changes, partly because they see them as legitimately part of the professional preserve, and partly because parents have traditionally had no say in the curriculum. They have disliked some aspects, but they have lived with them—all except one where developments in the curriculum were used to introduce the market. I refer to the proposal to introduce national testing for all pupils in P4 and P7 regardless of their readiness to take such tests.[8] Parents saw the aim of the tests as being to establish standards by which schools would be measured.

> Parents saw the aim of the tests as establishing standards by which schools would be measured. They reacted as they did to all market orientated changes, with fierce and successful opposition ... Parents discovered they had the power to influence policy by simply withdrawing their children from the tests and making them unworkable.

They reacted as they did to all market orientated changes, with fierce and successful opposition. The objection was never to testing *per se*—parents on the whole like the rigour of tests—but to the particular form of test proposed. Parents discovered they had the power to influence policy by simply withdrawing their children from the tests and making them unworkable.

Child-oriented changes

The final area of change is totally child-oriented and arises largely from the kinds of attitudes which saw the introduction of the panel system to deal with young offenders. School was looked at more from the child's perspective, and behaviour which in previous years had been accepted, like bullying, or merely punished, like truancy, came to be viewed in a new light. In recent years, bullying is not only seen as being unpleasant, it is also unacceptable and something which schools can take steps to minimise, hence the growth in anti-bullying policies. Part of this has seen successful parental pressure to have playground supervisors in primary schools. On the truancy level, the government may be busy collecting statistics for use in its market model of education but, more sympathetically, schools and authorities are devising ways of keeping truants at school by addressing the reasons for their truancy. In a similar vein, many authorities are attempting a more child-centred approach to disruptive pupils. There are youth strategy schemes which aim to keep children in their local schools and bring in other agencies such as social workers and child psychologists to address their problems. Although all parents like the new approach to bullying there are divergent views over truancy and disruptive behaviour. Parents of more law-abiding youngsters tend to regret what they see as the negative impact of the new policies on *their* children's learning. However, what objection there is remains at the 'grumbling' level with a request for more resources to implement the policies properly, rather than being openly hostile.

Parents have tended to like and support those changes—to the curriculum and school environment—which they perceive as being designed to improve their children's experience at school. Where they have objected to such changes, their objections have taken the form of constructive criticism rather than outright hostility. However, the government's attempts to introduce a market system into Scottish education through organisational changes have run into obstructive opposition which has been remarkably successful.

Notes

1. All Scottish schools serve local districts and every child has a right to a place at his or her local district school. However parents can request a place at a different district school and this has to be granted if there is room once all the local district children who want a place have been accommodated. Placing requests can be refused if the school is physically full or if it would be necessary to employ an extra teacher to accommodate the placing request child/ren. Where there are more placing requests than there are places, the authority grants them according to published criteria which include considerations such as special needs, a sibling already at the school, distance from the school, and so forth.

2. School boards were set up in Scotland in 1989. They are small committees of parents, teachers and community representatives but with an overall parental majority – who can discuss with the headteacher aspects of the running of the school. Boards' actual powers are mainly limited to being involved in the appointment of senior staff, including the headteacher, and the right to veto the headteacher's proposals for how the money for school books and equipment is to be spent. Boards have the right to seek extra powers, but none have. Most boards are content to act as informal forums for discussing school concerns and to lobby the education authority and/or government on behalf of the school.

3. The government publishes comparative tables of school statistics on examination results, per pupil costs, truancy rates and school-leaver destinations. These comparative tables are popularly known as 'league tables'.

4. School Boards can take over the running of the school from the education authority if such a proposal is approved first in a ballot of all parents at the school and secondly, after due consultation, by the Secretary of State for Scotland. The school board then becomes a board of management and is fully responsible for the school including the hiring and firing of staff.

5. Devolved school management is a scheme whereby schools have control of at least 80 per cent of their 'at school' costs, including staffing costs. In practice their 'control' is limited as there are strict guidelines on minimum staffing standards and building costs are only open to limited variation.

6. Local government reorganisation has involved the nine mainland regional authorities – and 53 district authorities – being replaced by 29 new unitary authorities on April 1, 1996. The regions have been responsible for education but this responsibility is now discharged by the new unitary authorities.

7. The self-governing schools legislation states that a school cannot be closed whilst it is in the process of holding a ballot on whether it should become self-governing. The Southside Parents Action Group obtained a legal ruling that the same applied if such a ballot was being held in any associated school – for example, a primary school which feeds into the secondary school or a neighbourhood school which would take the children from the school once it was closed. They then held a series of such ballots in all the schools associated with the school under threat of closure.

8. It was proposed that all children in Primary 4 (aged 8) and Primary 7 (aged 12) were to be tested, using nationally prepared tests, over a six week period, regardless of at what stage individual children were in the curriculum. The aim was to produce test results which could be compared in order to identify good and bad schools.

2.3 BLACK VOLUNTARY ORGANISATIONS WORKING WITH CHILDREN

SURVIVING THE NINETIES

Julia Sudbury

Director of Sia, the National Development Agency for the Black Voluntary Sector

For Black[1] families in the UK in the 1990s, survival is often a struggle. Families are faced with overwhelming problems as they attempt to nurture and educate their children in a hostile environment. As social divisions increase and safety nets are dismantled, Black families are disproportionately affected by unsuitable housing, unemployment, poverty and ill health. For example Black women experience an unemployment rate of 16 per cent compared with white women at 6 per cent; similarly Black men's unemployment rate is twice that of white men.[2] The rise and attempted legitimacy of Far Right activity and racist violence, is putting stresses on families which are largely undocumented.[3] Black children continue to be failed by and excluded from the education system.[4] Yet, despite these overwhelming odds, Black families continue to survive. It is in the context of this struggle that Black voluntary organisations offer hope and support to many families.

A profile of the Black voluntary sector

Black voluntary organisations arose in the UK as a direct result of the exclusion from mainstream services experienced by Black families.[5] In many instances, this exclusion took the form of a colour bar, whereby Black families were turned away from housing, education and social opportunities. In many more cases, the 'bar' was more subtle, such as council housing allocations which excluded people who had not been in the borough for a minimum period of years. At times it was based on a failure to provide services which were culturally appropriate, or a refusal to recognise non-European languages. At other times, services were simply inaccessible because to access them would involve entering 'no go' areas, where high levels of racist violence and abuse were known to occur.

> The diverse range of problems facing Black communities meant that many organisations took on more than one role. Rather than evolving as issue-based groups, they arose out of communities and addressed the diverse needs of that community.

As a result, Black voluntary organisations were established to address a whole range of needs, from pre-school care to supplementary education, training, housing, education, entertainment, cultural activities and caring for elders. The diverse range of problems facing Black communities meant that many organisations took on more than one role. Rather than evolving as issue-based groups, they arose out of communities and addressed the diverse needs of that community. This holistic approach means that Black organisations are often more effective at supporting the child in the context of family issues and problems. A Black Women's Centre offering childcare provision, will probably also be able to offer advice on immigration, racial harassment, racism at school or claiming benefits. Yet such a centre is often marginalised from mainstream children's services because it is not recognised as a childcare agency.

The holistic approach is not the only feature of Black voluntary organisations which differs from mainstream statutory and voluntary agencies. Black voluntary organisations grow organically out of Black communities. They are the result of a direct experience of exclusion and discrimination. As such, Black voluntary organisations have an empowering role. In inner city communities, where there are high levels of unemployment, and where the majority of those in work will not have got through the 'glass ceiling', Black voluntary organisations provide the opportunity for people to gain experience, to access resources and to manage staff, buildings and finances. This is an empowering experience, not just for those that sit on the management committee, but for parents and volunteers who will also have a say in how the organisation is run. This active involvement of Black people at all levels of Black voluntary organisations creates real accountability to the communities they serve. It also provides an important role model for Black children growing up in an environment where positive images of Black people in senior positions are largely limited to children's books.

Funded to fail?

As the UK's Black communities become increasingly impoverished and marginalised, Black voluntary organisations have a vital role to play in the creation of opportunities for children. Yet the sector is facing a funding crisis. This crisis is located not just in the shrinking of public sector resources, but in a restructuring of funding to the independent sector which is disadvantaging Black voluntary organisations. There is a number of trends which are indicative of this restructuring. The first is the move towards a colour blind approach. Section 11 of the Local Government Act 1966 was the first 'race specific' public funding provision. Under the Act, local authorities could claim 75 per cent of expenditure on initiatives targeted at 'new commonwealth' communities, particularly in the field of language provision. While it was introduced to subsidise local authority expenditure on what was seen as an unwanted burden, Section 11 nevertheless created an opportunity for many Black voluntary organisations to access funds to deal specifically with problems facing their communities. The amalgamation of Section 11 along with other targeted funds such as Ethnic Minority Grant and the Urban Programme, into the Single Regeneration Budget in 1994 was a firm step towards a colour blind approach. As was anticipated by Black organisations,[6] this change created a net loss as Black voluntary organisations were squeezed out by larger mainstream players.

> The contract culture ... rather than creating a wealth of opportunities for specialist childcare, has led to dilemmas and further exclusion for Black voluntary organisations working with children.

The second trend is the shift from grants to contracts. For Black voluntary organisations, contracting for care has created two key problems. First, they may find that the 'purchaser' is not interested in purchasing specific services for Black children. This may lead to pressure for groups to provide services to white children, so altering the client group and changing the self help nature of the organisation. Secondly, Black organisations simply do not have the resources and time required to submit tenders and may lose out when they do due to the lack of savings associated with larger bidders. The contract culture, then, rather than creating a wealth of opportunities for specialist childcare, has led to dilemmas and further exclusion for Black voluntary organisations working with children.

Finally, and linked to the above points, there has been a government-led move towards 'partnership' as an essential part of funding. Over the past three years, central government has introduced new competitive schemes for urban regeneration. City Challenge, the first such scheme was superseded in 1994 by the Single Regeneration Budget which amalgamates all existing urban funding into one programme. These initiatives require local authorities, Training and Enterprise Councils, businesses and voluntary organisations to produce joint bids which then compete for a large investment into a given area. This requirement to work in partnership to access funds has led to the overnight creation of 'partnership consortia'. However, such partnerships have rarely looked at the unequal status of those around the table and have ignored those who have not been involved. Black voluntary groups have found themselves unable to influence the nature of bids or to access significant funds. The rhetoric of 'partnership' has clearly failed to deliver.

The pressure to conform

At a time when funding is threatened and Black children are subjected to poverty, racism and exclusion, Black voluntary organisations have a crucial role to play in campaigning for change. Historically, Black organisations have been instrumental in campaigns against bussing of school children, and more recently in the successful campaigns to prevent large cuts in Section 11 funding of work with children. Yet the current trend is toward one of conformity.

If the 1980s saw an upsurge in protest, as was witnessed in community uprisings in Toxteth, Handsworth and Brixton, the 1990s have seen Black communities taking a lower profile. Ironically, at a time when the Charity Commission is publicly recognising the validity of campaigning, many Black groups feel that their charitable status means that they cannot be seen to be involved in local politics. Similarly, the pressure to be seen as non-threatening in the context of competition for contracts has led to further conformity. The increasing professionalisation of childcare, and in particular the Children Act means that many organisations are taking on National Nursery Examination Board trained staff who may have little knowledge of community struggles and little inclination to become involved in local politics.

Meeting the challenge

Black voluntary organisations continue to meet the challenge of meeting the needs of Black children and families in an increasingly hostile and competitive environment. Yet the services which these organisations provide and, perhaps more importantly, the opportunity they offer for Black people to have a stake and a say in their local communities is under threat. Black groups are unique in the way in which they combine accountability, empowerment and essential services. This unique combination should be recognised and promoted by policymakers, funders and purchasers. It is an approach to working with children and families which many organisations have a lot to learn from.

Notes and References

1. Throughout this article I use 'Black' as a political colour which describes communities, in the UK context primarily African, Asian and Caribbean, which experience racism and exclusion. This term is not used to imply a supposed homogeneity of culture, language or background, but rather to capture the notion of a common cause within diverse experiences.
2. Equal Opportunities Commission, *Black and ethnic minority women and men in Britain 1994* (Manchester: EOC, 1994).
3. The figure for racial attacks in the UK varies from 80,000 (Commission for Racial Equality) to 130,000 (British Crime Survey). Both are likely to be underestimates given the very low level of reporting of such incidents. In any case, 'low level' racist abuse, graffiti and intimidation are certainly not included in such a figure. Hasnah Sheriff (VOLCUF, 1993) has given a revealing account of the impact on children of racial violence targeted at families.
4. Maud Blair has carried out revealing work on this issue and finds that while African Caribbean boys are more likely to be permanently excluded than white children, explanations given by school staff tend to blame the child's behaviour or background (Blair, in *Equalities News,* March 1995).
5. For an in depth exploration of the origins and nature of the Black voluntary sector, see Sika Valery Small, *From arts to welfare: a bibliography of the Black voluntary sector,* (London: Sia, 1994).
6. Medas, M., *From City Challenge to Single Regeneration Budget* (London: Sia, 1994).

2.4 REORGANISATION

TRENDS AND ISSUES IN NORTHERN IRELAND

Lynne Peyton

Assistant Director of Social Services, Southern Health and Social Services Board, Northern Ireland

Children's services have been caught up in organisational changes over two decades and have struggled to meet the very considerable needs of children in Northern Ireland. A new note of optimism has been introduced in the form of the Children (Northern Ireland) Order, due for implementation in late 1996. This major legislative reform should herald the most substantial investment in children's services for many years. It comes at a time of relative political stability following the cease-fire and when new opportunities to promote social inclusion and economic progress are being promoted by the European Union Peace and Reconciliation Initiative. The challenge is to ensure that developments are co-ordinated both centrally across government departments and by service providers and that local communities are fully involved to ensure that schemes and services consider local needs and issues.

Demography and social indicators of child care in Northern Ireland

In considering the challenge posed by the Children Order it is important to have a sense of the demographic and social indicators of child care need in Northern Ireland. With almost half a million children under 18 in a total population of 1.6 million, children represent a higher proportion of the Northern Ireland population than is the case in other parts of the UK.[1] Social factors influencing the delivery of services to children and families include changing family structures, low income and rural isolation. The numbers of children in lone parent households is estimated at 95,000, with an increase from 13 per cent in 1985 to 18 per cent in 1992 of families headed by lone parents.[2] Gross weekly household income in Northern Ireland in 1993 was only 86 per cent of the UK average level and within the Province there is a higher dependence on social security benefits.[3] Many families with young children live in thinly populated rural communities with consequent implications for resourcing and providing services.[4] Levels of day care provision are lower than in other European countries and there is heavy reliance on informal caring arrangements.[5] The average per capita expenditure on child care for Northern Ireland at £83, is lower than the average England local authority rate of £94 in 1991–2.[6] While there have been increases in the total housing stock and in the quality of provision during the 1990s, the Province compares unfavourably with England.[7]

Service delivery structures

There are also regional characteristics of the public sector in Northern Ireland that need to be understood. Throughout the UK there is growing concern about the

> It was assumed that Northern Ireland's model of integrated health and social services boards, unique within the UK, would secure the most effective use of available resources, but despite integration the service continued to be managed along professional lines and remained dominated by a health agenda and by acute sector spending.

impact of local government reorganisation, given that the trend generally is towards breaking service delivery structures up into smaller units. While the issues are similar, the Northern Ireland restructuring took place within a fundamentally different context. In Northern Ireland there are 26 district councils, made up of elected representatives, with responsibility for a range of public services including recreation and leisure, environmental health and building control functions. Most councils also have a community relations officer with responsibility for promoting activities on a cross-community basis by involving local people from both religious traditions. Unlike their counterparts in Scotland, England and Wales, they have no responsibility and little influence over social services, education and housing, all of which are provided by public bodies accountable through various governmental departments to the respective Minister. Until 1973, health services and personal social services were provided separately through a hospitals authority, a special care authority and through the health committees and welfare committees of six county councils. Since reorganisation in 1973 four integrated area health and social services boards, which are agents of the Department of Health and Social Services, have been responsible for providing the whole range of these services within a regional strategic plan. Public accountability was assured through the inclusion of elected representatives of district councils, churches and local communities on the area board. The personal social services committee of each board had a particular responsibility for discharging the board's statutory obligations with regard to children and young people.

It was assumed that Northern Ireland's model of integrated health and social services boards, unique within the UK, would secure the most effective use of available resources, but despite integration the service continued to be managed along professional lines and remained dominated by a health agenda and acute sector spending. The proportion of expenditure dedicated to personal social services (excluding monies transferred from social security to fund private residential care) has remained virtually unchanged over the past 10 years and represents less than 20 per cent of the Boards' total budgets.[8] The structure has been subject to numerous revisions leading to continual organisational change. Boards appointed general managers in 1986 and similar arrangements for general management were subsequently introduced at unit level, hence fragmenting the professional reporting arrangements and creating new lines of accountability.

Establishment of Trusts

Paradoxically, however, it was the attempt to achieve greater consistency in health care legislation between England and Wales and Northern Ireland that has created further unique arrangements for the delivery of personal social services within the Province. The model for trusts proposed in the White Paper *Working for Patients* was designed for health organisations in Great Britain and attempts to import it to Northern Ireland had a direct effect on child care services because of the integrated health and social services arrangements.[9] This raised issues as to how the statutory accountability for children's services could be effectively discharged within self-governing trusts whose members are not democratically elected and within which there could be tensions between a business culture and children's needs. Child care professionals also identified concerns with regard to potential inequality of service provision, inconsistency of practice across trusts, and more difficult liaison with universities, voluntary organisations and other statutory agencies. Consequently an appropriate amendment to the legislation was made in 1994 which built in a number of safeguards.[10]

In order to safeguard the interests of children and other vulnerable individuals each area board must appoint a director of social services who is a qualified social worker and a qualified social worker must similarly be appointed as an executive member of each Trust board. Appropriate schemes for the delegation of statutory functions by Trusts have now been approved by boards who retain the strategic responsibility for the devolved functions and a responsibility for monitoring the effectiveness and quality of the service in line with the board's responsibility as commissioner and purchaser of services. Directors are expected to assess the needs of the population in their area and prepare an annual report which includes their response to any identified needs. Trust chief executives are required to provide boards with evidence of their adherence to agreed schemes, including the outcomes of monitoring activity.

Children's legislation in Northern Ireland

> Responsibilities of local authorities to support children in need cannot be directly translated to heath and social services boards and the potential exists for social services departments to be isolated in attempting to discharge these responsibilities unless there is a strong central government inter-departmental lead, multi-agency ownership and substantial additional funding.

The Children Act (England and Wales) 1989 has greatly altered the shape of children's services with its emphasis on parental responsibility and family support, and only resorting to care proceedings when all other options have been exhausted. Its provisions did not however extend to Northern Ireland, where existing legislation in the form of the Children and Young Persons Act (NI) 1968 still applies. The Children (NI) Order 1995, closely follows the 1989 Act, and while there is broad support for the underlying principles, designed to ensure that the welfare of the child is paramount by ensuring that both the needs of children and their rights are respected, there have been difficulties in transferring legislation to the fundamentally different organisational structure. Clearly, responsibilities of local authorities to support children in need cannot be directly translated to health and social services boards and the potential exists for social services departments to be isolated in attempting to discharge these responsibilities unless there is a strong central government inter-departmental lead, multi-agency ownership and substantial additional funding. In recognition of this, an inter-departmental project board has been established to ensure co-ordinated implementation of the Children Order, accompanied by a 5 year package of financial investment geared mainly towards children who are most vulnerable, including those with disabilities. Evaluation of the Children Act has facilitated additional benefits for children within the Order, including the regulation of daycare services for children up to the age of 12, as opposed to age 8 in England and Wales and an independent guardian *ad-litem* service established as an agency which is separate from boards and Trusts. Professional staff from boards, Trusts, voluntary organisations and professional associations have also co-operated with the Department of Health and Social Services (DHSS) in drawing up the regulations and guidance which accompany the Order.

Co-ordination and partnership policy

Since the early 1990s agencies with an interest in children's services have examined opportunities for closer co-ordination, particularly with regard to early years services and their crucial role in the development of young children and in family support. The consequent joint policy document on 'Early Years' requires inter-agency co-operation in service planning, standard setting, monitoring and training.[11] It recognises and values the role of a thriving voluntary sector whose impact has been maximised since they organised under the umbrella grouping of Child Care Northern Ireland, a representative organisation involving more than 50 childcare voluntary agencies. It is now crucial that the DHSS, boards, Trusts and statutory bodies with responsibility for education, housing and other public services and voluntary organisations can co-operate and work in partnership to ensure improvements in the social and health status of the population, and particularly of children and families.

The Southern Health and Social Services Board provides an example as to how one purchasing authority is attempting to forge partnerships and networks which will assist its assessment of need, inform its purchasing strategy and monitor the standard and effectiveness of services within the new legislative and structural arrangements. The Board's long-standing tradition of collaboration is evidenced by its formal partnership with Child Care Northern Ireland and its strong and energetic multi-agency committees on child protection and early years services. Specialist child care committees focusing on foster care, adoption and residential care include representation from trusts and appropriate voluntary agencies. The need for collaboration with district councils and for accountability to its resident population across all programmes of care, has led the Board to establish a number of locality-sensitive purchasing teams which aim to establish close links with other service providers and create links whereby community opinions can be channelled back to the purchaser.

Since the establishment of the first Health and Social Services Trusts in April 1994, tensions between the purchaser and providers have been continually addressed and attempts made to complement the contracting process, which is not in itself sufficient to ensure full implementation of statutory child care responsibilities and the promotion of high quality family support programmes. Additional mechanisms have been agreed for monitoring schemes, setting and maintaining standards and for formal and informal collaboration on child care issues. These include joint assessments of local need and a corporately developed child care strategy which will form the basis of each trust's children's services plan.

The experiences of the Southern Health and Social Services Board and that of other boards in developing their individual arrangements, clearly demonstrate that collaboration and co-operation are the cornerstone on which to build future services.

There is energy, commitment and capacity at all levels to meet the challenge posed by the Children Order. Children are at last on the agenda. The issue now is how best to ensure their needs continue to be a priority in Northern Ireland.

Notes

1. Northern Ireland Office, Northern Ireland Census (Belfast, 1991).
2. Department of Health and Social Security, Northern Ireland Social Security Statistics (Belfast, 1993). Northern Ireland Continuous Household Survey.
3. Policy planning and research unit, Belfast, 1993. Family Expenditure Survey (1993), DHSS, Northern Ireland Social Security Statistics (Belfast, 1993); DSS Social Security Statistics (London, 1993).
4. K. F. McCoy, *Promoting Social Welfare. Second Annual Report of the Chief Inspector of Social Services in Northern Ireland*, (DHSS, 1995) p. 10.
5. Policy Planning and Research Unit, 'The Use and Demand for Child Care Services and Nursery Education among the Parents of Children Aged 0–7 in Northern Ireland' Occasional Paper No. 27 (Belfast, 1994).
6. Policy and Accounting Unit, Key Indicator Package 1991–92.
7. Northern Ireland Housing Executive House Conditions Survey (Belfast, 1991); English House Conditions Survey (London, 1991).
8. DHSS (NI) Summary of Health and Personal Social Services Accounts (Belfast, 1982/3–1990/1).
9. Department of Health and Social Services, Management Executive 'Working for Patients' (1991).
10. Health and Personal Social Services (NI) Order (Belfast 1994).
11. Department of Health and Social Services and DENI, *Policy on Early Years Provision for Northern Ireland* (Belfast, 1994).

Chapter 3

◆

PERSPECTIVES ON CHANGE: SCANDINAVIA

3.1 YOUTH POLICY IN TRANSITION
A SCANDINAVIAN REVIEW

Ola Stafseng
Senior Researcher, Norwegian Youth Research Centre

Young people: changing perceptions

In the immediate post-war era, the status of young people was very high because of the significance of their wartime role in the resistance. In all the Scandinavian countries this period saw young people becoming much more involved in public affairs and the political system and as a consequence, youth policy became a major focus as peace and democracy were rebuilt. Nordic institutions were established and the Council of Europe became an important body for educating youth and youth leaders.

Adolescence in the modern sense became visible during the 1950s. The first signs were a rapid growth in juvenile delinquency and serious riots in Oslo in 1956 when *Blackboard Jungle* (with its rock and roll soundtrack) was screened. Adolescence became a mythical, urban phenomenon, a lifestyle brought into Scandinavian communities by young sailors returning home with a capacity for conspicuous consumption. The majority of young people aged between 15 and 19 were at that time in paid employment.

The great transformation of adolescence took place in the early 1960s when government reforms made full-time education a majority activity. A parallel development was the emergence of 'leisure', defined as time and space for hedonistic pursuits. At the same time the traditional Calvinist view of free time was largely consigned to history as belonging to older generations.

Young people in the '60s had easy access to the labour market, marriage and housing … Post-war adolescence in Scandinavia enjoyed new and increased resources as well as age-appropriate institutions, and this led to its acceptance as an independent and distinct life phase.

Awareness of the underlying demographic factors regulating adolescence is a phenomenon of recent years. From 1950 to 1970 the proportion of young people changed from nearly 1:6 to almost 1:4 of the overall population,[1] which might explain why the 1960s is regarded as a particularly youth-centred decade. The economic importance of young people grew even faster during the same period. Young people in the 1960s had easy access to the labour market, marriage and housing. Large increases were also observed in the numbers of young people taking some form of further or higher education. Post-war adolescence in Scandinavia enjoyed new and increased resources as well as age-appropriate institutions, and this led to its acceptance as an independent and distinct life phase. These trends continued until the 1980s, boosted by the increased birth rate of the 1960s.

This pattern changed as the increase in women in employment led to young people's declining demographic importance, reducing their priority in relation to welfare benefits. By 1990, due to the low birth rates of the 1970s, the number of adolescents within the population returned to its former proportions. This trend looks set to continue towards the year 2000.

Changing patterns of participation in society

Changing interactions between family, education and work have now led to a shift from a psychological perspective on adolescence to a broad cultural view, and from vocational guidance to the study of adolescents as consumers and a focus on adolescent lifestyles.

This change of emphasis stems from the attempt to understand the nature of young people's participation in society in responding to current issues. Early entrance into adulthood through employment, personal income and early marriage has now been transformed into an extended period of dependency on family and/or state subsidies (such as study loans or social benefits). Young people's lives today are much further removed from independent economic activity than previously, leading to a sense of alienation and a lack of adult responsibility.[2]

There is a wide range of formal and informal clubs and associations whose primary focus is young people. Most of the formal associations—Christian and secular as well as occupational and leisure—have traditions going back to the last century, whilst other organisations (sports clubs in particular) developed mainly after the First World War. Towards the end of the 1940s the term 'non-organised youth' was introduced to refer to a potential problem group. Youth associations and the state co-operated in promoting the value of organised activities for young people. The more recent concept of 'youth clubs' has mainly developed with support from the public sector. During the last decade other concepts of organised group activity have been recognised, including *ad hoc* and informal 'get-together' groups and youth subcultures.

At present 65 per cent of 16–24-year-olds are members of one or more formal associations, and 50 per cent of these are active members. Both membership and

> As many as 95 to 97 per cent of Norwegian teenagers have experienced being a member of a youth association ... The exception to this pattern is to be found among immigrant youth in the larger towns

activity decrease with age, and the decline is sharper among young women than young men. Differences in local ecologies mean that opportunities for organised activities vary from region to region. A comparison of 15-year-olds in various local communities shows that between 70 and 74 per cent are members of organisations, while an additional 21–4 per cent have at some time been members. This indicates that as many as 95–7 per cent of Norwegian teenagers have experienced being a member of a youth association. The figures highlight the large turnover of members, and the change in membership with increasing age.[3] The exception to this pattern is to be found among immigrant youth in the larger towns.

New technology and the mass media have further established the characteristics of modern adolescence. Informal group activity has been – and still is – important to young people as can be seen from the numbers attending cinemas, pop concerts and discotheques. Young people also make up the largest user group for more traditional facilities such as libraries and museums. Together with personal computers and pop music, these cultural activities have blurred the edges of the transitional stage between childhood and adolescence. Children aged between 7 and 10 are already familiar with many of the activities mentioned, and they have acquired many of the skills and symbols that have hitherto been a distinguishing factor of young people, their culture and lifestyle.

A history of youth policies

Between 1945 and 1960, youth associations and sports activities combined to occupy a very strong position in society, and the Social Democrats were of particular importance in this respect during the rebuilding of the society at this time. In Norway, youth and sports schemes were funded through the introduction of state football pools from 1949. There were similar arrangements in the other Scandinavian countries. The grants made it possible to develop a municipal infrastructure for youth and sport services. Sports facilities were built locally in schools, the premises of local associations and community centres. This policy was generally successful, and by establishing such an infrastructure, Scandinavian countries were to prove able to cope with the challenges ahead.

Youth policy was linked from the start with leisure and recreational policies. From the beginning, sports clubs and voluntary associations collaborated with the state through the National Youth Councils in developing youth policies. Initially, voluntary associations refused any financial support from the state, regarding it as a threat to their autonomy, but from the 1960s onwards state support became increasingly important for their survival. The same model has been applied throughout Scandinavia.

The modernisation of youth policy and new methods of youth work at the municipal level were introduced within a social policy perspective. The first clubs for non-organised youth were established during the 1930s, with the prevention of youth delinquency as a main aim. In the late 1960s such initiatives included prevention of anti-social tendencies, new methods in the promotion of mental health, and drug abuse prevention. The non-organised activities included street outreach work, community action and night shelters.

Further experimentation and consolidation of policy continued until the end of the 1970s. Government co-operation across Scandinavia resulted in a high degree of co-ordination of work with young people, and a broader youth-policy concept developed during the next decade. At both national and local level there was a need for a holistic political and administrative approach to young people. Administrative and professional specialism tended to divide young people up and label them as drug addicts, drop outs, jobless or homeless and turn them into clients of functionally appropriate agencies, regardless of any abilities or talents they possessed in other parts of their lives.

> Existing schemes were developed to meet the needs of teenagers, but there is now an increasing number of young adults finding it difficult to move on from adolescence since they lack the economic advantages of their predecessors when entering adulthood.

The shift from Social Democratic to Conservative governments in Norway and Sweden in the early 1980s did not change the basic assumptions underlying modern youth policies. Both governments constructed schemes to bring about an integrated state youth policy. The social welfare services were asked to co-operate with traditional youth organisations as well as agencies like the police and environmental authorities.[4] This strategy of integration created opportunities for socialisation and learning. However, in retrospect, it has become evident that the main aim was to modernise the state administration through responsibility being given to one Youth Minister who would promote the integration of policies on welfare, education, work, leisure, and so on. This move has also been strengthened by co-operation within the Nordic Council of Ministers and, since 1985, by regular ministerial-level conferences on youth within the Council of Europe. This international infrastructure encouraged public investment in promoting research relating to young people.

Despite these developments and increased resourcing, youth policy today is finding it difficult to respond to the problems resulting from the extended period of dependency experienced by a growing number of young people. Existing schemes were developed to meet the needs of teenagers, but there is now an increasing number of young adults finding it difficult to move on from adolescence since they lack the economic advantages of their predecessors when entering adulthood. The current agenda on youth policy is dominated by housing, taxes, the division of welfare between generations, cheap loans and plenty of well-paid work for young people.[5]

Youth policy development

Two main developments in the modernisation of youth policies can be identified. The first relates to the nature of the system under which such policies are implemented, and the second concerns the way in which the problems to be addressed have changed.

Local authorities have a strong legal and political tradition in Scandinavia. Since the mid-1970s, all Scandinavian countries have developed a programme of decentralisation, dividing responsibilities for public policy between municipal, county and national governments.

The process of decentralisation has been led by the principle of 'subsidiarity', meaning that no decision making takes place on a higher level than necessary for its own efficiency. The structure of the administrative system in Scandinavia is thus the result not of bureaucratic diktats, but of ideas about local democratic control and decision-making in the public sector.[6] It also reflects ideas about the efficient structuring of public services, starting with general competence at the lower levels and moving on to specialised services higher up. This model leads to the principle of 'lowest-efficient-service-level', applied for example to the health service at the beginning of the 1970s.

Youth issues and services are handled at all administrative levels although the municipality acts as the main provider with primary responsibility. Youth organisations provide an example of how this works: basically, they are local associations with additional regional and national branches which in some instances serve as 'umbrella organisations'. The principal level at which they function is locally, supported by the municipality, while the county may support training for youth leaders and the state supports national and international policy activities.

Another illustration is the changing nature of state involvement following the closure of the National Youth Councils. Development schemes and projects are often partly financed by the state, with the aim of developing models for use in monitoring other areas of work with young people.

The need to modernise administrative systems grew out of the changing nature of the now pressing problems affecting young people. Three types of problem illustrate this particularly well.

The first, *youth unemployment,* was perceived in the 1970s as a problem to be handled by the labour market authorities alone. The phenomenon was later seen in terms of changes in the transition between work and school, which meant that youth unemployment should not only be examined by departments of employment, but perhaps primarily by the education authorities.

Secondly, *child abuse, juvenile delinquency or inadequate parenting* might be picked up by child welfare agencies or the police. Traditionally, decisions relating to these areas were made by the courts or child welfare committees since the responses frequently involved specialised use of foster care, special schools, juvenile rehabilitation institutions and so on. During the 1970s and 1980s a new strategy developed: whereas traditionally the child or young person was transferred *out* of the community, continuity of community life became a basic principle. Specialised agencies then became dependent on nurseries, schools, local probation officers or leisure associations, which led to the need for inter-agency and multi-disciplinary co-operation.

Thirdly, the concept of leisure as *recreation time*, in contrast to working or schooling, has changed. Analysis of modern youth cultures revealed that the traditional monopoly of the school in relation to knowledge was decreasing – or changing. New and important skills and abilities were developed by young people themselves, through music, satellite television, micro-electronics or peer group interaction.[7] The educational system needs to consider the increasing importance of informal learning and self-education. However, the barriers which often exist between communities, educational institutions and leisure activities can make this difficult.

The way forward

> The varied nature of problems and issues relating to young people requires a wide ranging integrated administrative and professional approach.

Other examples underline the direction in which youth policy is currently moving. One of the main problems lies in the increasing specialisation of professionals and administrators. The varied nature of problems and issues relating to young people requires a wide-ranging integrated administrative and professional approach, but state youth policy has neither the capacity nor the ability to organise it: the state could, however, use its authority and financial resources to encourage integration at the municipal level, which is already geared to this way of working. A framework for a higher degree of integration might be described as *horizontal*—between sectors—and *vertical*—between levels—aiming at a comprehensive and flexible youth policy.

Regardless of state activity, young people in Scandinavia—as in most Western countries—have tended to see more opportunities in the workings of market forces, at least in relation to the cultural affairs that affect them most.[8] This phenomenon led to interminable inquiries and studies of the welfare state, not all of which were focused on youth issues. Social sciences departments joined in, and there were a number of outcomes that influenced further modernisation of the public sector in general and youth policy in particular.

As the Scandinavian welfare states have been reformed, there has been a move toward 'civil society' and the encouragement of 'citizenship'. For example, 10 to 15

> A reduction in professional power is highly appropriate for youth policy, since the autonomous life world of the young person's community is one of the basic and enduring ideas in theory and practice.

years ago the state of the art treatment for young drug addicts was psychiatry, leading to a considerable strengthening of the profession. The ideal method for treating mental illness was individual analysis within a closed institution. Today, these methods have changed, tending towards educational training of the whole person, challenging the individual with an emphasis on group work through social and physical activities. And the training is not isolated from the community, it is visible; further, a background of drugs is not kept as a secret.

All these developments have had an illuminating effect both on policies and on the social sciences. In policy terms, there is a new focus on the voluntary sector, now defined as the 'third sector'. In the social sciences analytical concepts such as 'life world' and 'system' have arisen in tandem with a new community/society distinction, influencing many familiar approaches to welfare today. More fundamentally perhaps, a reduction in professional power is highly appropriate for youth policy, since the autonomous life world of the young person's community is one of the basic and enduring ideas in theory and practice.

Notes and References

1. Norwegian data, but typical for other Scandinavian countries. Hurrelmann, K. (Ed.) *Handbook on Adolescence* (London: Greenwood Press, 1994).
2. Christie, N., *Hvor tett et samfunn* (Oslo: Universitetsforlaget, 1975).
3. Ungdata, unpublished figures from database (Oslo: Norwegian Youth Research Centre, 1992).
4. Kirke-og undervisningsdepartementet, *Ungdommen og samfunnet. Rapport nr. 9 til Stortinget* (Oslo, 1982–3).
5. Østeraas, B. T.m *Motvindgenerasjonen* (Oslo: LNU, 1992).
6. This is an important reason for the sceptical resistance towards the European Union in Scandinavia because the EU is conceived as a bureaucratic mammoth with small democratic ambitions.
7. Stafseng, O., *Ungdomskultur og språksosialisering,* in H. Hansson et. al., *Barns Bildspråk* (Stockholm: Carlssons, 1991).
8. Stafseng, O., 'Ungdomskultur og språksosialisering', in H. Hansson *Barns Bildspråk* (Stockholm: Carlssons, 1991).

3.2 REFORMING SOCIAL WELFARE

GOVERNMENT INITIATIVES IN DENMARK

Annette Poulsen

Head of Child and Family Policy, Ministry of Social Affairs, Denmark

Many changes are now taking place in the social welfare provisions of Danish municipalities and counties. The social sector is faced with huge challenges. It will be necessary to find new and more efficient ways of solving problems with limited public resources as well as developing new ways of interacting with users, professionals in many fields and administrative sectors. This need for renewal is reflected in a number of centrally initiated and supported projects implemented by counties, municipalities, voluntary organisations, enterprises and local communities.

Local political responsibility and user participation

In the mid-1990s, the decentralisation process has widened and stretches further down; some areas of decision making and more responsibility are being transferred from county and municipal councils to institutions, personnel groups, staff, user groups and individuals.

When decentralisation was introduced to the public sector in the mid-1970s it was mainly a matter of transferring functions from the national government to counties and municipalities. In the mid-1990s, the decentralisation process has widened and stretches further down; some areas of decision making and more responsibility are being transferred from county and municipal councils to institutions, personnel groups, staff, user groups and individuals. The traditional administrative processes, in which *politicians* allocate funding, *professionals* determined the nature and form of services, and *the users* only received services, no longer applies. Today, both the nature and content of services are informed by the views of users as well as being more directly the responsibilities of politicians at a local level. This shift in power places new demands on politicians, in the municipalities and counties as well as centrally at the level of national government.[1]

Within services to children and young people, decentralisation has been reflected in new legislation involving parent boards and young people's participation in youth clubs. Living conditions for parents of children with special needs have also been strengthened considerably through public welfare measures.

Decentralised provision and centralised initiatives

Denmark's 14 counties and 275 municipalities are autonomous, politically governed administrative units, with their own tax base. County and municipal councils are elected through democratic elections every four years. Local councils, that is municipalities, provide services addressing locally perceived problems. They are responsible for a wide range of social welfare services including early years services, rehabilitation and care of the elderly as well as retraining; they are also responsible for supporting the non-insured unemployed in addition to primary and lower-secondary education. All municipalities, regardless of size, have similar political, economic and practical responsibilities concerning the implementation of social policy. More than half of the municipalities have a population of less than 10,000, whilst the smallest ones have about 3000 and the largest one has almost 500,000.

County councils administer functions requiring overall regional solutions or specialised knowledge. Counties advise municipal authorities on the treatment and support of vulnerable groups and on professional development in various fields. Counties also provide counselling, for example, for parents with disabled children. Finally, vocational training for young people is a county responsibility.[2]

'Pools' are strategic government programmes which bridge a centrally perceived gap between national government and county and municipal councils. Funding is made available by the central government, for which public authorities at lower levels can apply in order to develop local projects.

Throughout the 1980s framework legislation and delegation of functions downwards from the national level have been supplemented by government *puljepolitikk* (pools), covering several areas within public administration. Pools are strategic government programmes which bridge a centrally perceived gap between national government, county and municipal councils. Funding is made available by the central government, for which public authorities at lower levels can apply in order to develop local projects. The projects must conform with a set of centrally set criteria, and in most cases the successful public authority applicant must put as many resources into the project as they receive through the 'pool'. However, the funding made available to the pools is relatively small compared with the resources administered by county and municipal councils. The pool policies promote a wide range of centrally determined political goals, without undermining the autonomy of the counties and municipalities. The pools of the Ministry of Social Affairs have always had the purpose of promoting explicitly stated strategies affecting local service provision and developing new methods in service delivery; they usually involve targeted groups. The central 'pool' policies are meant to be seen as a supplement to the framework legislation, enabling the government to influence the quality of service provision and signal areas which should be given priority.

Child and family policy: inter-ministerial collaboration

In Denmark, general child and family policies are developed at a national level. The Ministry of Social Affairs lays down the general framework and conditions. Specific

The Inter-Ministerial Committee on Children (IMCC) was set up in 1987 as an interdisciplinary co-operative body and currently has 16 ministers represented. The establishment of the IMCC reflects the decision made in Denmark not to let just one ministry act as the competent body to deal with child and family affairs.

measures and services are implemented and resourced by the county or the municipality. The Inter-Ministerial Committee on Children (IMCC) was set up in 1987 as an interdisciplinary co-operative body, currently with 16 Ministers represented. The establishment of the IMCC reflects the decision made in Denmark not to let just one ministry act as the competent body to deal with child and family affairs. The present policy is to involve several ministries, drawing on their respective areas of competence. The main objective of the IMCC is to create coherence and unity in areas relating to children and families, and to take initiatives across sectors to improve the living conditions for children and young people. The Minister of Social Affairs chairs the IMCC and has the secretariat function.[3]

The municipalities and counties in Denmark are currently implementing an *Action Plan for Children and Young People Most at Risk*.[4] This is but one example of the pool policies, and additional resources are made available to the councils through applications from 1995 to 1998. The government's IMCC has agreed on the plan which has been prepared by an inter-ministerial group of civil servants. The starting point for the Action Plan is that children's own natural capacity to cope with stress and difficulties must be strengthened through support. This sometimes involves very intensive support from adults in care-taking roles. Ten concrete initiatives for developing new methods of such service provision are outlined in the Action Plan. Central to the Action Plan is the development of multi-disciplinary work and collaboration between services. Several projects are to be set up all over the country during the late 1990s. All projects will be evaluated and the results will be made available to all public authorities.

Unemployment: the ultimate challenge

Research indicates that the majority of children in Denmark today are growing up under materially good conditions.[5] During the last couple of decades, however, industrial and social developments have taken their toll. Unemployment has left its traces on the social fabric of the country. Therefore, the future of today's children is much less predictable than it was only one generation ago. Children are expected to be adaptable and parents are expected to provide parenting which ensures that they provide a 'holistic' and safe environment for their children—adults providing a stable framework for children in an unpredictable world. A relatively small group of children and young people, approximately 10–15 per cent, do not benefit from such stable and predictable circumstances.[6] This socially disadvantaged group has not grown smaller in recent years. Many of them are young parents who have never had a job. Through the pool policies there is a growing public commitment to bring adults and children's needs into focus, trying to avoid further marginalisation of this group.

References

1. Sociale Tendenser 1995. *Det Sociale Informations—og Analysesystem* (København: Socialministeriet, April 1995).
2. Ministry of Social Affairs. *National Report. World Summit for Social Development* (Copenhagen: Denmark, 1995).
3. Regeringens Børneudvalg. *Handlingsplan for de svagest stillede børn og unge* (København: Socialministeriet, February 1994).
4. *SIBU – puljen* and *KLUB – puljen.*
5. The Inter-Ministerial Committee on Children. *Children and Young People in Denmark. Growing Up in the 1990s* (Copenhagen: Ministry of Social Affairs, May 1992).
6. Per Schultz Jørgensen *et al. Risikobørn. Hvem er de – hva gjør vi?* (København: Socialministeriet, 1993).

3.3 TRANSLATING GOOD INTENTIONS INTO PRACTICE

IMPLEMENTING THE UN CONVENTION ON THE RIGHTS OF THE CHILD IN SWEDEN

Louise Sylwander
Children's Ombudsman, Sweden

As a signatory of the United Nations Convention on the Rights of the Child (the UN Convention), Sweden has committed itself to providing greater respect for the child as an individual. The Children's Ombudsman Office (*Barnombudsman*) was established on 1 July 1993 as part of the process of strengthening the rights of Swedish children and young people under the Convention.

The Children's Ombudsman was given the task of monitoring children's and young people's rights, and especially those of children at risk. The Ombudsman has three main duties:

- representing the views of children and making their voices heard;
- showing how the needs of children, as expressed by children, can be better provided for in different sectors of our society; and
- monitoring Sweden's ability to implement its obligations to children and young people in respect of the UN Convention.

This contribution outlines the context in which the Ombudsman's office operates in Sweden and some of the early areas of work.

Services to children and young people in Sweden

Viewed internationally, children and young people in Sweden have a relatively high standard of mental and physical health, free access to medical and social services, a variety of cultural and recreational amenities, good housing and educational opportunities. For some groups in Sweden, however, the improvements in general welfare during the second half of this century have come to a standstill, or even receded. The main reasons for this lie in the economic changes in the 1980s and 1990s, coupled with rising unemployment. As a consequence governments at national, regional, county and local municipal levels lost tax revenue. Sweden has also seen a growth in social segregation between ethnic minorities and the Swedes, and between different housing areas. The losers are often the youngest section of the population, especially those already at a disadvantage, for example, immigrants, families hit by unemployment and those in need of special support, including those with physical or mental disabilities. In addition there is an increasing number of children at risk, for example, refugee children, children subjected to sexual abuse and maltreatment, and children from families where parental care fails for various reasons.

Maternal and child health services are a county council responsibility, whilst the main responsibility for providing services to children and young people remains with the municipality—pre-school and after school services, education, leisure centres, youth clubs, schools and social services. Municipal and county council services are financed mainly by taxation revenue with additional user charges. A small number (around 10 per cent) of pre-school services and schools are run by non-governmental organisations or groups of parents, and they too receive national or municipal grants. In addition there are many voluntary and religious organisations which arrange leisure and sporting activities, as well as providing supportive and advisory services for any member of the family. Many of these activities are also financially supported by the municipalities.

The work of the Ombudsman

> The Ombudsman has recognised the need to direct more effort towards the municipal councils, because that is where the power rests in deciding whether or not the principles and requirements of the UN Convention will make a real and sustainable impact on Swedish society.

The UN Convention has acquired a certain currency in Sweden but, if it is to be properly implemented, it needs to be better known. One of the first actions undertaken was therefore to establish an information service. An information leaflet and statistical folder on children and young people are widely distributed, free of charge, as well as a wide range of reports which aim to promote discussion on a variety of children's issues and children's rights.

Several of the articles in the Convention may provide the basis for adopting a child's perspective within legislation and services. Among the important articles are: Article 2, the principle of non-discrimination; Article 3, the principle of the child's best interests; Article 12, the right of children to express their own views and to have them respected; and Article 4, laying down that the Parliament shall use all resources available to provide for the rights laid down in the Convention.

Unlike many other countries, Sweden has legislation which asserts children's rights and society's obligations towards children's need for help and support. However, some aspects of current legislation are inadequate in relation to the requirements in the Convention. The Ombudsman's office has therefore given priority to work related to drawing attention to such deficiencies in the Swedish legislation. One such area is the handling of refugee and asylum-seeking children and the need to strengthen the rights and principles of the UN Convention in relation to these children within the Swedish Aliens Act. Amendments were prepared for the Act but failed to become law. In addition, legal possibilities are still lacking for children and young people to influence public decision making, at both a national and local level where services are provided.

Some legislative amendments initiated by the Ombudsman have already been put into effect or are being processed by the government or the Parliament. Examples of legislative changes, stressing the principles of *the child's best interest* and *the right to be given a hearing*, include the Social Services Act and the Code of Parenthood and Guardianship.

The Ombudsman has no formal powers to make recommendations, but proposals include:

- making it a criminal offence to be in possession of child pornography
- requiring municipal authorities to consult children and young people in matters that directly concern them
- giving municipalities clearer guidelines on how to implement the principles in the UN Convention
- the government should draw up a separate Child and Youth Affairs Appendix to its annual Budget Bill
- children and young people should be entitled not only to information but also to protection from information potentially harmful to them, such as media violence
- children and young people should be entitled to be protected from victimisation or other degrading treatment.

Whilst legislation is the responsibility of government, services to children, young people and their families are mainly a municipal responsibility. Increasing autonomy as a result of decentralisation has given the municipalities more discretion in the allocation of resources and the planning of service delivery. These changes have led to services being reorganised, priorities redefined and expenditure reduced. The Ombudsman has recognised the need to direct more effort towards the municipal councils, because that is where the power rests in deciding whether or not the principles and requirements of the UN Convention will make a real and sustainable impact on Swedish society.

A survey undertaken by the Children's Ombudsman in the spring of 1995[1] on the implementation of the UN Convention at a municipal level revealed that so far only a few municipalities have acted explicitly on the recommendations in the Convention in formulating policies and delivering services to children and young people. However, the majority of municipalities are showing a great deal of interest in acquiring information and knowledge about the Convention and ways of translating it into practice in actual service provision.

In its first report to the Swedish Government in 1994, the Ombudsman's office has proposed that the municipalities should now conduct their own surveys, focusing on the needs of children and young people with a view to developing a considered policy approach based on the child's perspective. This should involve the municipalities drawing up special action plans for children and young people, describing their situation and proposing ways of developing and improving their conditions. The Convention has already been used to put pressure on groups such as school management, teachers and recreation leaders, to fulfil their responsibility in informing children and young people about their rights.

> Whilst the adult world appears to be increasingly willing to listen to and respect the views of children, regarding them as individuals in their own right, it remains to be seen whether society has adequate resources to cater for children's needs and give sufficient priority to children's services.

Looking ahead

The situation for children and young persons today and for the immediate future is likely to be dominated by two conflicting lines of development. Whilst the adult world appears to be increasingly willing to listen to, and respect, the views of children, regarding them as individuals in their own right, it remains to be seen whether society has adequate resources to cater for children's needs and give sufficient priority to children's services.

The Ombudsman aims to increase awareness of the UN Convention in order to improve the conditions of children and youth. The main strategy, in addition to initiating legal amendments, is to disseminate information on the Convention to all municipal authorities, enabling them to rethink and replace insufficient service structures, practices and attitudes. This is a process demanding both time and energy. The Children's Ombudsman, together with many other agencies in Sweden, has an important part to play in this process, both today and in the future.

Reference
1. Barnombudsmannen. *På spaning efter barn konventionen – En kommunstudie* (Stockholm, 1995).

3.4 REFORMS IN THE NORWEGIAN EDUCATIONAL SYSTEM

A TEACHER'S PERSPECTIVE

Arna Meisfjord

Pedagogical Section, Norwegian Union of Teachers

This contribution presents some of the main features of the extensive and wide-ranging reforms which are currently being introduced in the Norwegian educational system. It also focuses on some traditional educational values, which in my view should be preserved and developed further to strengthen the quality of the school system. The comments on the changes will be made from the point of view of the Norwegian Union of Teachers.[1]

Educational reforms

At present, the entire Norwegian educational system, from daycare through to university, is undergoing major change. The reforms comprise changes relating to organisation and administration as well as financing. All legislation concerning daycare and education is being revised. New national curricula[2] are being developed both for primary, secondary and upper secondary education. Through these reforms, young people (age 16–19) have been given the *right* to three years upper secondary education (Reform 94).[3] From the school year 1997–8, the age at which children start school will be lowered from seven to six. The period of compulsory education will therefore be extended from 9 to 10 years (Reform 97).[4] The new national curriculum will take effect from the same date.

The school day is relatively short in Norway (20 hours a week for the younger pupils). Schools will now be expected to establish activities in the afternoon for all children in the age groups 6 to 10. The national government is putting extra money into this scheme, which is considered to be an important family policy reform with the main objective to take care of children while parents are at work. So far, the focus has been on establishing places for all children, but it is the government's intention to build some pedagogical qualities into this service.

Norwegian tradition of comprehensive education

In Norway, the majority of children and young people living in the same district attend the local school. All public schools have the same overall objectives and their

> Educational opportunities should not depend on whether the family is rich or poor, whether they live in a town or in the countryside, or whether the children are boys or girls.

work is based on a common national curriculum. This is what is meant by the term 'comprehensive school'. This educational system has been developing over a long period of time, based on a strong popular wish as well as a broad political agreement that all children should have equally good opportunities for schooling and learning. In Norwegian educational policy it has, therefore, been important that all schools should have good and, as far as possible, equal economic and material conditions to carry out their activities. Educational opportunities should not depend on whether the family is rich or poor, whether they live in a town or in the countryside, or whether the children are boys or girls. Also, disabled pupils should have the same opportunities as others. Recent reforms have given all children with special needs the right to go to the ordinary local school. Teachers have supported this reform, although both parents and teachers often have to fight to get the resources necessary to give adequate education to these pupils. It is also seen as important that children and young people from ethnic and language minorities should receive just as good schooling as other children of the same age. In this way, the school has been regarded as a means to eliminate social differences and create greater justice in society.

There are very few private schools in Norway, compared with most other European countries. Thus, less than 1.5 per cent of the compulsory school age population attend private schools. The private schools which do exist, are based either on an alternative pedagogical philosophy, such as Waldorf schools or on a religious foundation other than the Evangelical Lutheran doctrine of the Norwegian State Church.

Decentralisation/centralisation trends

The changes being made represent conflicting tendencies. The revision of the legislation has a primary objective to bring the Education Act in harmony with the newly revised Municipal Act (1994), giving priority to ideas of decentralisation and greater local freedom. Thus, in the areas of budgeting, organisation and administration nearly all decisions are to be made at the municipal level.

The revision of the national curriculum, on the other hand, is based on a belief that there is a need for stronger national control over the *content* of the teaching, and a more prescriptive national curriculum. The professional freedom given to teachers in the present *Mønsterplanen* 1987—National Curriculum (M87)—is now being substantially restricted. The M87 was presented as curriculum guidelines, outlining both the overall and general objectives, and the subject specific objectives. In these curriculum guidelines the subject matter is presented in 3-year blocks, with a progression in each subject based on the 'spiral' principle – topics and subject matter are being repeated several times, with increasing degree of difficulty according to the intellectual development of the pupils. Within this framework, the teachers have a common responsibility to select topics and decide on progress and working methods, based on an assessment of the capabilities of the pupils, and of course taking into consideration that the teaching should be interesting and relevant, and have a bearing on the local community surrounding the school. These are all aspects of the locally organised curriculum work, which was introduced in the M87.

The new national curriculum document is divided into three parts: one general part, comprising both compulsory and upper secondary education, outlines the common basis and the overall objectives, and is called 'the Core Curriculum'; the second part, referred to as 'the Bridge', specifies the general principles applicable to compulsory education; and the third part presents the subject specific curriculum. The curriculum is no longer presented as guidelines. Instead of 3-year blocks there are now specifications of content matter and progression for each school year, with educational objectives being changed from 'open' objectives, giving direction to the work, into specific requirements of what the pupils should have learned each year.

Seen together, the changes mean that the local authorities will have more freedom to run the schools as they choose, while the teachers will have less freedom to adapt their teaching to suit the needs of the individual child, or to take local conditions into consideration. Also, a national curriculum that is both detailed and prescriptive will change the role of teachers into that of a technical functionary rather than a responsible professional. To be able to adapt the teaching to the needs of the pupils, and make use of their experiences in learning, the teachers must be given a certain freedom within the framework of the common curriculum.

> Data collected by the Norwegian Union of Teachers show that decentralising decisions concerning financing and organisation of schools lead to increased differences between local schools.

Therefore, the changes which are being made may well weaken the Norwegian comprehensive school, and lead to larger differences among pupils, schools and different parts of the country. In my view, the Norwegian tradition of national control of the economic foundation of the schools and national legislation securing basic equality regarding resources and organisation, should be carried on as a necessary foundation on which to further develop equity in education. Many local authorities have economic problems. Accordingly, they are bound to use their new freedom to try and save money, rather than try to develop a better school. This is the background to why the Norwegian Union of Teachers demands that the extra costs of the reforms should be borne by central government, and not depend on the varying local economies.

The changes in educational policy that can now be observed in Norway must be seen in light of the ideological shift that started in the early 1980s. Gradually, child-centred educational ideas have been replaced by 'management by objectives'-thinking. Increasingly, education is being considered as a means to strengthen the ability of our country to compete in the international market. There is also a belief that market orientation and competition will strengthen the quality of education.

Data collected by the Norwegian Union of Teachers show that decentralising decisions concerning financing and organisation of schools lead to increased differences between local schools. We fear that the proposals presented will further strengthen this development.

- The Act will no longer indicate the exact maximum class size.
- There will no longer be a legal requirement as to the total number of allocated teaching periods per class.
- There will be no national requirements regarding which teaching and other positions there should be on the school staff (apart from the head teacher).
- There will be no national standards regarding school buildings, equipment and teaching material.

Instead of binding national standards, terms like 'sufficient' and 'appropriate' are being used. In our view, this does not provide a strong enough basis to secure equitable conditions for all. The Norwegian Union of Teachers is critical of the present development. We think that market orientation and competition will only strengthen those already strong, and thus create larger differences between people individually and socially. Co-operation and solidarity must be the ideological foundation of an equitable school. This thinking must be the basis for the development of the school even in the future. We want a school where all children, irrespective of social or ethnic background, gender or personal abilities, will be given the best conditions for learning, growth and development. To further develop the school in this direction, we need the active participation and co-operation of school authorities, teachers' unions as well as parents and local communities. We want a school which is active in society, has high quality, and demonstrates efficient use of available resources. A school based on these ideas will be able to contribute towards more equality and greater social justice, both in our own country and in relation to the rest of the world.

Notes and References

1. The Norwegian Union of Teachers, *No-one left behind to idle*. Policy document on education (Oslo: NLL, 1994).
2. Stortingsmelding nr. 29 *Om prinsipper og retningslinjer for 10-årig grunnskole – ny læreplan* (Oslo: 1994–5).
3. NOU 1995: *18 Ny lovgivning om opplæring*. (Oslo: Kirke-, utdannings- og forsknings-departementet).
4. *Prinsipper og retningslinjer for den 10-årige grunnskolens oppbygning, organisering og innhold.* Oslo: Kirke-, utdannings- og forskningsdepartementet (1994).

3.5 THE REORGANISATION OF EARLY YEARS SERVICES FOR YOUNG CHILDREN

A SCANDINAVIAN PERSPECTIVE

Oddbjørn Knutsen

Professor of Political Science, University of Oslo

Over recent decades all Scandinavian countries have seen considerable changes and developments in services for young children. The changes have included the development of a range of parental and family leave entitlements in addition to radical restructuring of daycare and education services for young children, integrating publicly-funded services within the welfare system. The changes have placed early years services at the heart of the Scandinavian universal welfare model.

This contribution is based on a study[1] of developments in early years services in Scandinavian[2] countries from 1985 to 1992. It finds that, whilst there are similarities, there are also significant differences in the systems. The main features of services in Scandinavia are described, followed by an examination of how general decentralisation within the public sector has influenced the provision of services for young children in the different countries and the effect it has had on patterns of provision.

> Such reforms mark the transformation of daycare from a residual welfare service to a service which conforms to the universal welfare state model which characterises the Scandinavian countries.

Denmark established state support for daycare centres in 1919. Regulations concerning daycare institutions in Denmark were incorporated into legislation in the 1930s. Norway and Sweden followed. Sweden established state support in 1944–5 and Norway gradually established it from the late 1940s until 1963, when state support was introduced fully. In this early period early years services were divided into two separate types of institutions with children generally drawn from different socio-economic groups. One set of institutions was pedagogical with relatively short opening hours, and the other—social institutions—had long opening hours. There was wide agreement in Scandinavia over the need to bring together these services within the same regulations. Pedagogical and social functions should be exercised within the same institution and the children should be from mixed socio-economic groups. Legislation and special reports which have been decisive for the structural development of daycare services in accordance with the universal welfare state model can be identified in all Scandinavian countries. Such reforms mark the transformation of daycare from a residual welfare service to a service which conforms to the universal welfare state model which characterises the Scandinavian countries. Denmark was the first Scandinavian country to pass such an Act in 1964–5. In the other countries new regulations were issued during the mid–1970s.

Growth and reorganisation of provision

From about 1985, Scandinavian welfare states have experienced some general problems in fulfilling government social welfare commitments requiring the reformulation of policy objectives. Despite this, there have been significant developments in services for young children. In all three countries priority has been given to increasing the number of daycare places.

A comparative analysis of the growth of daycare centres, shows that Denmark and Sweden had the highest coverage in the 1950s and 1960s (see Table 3.1).[3] The growth in childcare places started earlier in Denmark and Sweden, compared with Norway where provision did not expand until the last part of the 1970s. However, childcare arrangements in Denmark and Sweden were different in form. In Denmark full day social institutions were dominant during the whole post war period, while pedagogical part-time arrangements were prevalent in Sweden until 1970. Subsidised family daycare played an important part in providing daycare services both in Denmark and in Sweden, while this form of care was not considered relevant in Norway. As shown in Table 3.1, during the last three decades coverage has been much higher in Denmark than in the other countries, with Norway still behind at the beginning of the 1990s.

From around 1985 the Scandinavian welfare states have experienced some general problems in fulfilling government social welfare commitments requiring the

TABLE 3.1   Children in early years services: 0–6 years (coverage in percentages).

Country	Daycare	Family daycare[a]	Total coverage
Denmark			
1960	6	–	6
1970	11	1	12
1981	30	13	43
1992	43	16	60
Norway			
1960	2	–	2
1970	3	–	3
1981	23	0.5	16
1992	38	2	40
Sweden			
1960	1	0.5	1.5
1970	4	4	9
1981	21	13	34
1992	38	12	50

NOTE
a. Subsidised, i.e. publicly-funded and controlled.

SOURCE: Knutsen (1991: p. 247), Table 12.4, and Knutsen (1994: pp. 23–4) Table 1.1.

reformulation of policy objectives. Despite this, there have been significant developments in services for young children. In all three countries priority has been given to increasing the number of daycare places. While the biggest increase in coverage and number of places is seen in Norway and Sweden, there has also been substantial expansion in Denmark. The expansion in Norway is remarkable given that for many years they lagged behind their neighbours. New forms of services, such as family daycare and the integration of 6-year-olds into schooling, are also increasing.

A detailed study[4] of the organisation of childcare provision in the 1980s revealed that the Swedish institutions had very generous organisational patterns compared with the other Scandinavian countries. They had longer opening hours, smaller numbers of children per group, better staff-child ratios, and nearly all the staff were trained childcare workers.[5]

Further reorganisation of childcare services is evident in Sweden in the 1990s; the changes have led the Swedish system to become more like the other Scandinavian systems. So far we have seen a move in the direction of fewer staff and an increase of children per group compared with the two previous decades. However, this change has brought Sweden in line with the staffing levels in Denmark and Norway. The expansion of daycare institutions in Sweden has been at the expense of family daycare which has come to be seen as providing poorer quality care. At the same time high aspirations are being maintained in relation to other variables seen as central to the Swedish early years system. This is particularly evident in respect of the educational content, opening hours, and the proportion of young pre-school children.

Decentralisation

Planning and implementation responsibilities at the level of municipalities for national policies for expanding childcare services show clear differences between Sweden on the one hand, and Denmark and Norway on the other. In Sweden national planning requirements for expanding provision have been more evident, and it is not by chance that Sweden was the first to formulate the goal of childcare as a right for selected groups of children/families. Such rights imply that national policy can considerably influence municipalities in expanding services. However, during the 1980s, there has been considerable decentralisation from the state authorities to the municipalities in all countries. Denmark was the first country to decentralise its childcare in the mid-1970s with the implementation of the Social Assistance Act.

Decentralisation, from the central municipal administration to the individual institution, has also taken place within the daycare services. Data from 1992–3[6] show that the process of decentralisation to the institutional level has gone much further in Denmark and Sweden than in Norway.[7] In Denmark and Sweden the institutions had more opportunities to carry over money to the next year's budget, to transfer between various items in the budget and control over more items. The initial decentralisation process in Denmark and Sweden took place during the years from 1975–84 to 1985–9 respectively.[7]

The public-private mix

The proportion of privately-owned institutions varies considerably among the countries. Whereas private ownership of daycare institutions is still relatively uncommon in Sweden, about 45 per cent and 35 per cent of daycare institutions in Norway and Denmark respectively had private owners in 1992–3. The corresponding percentage for Sweden was less than 10 per cent. These differences have been stable since the 1960s. However, privately-owned institutions in Norway are increasing in the 1990s. Owners of private childcare institutions in Norway are mainly religious organisations and congregations, voluntary organisations such as the Women's Institute (*Husmorlag*), parents' co-operatives and single owners, of whom a small but increasing number are operating on a 'for profit' basis. Institutions owned by religious and voluntary organisations have decreased over time whilst parents' co-operatives and single owners are on the increase.

An important difference between the privately-owned institutions in Denmark and Norway is that far greater public control is exercised by local authorities in Denmark than in Norway. In Denmark the Social Assistance Act of 1974 provides for strict control of the private institutions. The privately-owned institutions are included in the municipality daycare plan, and the municipality decides the intake of children. In Norway the privately-owned institutions generally have greater autonomy in relation to the local public authority, although the relationship varies greatly between municipalities.

Services for young children have been given high priority in the three Scandinavian countries in the 1980s and 1990s. The most striking trends are the continuing increase in the number of places and the changes in the organisation of the services. Coverage and organisational patterns have become more similar over time.

Notes and References

1. Knutsen, Oddjørn, *Mer lik, men stadig forskjellig. En komparativ studie av barneomsorgen i de nordiske landene 1985–1992*, INAS-rapport 94:7 (Oslo: Institutt for sosialforskning, 1994).
2. Finland, which was part of the study, is not included in this chapter.
3. Knutsen, Oddbjørn, *Offentlig barneomsorg i Norden: En komparative studie av utviklingen i de nordiske land*, Rapport 91:12 (Oslo: Institutt for sosialforskning, 1991).
4. Knutsen, Oddbjørn, *Organiseringen av barneomsorgen og skolebarnomsorgen i de nordiske landene. En komparative studie av institusjoner, utdanninger og personell*, INAS-rapport 90:4 (Oslo: Institutt for sosialforskning, 1990).
5. Pre-school teachers, child nurses or the equivalent from higher or further education institutions.
6. Knutsen, Oddbjørn, *Organiseringen av barneomsorgen og skolebarnomsorgen i de nordiske landene. En komparative studie av institusjoner, utdanninger og personell*, INAS-rapport 90:4 (Oslo: Institutt for sosialforskning, 1990).
7. Difficult to establish any significant decentralisation in Norway.

PART II
COLLABORATION

Chapter 4

◆

COLLABORATION: UK

4.1 'ALL IN THE SAME BOAT—ROWING IN THE SAME DIRECTION?'

INFLUENCES ON COLLABORATION OVER CHILDREN'S SERVICES

Paul Sutton

Lewisham Education Department

In the last years of the millennium, there is a sense of frustration amongst those responsible for services for the well-being of children and families in the UK. Despite the introduction of wide-ranging legislation on child care,* the implementation of far-reaching reforms in education and health services, and the adoption by the UK of the UN Convention on the Rights of the Child, there is a sense that services are more fragmented than ever, and those which view the child holistically are achieved despite rather than because of the law. Furthermore, some commentators would argue that the social fabric of the UK has unravelled over the past 15 years, so that the comprehensive intentions of the Children Act 1989 have been undermined by the limitations of the socio-economic structural changes at work.[1] Meanwhile, central government policy has concentrated on experimentation with the forms of local government and its own relationship with local government. This chapter will examine some of the forces which have influenced the trend towards the fragmentation of services and will describe some of the opportunities for more effective, child-centred, cross-agency working.

Why collaborate?

Health and welfare legislation for children in the UK tends to be prepared by individual government departments working to different ministers, and on the whole affects

---

* The Children Act 1989 in general applies to England and Wales only, and references to specific sections are applicable accordingly. Similar legislation has been introduced in Scotland in the Children (Scotland) Act 1995, and in Northern Ireland through the Children Order. Education legislation referred to is also specific to England and Wales.

> Recent legislation has in effect created gaps between the services of different agencies which have to be filled through new planning and policy partnerships and new forms of co-operation.

single agencies charged with specific statutory duties. Legislation which spans the responsibilities of, for example, different local authority departments is rarer. It is left to the different agencies to ensure that their services are dovetailed to form a close fit. Of course, co-operation between agencies is not new, especially when it concerns the delivery of a specific service to a specific user. However, recent legislation has in effect created gaps between the services of different agencies which have to be filled through new planning and policy partnerships and new forms of co-operation. These gaps have become all the more evident as the income differentials between the rich and the poor have created greater relative poverty than in almost any other developed nation.[1] This has brought about a need for more services in some areas, and has highlighted both the need for inter-agency collaboration and the targeting of some universal services such as health visiting.[2]

There are many forms of co-operation; these might be described on a continuum:[3]

- Communication of one agency's position to another.
- Consultation by one agency with others over proposals.
- Collaboration between agencies where agencies reach agreement about the extent and limits of their services, make adjustments, and then provide services independently.
- Joint planning in which planning is conducted as a single joint activity.
- Joint commissioning, in which joint planning results in the joint provision of a service.

For the most part this chapter will address the need for agencies to do more than communicate and consult about policy, and rather operate at the collaboration/joint planning/joint commissioning end of the continuum.

The Children Act 1989

The Children Act 1989 passed through Parliament with all-party support, though not without substantial debate about some of its key provisions, and was intended to be a comprehensive piece of legislation. It brings together private and public law on children for the first time, and requires that the support of children in their families, in the widest possible sense, (rather than prevent more intrusive interventions which was the thrust of previous legislation) should be a major local authority responsibility, and that the social services department should be able to call upon the assistance of local education authorities and health authorities in the exercise of their duties.[4] Furthermore the local authority has a duty to publish information about services provided by themselves and others, identify possible service users, and ensure that they are aware of the information about services which might help them.[5]

The Act is unique in child welfare legislation in viewing a request for help as 'normal', the action of a responsible parent, and was clearly, by implication at least, intended to dispel some of the stigma associated with the receipt of social work and associated services.

Divergent legislative agendas

However, almost simultaneously, central government embarked upon reforms in two other key sectors with a crucial bearing on the life of children. These reforms can be seen as undermining the collaborative messages of the Children Act.

The Education Reform Act (1988) and subsequent measures introduced a standard annual norm for contact hours between teachers and children (1265 hours over 195 days), and a National Curriculum based squarely on academic attainment in key subject areas, with performance based on published league tables of school-by-school comparisons, despite the inclusion of so called 'cross curricular' themes loosely based on notions of emergent citizenship. More importantly, the Education Reform Act devolved the responsibility for the management and financial running of schools to local governing bodies, and eroded the power of the local education authority strategically to direct activity or policy. In part, these changes reflected a sustained drive towards consumerism, with parents in this case perceived as the final arbiters about the quality of education through the exercise of choice over which school their children attended.

The National Health Service and Community Care Act (1990) introduced market-style reforms into the NHS by separating the roles of purchaser and provider. Health authorities or commissions became the main (but not unique) purchasers, and self governing NHS Trusts were established for both hospital and community services as the main providers, whilst general practitioners could opt to become fundholders and purchase services. The relationship between purchaser and provider was established through the use of contracts.

Housing authorities do not have to consider homeless 16–18 year olds as priorities for rehousing, whilst the general entitlement to income support for young people aged 16–18 was withdrawn in 1988 in favour of a small living allowance which was payable conditional upon attendance on a variety of vocational training courses.

It has been argued that these reforms are essentially contradictory in effect.[6] On the one hand, legislation has given to local authorities the duty to provide a wide range of services to support children and families in need and co-ordinate the activities of other agencies to ensure that the Children Act's broad ambitions are fulfilled; on the other it has taken away the ability of those other agencies to collaborate by a significant reduction in their powers to direct compliance with such requests, and has eroded the financial and housing framework which might prevent young people from falling into homelessness and poverty.

Demographic and local government changes

Two other significant forces can be identified which have impacted upon the ability of agencies to provide a holistic service for children and families. First, the proportion of children aged 0–16 in the general population, in the UK, currently about 20 per cent has fallen from 25 per cent in 1961 and is predicted to fall further until the year 2021, when this age group will make up only about 18 per cent of the population. The proportion of the population aged 65 and over has risen from 12 per cent 1961, and will continue to rise to about 20 per cent in the year 2021.[7] It is likely that these demographic changes will diminish the political priority accorded to children's services and will squeeze both central and local government spending on children, which is already held to be less favourable than spending on older people.

> For the most part, in the past, agencies operated in isolation, perhaps confident that the boundaries of one service agency provided a close enough fit with those of adjacent services.

Secondly, central government has embarked on a series of reforms of the structure of local government intended to reduce the complexity of multiple tiers, make local government more responsive, reduce bureaucracy, and bring services and control of them closer to 'the people'. The effects of these reforms are only just emerging, but they have three main facets. First, they have been partial, in that in some parts of the UK unitary authorities have been comprehensively introduced, whilst in others responsibility for running services still rests with a number of different tiers. Furthermore, they have done nothing to reconcile the problems of co-terminosity between local government and health authorities, and in some cases have exacerbated them. Secondly, they have created some authorities with populations so small, and infrastructures so fragile that their ability to deliver the full range of services has been questioned. Thirdly, experiments with arrangements for central government funding of localised regeneration initiatives in parts of some of the larger cities (for example, City Challenge, Single Regeneration Budget, Housing Action Trusts and so forth) have created tensions and competition between the traditional central democratic committee and management structures of local government, and local appointed boards of management and in some cases localised political structures based on the constituency, ward or neighbourhood level.

Against this background, some rather uncoordinated and geographically scattered strategies are emerging which might enable agencies to collaborate to promote children's well-being on a 'whole child' basis. To some degree, this new found desire to collaborate has been forced upon agencies which have had to depart from traditional methods of communicating their objectives and strategies to one another.

The new realities

For the most part, in the past, agencies operated in isolation, perhaps confident that the boundaries of one service agency provided a close enough fit with those of adjacent services. The most prevalent forms of co-operation were those which entailed one agency communicating its objectives and strategies to another, or consulting on them. Where agencies tended to share responsibility for a particular group of children, for example disabled children or children with mental health problems, some forms of collaboration emerged, sometimes resourced through joint finance, usually delivered through health, education and social services agencies, and sometimes voluntary organisations. Often this collaboration took the form of joint teams, yet this was seldom based on a rigorous strategic joint assessment of the extent of the needs to be met, and the rational deployment of resources to meet that need. Rather, these initiatives were opportunistic and were frequently generated by practitioners rather than commissioners of services.

In 1994, the Audit Commission published a report which examined the co-ordination of child health and social services for children in need—the central territory of the Children Act.[8] That report was important for its focus on the 'new realities' of the reforms in education, social services and health, its consideration of the broad social context of poverty, morbidity and housing, and on the management of service boundaries rather than the response of individual agencies. The conclusions of the Audit Commission urged better joint-strategic planning between agencies, better monitoring of effectiveness and joint-service delivery strategies, noting that 'the potential for duplication, confusion and waste is considerable unless these changes are managed effectively'. The underlying message is that agencies will have to do more with less, and do it jointly in order to respond to public demand and legislative imperatives for both quantity and quality.

Children's services plans—a new prompt to collaboration

In 1992, central government had already advised all local authorities in England to produce children's services plans, intended to be the counterpart of community care plans, setting out the local authority social services department's strategic plans for children's services in their area. This guidance advised social services departments to consult with other agencies in the formulation of their plans. It is likely that these plans will be made mandatory in the near future.[9]

What is the evidence that agencies have taken this advice to heart in the UK? Early years services provide perhaps the clearest example of the intention, though not yet fully the ability, to collaborate. Depending on one's view, these services are marked by the fragmentation referred to earlier, or (in the government's view) provide a rich diversity of service provision. They are provided by private, voluntary, education and social services sectors, there are different entry requirements, different stated purposes and thus curricula or programmes of activity and different charging structures. Comprehensive information for consumers is poor, and coverage is extremely patchy. The status, training and remuneration of staff is as varied as the provision itself. Compared with nearly all other EU countries, the UK has a very low level of provision. Partly driven by the requirement in the Children Act 1989 to review such services every three years, some local authorities are beginning to develop strategies both to provide a single unified service on the one hand, or to develop ways of working which seek to accommodate the structural differences rather than overcome them entirely. A recent study undertaken by the National Children's Bureau of 11 English local authorities identified a range of collaborative responses to the problem.[10] What these responses have in common is that they seek to operate against the backdrop of a lack of a coherent national strategy to meet the needs of children aged under five.

> It is in the provision of 'family support' services where collaboration appears to be most problematic and patchy, despite the strong advice from the Audit Commission and the intentions of the Children Act 1989.

By the end of 1994, the vast majority of local authorities in England had produced their first children's services plan.[11] Whilst most of them were simply, if not entirely simple 'stocktaking' exercises, some plans did start to demonstrate that local authority social services departments were beginning to take the need to collaborate with other service providers seriously. For the most part, where local authorities were collaborating, they were doing so around services to a particular group of children. The more easily identifiable, the more likely was that collaboration, especially if it coincided with traditional areas of cross-sectoral co-operation. For example there is growing evidence that services for children with disabilities, or mental health problems are not seen as the prime concern of one single agency, but rather that they are perceived as fertile ground for an advanced form of collaboration—joint commissioning—with the possibility of new joint services emerging rather than more clearly delineated demarcations between old services. Of course, there is also a history of collaborative approaches in child protection and youth justice services. These seem set to continue with the added impetus of children's services plans.

Despite this evidence, some groups of children still seem to 'miss out'; for example those recently discharged from local authority care, where the need to address the holistic needs of a young person could hardly be more apparent, and children looked after by the local authority who still seem to suffer disproportionately from poor health and lack of educational attainment.

However, it is in the provision of 'family support' services where collaboration appears to be most problematic and patchy, despite the strong advice from the Audit Commission and the intentions of the Children Act 1989. There may be a number of reasons for this. First, broad preventive services are notoriously hard to evaluate not least because prevention is frequently sketchily defined; they are often 'open access' and their effects on behaviour may not be seen until much later when many other variables have intervened. Secondly, social services departments have been preoccupied with the task of child protection for 20 years now, despite the mounting evidence that services are expensive in terms of resources, poorly targeted in that they tend to draw in families who do not 'need' them, poorly evaluated and poorly perceived by users. Thirdly, the concept of 'children in need' is neither well understood nor used by agencies other than social services departments. Fourthly, the changes affecting schools which are described above have tended to value academic attainment and school attendance above the more nebulous achievement of schools in providing a social anchor for vulnerable children and families, if only because the former can be more easily compared with competitors in a quasi-market setting. Fifthly, primary health care services attract less attention and consequent funding than acute specialised services. Partly this is a result of the more intensive staff resourcing required by acute services, and partly a result of the still commonly held perception that health is to do with medicine and hospitals rather than community-based services. Finally, agencies lack the analytical tools to jointly identify either the parameters or the priorities of this group of children. A perverse rule thus seems to apply: the more residual the group of children, the more likely is the evidence for the beginnings of collaborative work.

Yet it is in this area where the beginnings of a changing agenda might be found. One of the effects of the socio-economic changes referred to above, and the consequent demand to meet increasing need is that all three of the main agencies charged with the well-being of children are beginning to rediscover their role in the broadly 'social' agenda. The welfare of children in the UK is fractured by poverty and inequality,[12] and their needs are unlikely now to be met by a response which is individually rooted in just one professional discipline. This movement might be predicted to lead to a blurring of roles and responsibilities of different professional groups, the emergence of new occupational roles or quasi-professions, and a new emphasis on work at the boundaries of organisational responsibilities rather than the retrenchment into 'core' activities which has characterised organisational responses in the recent past. Recent joint work between the housing, social services and education departments and the health authority in Birmingham has begun to sketch out the beginnings of a broad family support strategy which contains all of these elements.

Local government review

Although the consequences of the local government review are still emerging, and none of the new unitary authorities is yet in the position of actually running services, elected members in the areas covered by some of the new unitary authorities are beginning to consider how best to organise their services. For some, previously from the district councils, this is a process of discovery, since they may be unfamiliar with the legislation which they will have to administer, and may or may not have experience of serving on the relevant committees.

> Other local authorities have grasped the opportunity presented by children's services plans to attempt to view children as emergent citizens, by attempting to harness and reorientate services which are not the traditional preserve of education, social services or health.

Others, by virtue of the size of the population and the fragility of the infrastructure which they have inherited, are having to consider the potential of collaboration on service delivery across the new boundaries, and certainly with voluntary organisations. This is especially true of those new authorities which are mixed rural and small urban, where services in the old authorities had been concentrated in larger centres of population from which they are now divorced. Yet others, especially the newly created city unitary authorities show exciting signs of at least considering whether the traditional local authority committee structures could be realigned to provide more comprehensive services. For these authorities it will be essential to start with a clear vision for children in their areas, and begin the process of redesign around that vision. This need not entail the creation of large new bureaucracies but rather some more rational planning of those services which could benefit from merger (early years might be a good example), and those where clear bi- or trilateral arrangements could be built in from the outset.

A new agenda

Other local authorities have grasped the opportunity presented by children's services plans to attempt to view children as emergent citizens, by attempting to harness and reorientate services which are not the traditional preserve of education, social services or health. Such strategies have not only attempted to collaborate with leisure services to ensure, for example, that play and library services are hooked into an overall strategy, but have undertaken collaborative forays into the fields of urban planning, architecture, roads and environmental health, and in some cases the private and commercial sector, in a brave attempt at the creation of child friendly cities. For example, Leicester has declared itself Britain's first environmental city, and is engaging children and young people in a range of cross-departmental activities designed to stimulate both their evident interest in environmental issues and their status as important sources of intelligence about life in the city. Edinburgh City Council promoted itself as a child-friendly city and engaged the co-operation of a number of commercial concerns in initiatives designed to improve children's experience of city life. These projects are all at the experimental stage and certainly do not reflect as yet the longer experiences of working and thinking in this way which can be found in Emilia Romagna in Italy, or parts of Spain and Denmark.

The second strand to these experiments is located at an even more tentative point. Some cities are beginning to recognise that children under 16 might make up a quarter of the population, might represent, in a very literal sense, the future, yet have no formal say over the planning or management of agency policies. Again, much of the thinking around comprehensive ways of consulting with children and young people is small scale, often prompted by working with other agencies on children's services plans and derived from European initiatives. Nevertheless, it may not be too long before we witness the emergence of formal consultative structures which may start to view children as citizens with a range of valid views on the spectrum of local authority services.

What the new ways of working all have in common, is that they all recognise that needs are now too complex and sometimes too overwhelming for one local authority department or health authority to be able to meet alone; that the marked increase in relative poverty is giving rise to a demand to address the needs of children and their families in new ways, and that the old professional and departmental boundaries must become more permeable. The challenge to well established bureaucracies to collaborate effectively is not small. Very early experience of children's services plans demonstrates this. Whilst there may be a recognition that we are all in the same boat, we now have to learn to row in the same direction.

Notes and References

1. Wilkinson, R. G., *Unfair Shares: The Effects of Understanding Income Differences in the Welfare State* (Essex: Barnardo's, 1994).
2. Audit Commission, *Seen but not Heard* (1994).
3. Department of Health (1995a) Study of Children's Services Plans in 45 Local Authorities (forthcoming).
4. Children Act 1989, Section 27.
5. Children Act 1989 Schedule II, Part 1.
6. Jones, A. and Bilton, K. *The Future Shape of Children's Services* , (London: National Children's Bureau, 1994).
7. *Social Trends,* Central Statistical Office 1995.
8. Audit Commission, *Seen but not Heard* (1994).
9. Department of Health Draft Circular. Children's Services Plans (1995b).
10. McQuaid, S. and Pugh, G., *The Effective Organisation of Early Years Services* (National Children's Bureau,1995).
11. Department of Health (1995a) op. cit.
13. Wilkinson, R. G. (1994) op. cit., and Young, M. and Halsey, A. H., *Family and Community Socialism* (1995).

4.2 ACHIEVING HEALTH AND SOCIAL GAIN FOR CHILDREN IN WALES

A COLLABORATIVE APPROACH TO THE PREPARATION OF GUIDANCE

Catriona Williams
Director, Children in Wales
Paul Davis
Consultant Community Paediatrician, University of Wales College of Medicine
Marcus Longley
Strategic Planner, Welsh Health Planning Forum
Jo Sibert
Professor of Community Child Health, University of Wales College of Medicine
and
Dr Morton Warner
Executive Director, Welsh Health Planning Forum

This is an account of the approach taken in Wales to produce guidance for all relevant agencies on services to achieve health and social gain for children. It outlines the context in which the guidance was developed, the process undertaken and some examples of final recommendations.

Joint working in Wales

As part of the UK, Wales has a total population of around 3,000,000 people. In 1993 there were 668,000 children under 18, representing 22.5 per cent of the total population. Wales is a predominantly rural area, but its population is concentrated in the south and the northeast where the old heavy industries of the industrial revolution have only partly been replaced by new technology-based manufacturing. The average income of households in Wales is below that of the UK as a whole and significant sections of both the urban and rural population experience relative deprivation. There is a significant Welsh speaking minority and recent legislation reinforces the position of the Welsh language in public life.

The health services in Wales are under the remit of the Secretary of State for Wales who is a member of the UK cabinet and the Welsh Office, and is also responsible for most other government functions in the country. Locally, the health service is split into purchasers and providers. There are currently eight district health authorities which purchase health services and also hospital trusts and community trusts which provide them. General practitioners who work either individually or in group practices provide an increasing number of services and many hold their own budgets to purchase hospital care. Family Health Services Authorities (FHSAs) support and monitor the work of the GPs and are soon to be integrated into a reorganised health authority structure which will comprise five areas. Services such as education and social services are the responsibility of locally elected councils of which there were eight, but which were reorganised into 22 in April 1996. Given that so many different agencies and disciplines provide services which are crucial to children's well-being, it is clearly vital that their efforts be co-ordinated.

Wales starts with some natural advantages in this respect. For instance the Welsh Office has oversight of almost all relevant services for children and due to the small population professional networks have traditionally met on an all-Wales basis. Until April 1996 each health and local authority served the same population and in a number of important areas there is a history of successful joint working. For over 10 years the Welsh Office stimulated and funded the 'All Wales Strategy for Mental Handicap'[1] which provided a framework for local joint planning, which had led to a comprehensive range of community based, multi-disciplinary services and a much greater voice for the consumer. The Children Act 1989 (which applies to England and Wales) required considerable inter-agency collaboration in the delivery of children's services.

> Even within individual services such as health or education, it is becoming increasingly difficult to take a strategic view of service development as hospital and community health trusts become self governing and schools become locally managed.

There are however several barriers to successful joint planning. In addition to the different values and priorities of different professional groups and the differing and sometimes contradictory legislative frameworks within which they operate, Wales also has to contend with the fact that the health services are controlled by the Welsh Office whereas other services are accountable to locally elected politicians. Even within individual services such as health or education, it is becoming increasingly difficult to take a strategic view of service development as hospital and community health trusts become self governing and schools become locally managed.

The need for a common approach on services for children

Individual health authorities within Wales are being guided by '*Protocols for Investment in Health Gain*'[2] produced by the Welsh Health Planning Forum. The protocols concentrate on specific health problems such as cancers or cardio-vascular disease and define health gain as 'adding years to life and life to years' (reducing premature death and improving quality of life). From these protocols the health authorities produce '*Local Strategies for Health*'.

The Welsh Office recognised the need to clarify particular issues relating to the health and social well-being of children, and asked the Planning Forum to produce a separate document to supplement the protocols. The rationale was clear. Firstly, children are different—they experience illness in different ways from adults, childhood is a period of rapid growth and development and children are dependent on adults—and therefore services for them should be significantly different from those of adults. Secondly, services should address the needs of the child as a whole including physical, mental, spiritual and social well-being, usually in the context of the family. In recognition of this range of needs, the concept of health gain was broadened to become 'health and social gain'.

Finally there was the recognition of children's rights. The United Nations Convention on the Rights of the Child[3] reaffirms that children, because of their vulnerability, need special care and protection. It also recognises the right of the child to be involved in decisions affecting him or her.

The Convention also particularly recognises the right of the child to the enjoyment of the highest attainable standard of health and to the facilities for the treatment of illness and rehabilitation of health. In England and Wales the Children Act (1989)[4] has, as one of its principles, that the child's welfare is paramount. In the environment of the National Health Service, this inevitably leads to the question of how the rights of the child to this highest attainable standard of health could be achieved?

Achieving a common approach

The Welsh Health Planning Forum began the process by convening a panel of 20 people from around Wales, selected on the basis of their personal contribution and also their ability to represent the various philosophies and priorities on children's services. Membership included:

- from the Welsh Office: civil servants from the divisions responsible for health policy and education, social services policy and inspectorates, and medical and nursing advisors
- from the health service: paediatricians, a GP, a child and adolescent psychiatrist, a consultant in child dental health, a dietician and a representative from the Health Promotion Authority for Wales
- from social services: a principal officer responsible for children's services, and
- from other groups: an educational psychologist, representatives of parents' groups and the director of Children in Wales—Plant yng Nghymru.

The panel was chaired by Jo Sibert, Professor of Community Child Health in the University of Wales College of Medicine and Chair of Children in Wales—Plant yng Nghymru.

The timescale was almost impossible—to produce a document in four months—but it was achieved. This was primarily because of the high level of commitment from all those taking part and the awareness that it would inform the local strategies for health that would be produced at that time.

The work was divided between the various panel members who produced the source documents on their particular area of expertise either alone or with another panel member. These documents were circulated prior to panel meetings and were then discussed by the panel both in relation to their individual content and to the method of inclusion into the final document. Throughout the process Children in Wales, the national children's agency with a multi-disciplinary membership, consulted with its member agencies about issues of concern to them.

The collation and editing of papers was primarily done by the strategic planner and a community paediatrician. The work was felt to be of such significance to all concerned that it became a priority and time was given freely.

Completed in August 1993, the document sets out a coherent philosophical framework and a set of practical recommendations. It provides a compendium of all the advice already available for health authorities on children's health services. We hope it will encourage the development of services in areas that are child and family centred as well as resource effective and that our experience will assist others to develop clear guidelines of their own. We also hope that our methodology will be replicated locally in order to maximise the knowledge, experience and resources held by all the agencies concerned for the welfare of children.

The guidance document 'Health and Social Gain for Children: Guidance to Inform Local Strategies for Health'[5] is outlined below in the following sections.

Children are different

This sets out the basic framework for what follows by promulgating four sets of rights, derived largely from the UN Convention on the Rights of the Child and the Children Act 1989. They are set out in Figure 4.1.

By starting from this position, which could command the support of all those around the table, it became easier to relate the diverse range of children's services to a common core of 'standards'. This tended to emphasise what each had *in common* rather than their differences.

The guidance (action in relation to specific conditions)

Social and health aspects of specific issues occurring in childhood were identified which require specific strategies. Examples ranged from sudden infant death syndrome and childhood asthma to child abuse. Interventions were considered in relation to the following types: promoting health, fitness and well-being; preventing ill health; monitoring health and development and diagnosis and treatment.

A child and family centred service

Children are different and require to be regarded as 'children first'. They should be treated by professionals with special training in the needs of children. Users of health services should be encouraged and enabled to participate in planning of their services, often aided by consumer organisations such as Community Health Councils and the

FIGURE 4.1   **The rights of the child.**

General rights: all services should focus on the needs and wishes of the child
- non-discrimination
- the importance of the family
- the child's right to be heard
- protection from harm

Rights to health: all children have rights to
- life
- health
- full development of potential

Rights to health and social care: services should be
- effective
- equitable
- accessible
- relevant to the needs of the child and the community
- responsive
- efficient

Rights of children in need
- in addition to the rights set out above, health and other agencies should jointly adopt a proactive strategy to identify and meet the requirements of those children defined as being 'in need' by the Children Act 1989

voluntary sector. Good quality services are characterised by an emphasis both on prevention and treatment, which should be holistic and child and family centred.

The report of the National Association for the Welfare of Children in Hospital[6] contains valuable guidance. Purchasers may need particular guidance on ensuring access to appropriate care for children from ethnic minority groups such as that contained in the Action for Sick Children report.[7] We emphasised the need to have facilities appropriate for children and the desirability of caring for all children as far as possible within one department: within accident and emergency departments; outpatients; day units; intensive care and surgical units. Various documents have given guidance in this respect, particularly those issued by the British Paediatric Association.

We believe that the principles of the Children Act and the UN Convention can best be met by each health authority and FHSA designating 'a senior officer as Commissioner for Children', who would also have a key role in promoting integration among primary and secondary care, the community and hospital branches of secondary care, tertiary services and other agencies such as social services, education and voluntary organisations.

In particular this will facilitate the effective provision of services for 'children in need' under the Children Act. In this way the much-neglected needs of children in residential care as well as other groups would be effectively targeted. We also believe that the trend would then be for the development of services outside the hospital which would ensure that children are not inappropriately hospitalised.

Resource effectiveness

> Within a framework for investment in child health services, opportunities for disinvestment and redistribution of resources were identified. For example, the transfer of the child health surveillance and immunisation services from community child health to primary care has released clinical medical officer time.

Within a framework for investment in child health services, opportunities for disinvestment and redistribution of resources were identified. For example, the transfer of the child health surveillance and immunisation services from community child health to primary care has released clinical medical officer time, which in these areas has been utilised by expansion of the community general paediatric, special needs and child protection services, thus moving workload from hospital to community services and from community to primary care.

There may need to be an adjustment in the balance of resources to allow for changes in patterns of patient care, for example, as a result of better management of admissions, matching beds to demand, guidelines on acute admission, availability of experienced doctors for telephone advice, short-term observation facilities, wider health education and reduced average lengths of stay, boosted by quality services within the primary health care sector and community services.

Conclusion

We have presented a model for producing advice for purchasers of children's services. In each region such advice will consider local requirements of the service as well as local variation in the direction of clinical services emanating from relevant government or regional agencies. It is essential during this phase of NHS development that providers and health planners in each region draw together national and regional guidelines on children's health issues to identify current best practice and clearly advise purchasers of health services to ensure that they have the best possible information upon which to base and prioritise their decisions.

Perhaps the most significant aspect of this model is that it attempts to reflect the current reality rather than artificially compartmentalising services for children. It brings together four aspects that interact to form the whole—traditional health services (historically based); intersectoral issues (recent legislation, policies and practice); a rights based approach (UN Convention on the Rights of the Child); and current policy trends such as health gain targets.

References
1. Welsh Office, *All Wales Strategy for Mental Handicap* (Welsh Office, 1983).
2. Welsh Health Planning Forum, *Protocols for Investment in Health Gain* (Welsh Health Planning Forum, 1993).

3. *United Nation Convention on the Rights of the Child*, (London: HMSO, 1992).
4. Department of Health, *The Children Act 1989* (London: HMSO, 1989).
5. Welsh Health Planning Forum, *Health and Social Gain for Children* (1993). Primary sources for the health and social gain document: The Audit Commission for England and Wales, *Children First: A Study of Hospital Services* (London: HMSO, 1993). Standing Committee of Voluntary Organisations, *Parents Deserve Better* (SCOVO, 1989). Department of Health and Welsh Office, *Working Together with the Children Act 1989* (London: HMSO, 1991).
6. *Caring for Children in the Health Services, Bridging the Gaps*. This is an explanatory study of the interfaces between primary and specialist care for children within the health services (London: Action for Sick Children, 1993).
7. Action for Sick Children, *Health for all our Children: Achieving Appropriate Health Care for Black and Ethnic Minority Children and their Families*, Quality Review Series, (London: Action for Sick Children, 1992).

4.3   CREATION OF A CHILDREN'S SERVICES DIVISION

A PRACTICAL CASE STUDY

Roy Jobson

Chief Education Officer, Manchester City Council, England

Historically Manchester has always been, and has always seen itself to be, at the cutting edge of social and economic change and development. Although the city took more than its fair share of blows in the late 1970s and early 1980s as old industries collapsed, and with them their communities, since the mid-1980s the city council has been implementing a vision of Manchester as a major European city. This is witnessed by major developments such as the Olympic and Commonwealth Games bids, large scale building projects, such as a new concert hall and velodrome and complete revitalisation of parts of the city.

It was also realised, however, that the regeneration of Manchester's economic position will serve little purpose unless it is accompanied by providing opportunities for the whole of the community, with an emphasis on redressing current inequalities and disadvantages. It is within this context that the needs and aspirations of children, young people and their parents were considered as a high priority within the city council's organisation.

The creation of an integrated Children's Services Division within the education department has at its heart a philosophy which is based on the city council's commitment to a comprehensive programme of services for children and that the ultimate goal is to provide, as a basic right, good quality childcare provision which meets the needs and aspirations of all parents and children in Manchester. Whereas the achievement of that goal is clearly a long way off, and it will certainly take a massive shift in government policy on issues such as childcare and nursery education, the city council does have that goal in mind and does consider it to be achievable in the long term.

Early years services in Manchester

The local elections of May 1984 provided a council of a different political complexion and although Manchester was always a high under-fives provider, the new leadership were committed to expansion. During 1985 and 1986 therefore, the number of nursery class places was increased dramatically, nursery provision was both extended and improved and an 'in principle' decision to expand the number of day nursery places was taken (see Tables 4.1 and 4.2).

The approach in Manchester, like many other parts of the UK, had resulted in:
- divisions between services and service providers, often leading to ill-conceived competitiveness and negative attitudes

TABLE 4.1 **Under-fives provision (1993–4).**

Total under-fives (No.)	(%)	In nursery education (No.)	(%)	Daycare (No.)	(%)	Part-time play (No.)	(%)
32,500	100	20,000	61.5	3640	11.2	3835	11.8

Source: Manchester City Council database.

TABLE 4.2 **Early years provision (1993–4).**

Type of provision	Number of places	Increase since 1985–6 (%)
Nursery class/school	5995	20
Creche or play	1000	60
Daycare	1484	20

Source: Manchester City Council database.

- different training backgrounds and perceptions of staff 'values', and
- different management approaches, leading to differing cultures and modes of service delivery.

Setting up of officer working party

As a result, an officer working party was set up (which I chaired) and a parallel under-fives committee was formed. One of the first tasks for the working group was to produce a philosophy for childcare, bearing in mind that many of those involved came from differing backgrounds and approaches. This was true not only of the differences between social services and education, but also with other services such as architects and design work in relation to equal opportunity policies. The immediate practical realisation of this philosophy was the creation of children's centres as new build multi-purpose establishments. The fundamental principles which were established were as follows:

- community based, flexible childcare offered as a right
- parental choice
- parental involvement in decision making
- services offered on a neighbourhood basis
- a range of services to be offered
- the centres to be a community resource
- anti-sexist and anti-racist childcare
- integration of all children, including those with special needs, and
- affordable services for all who want them.

The first four centres were completed by 1988 with the following facilities:

- nursery provision for 50 children
- parent and toddler group
- before and after school and holiday provision
- accommodation for community use
- creche facilities, and
- outside play areas.

Clearly a number of changes have occurred in respect of both the principles and the range of provision either because of resource difficulties or the development and refinement of the policies, and the changing nature and requirements of society. The reason I have described the creation of these centres is to emphasise that their creation and the development work which took place alongside, fundamentally shifted the balance of thinking with respect to children's services. The officer and member groups which were brought together consisted of people from a variety of backgrounds—education, social services, play (recreational services), planning, architects and so forth. In that respect it represented the first steps down the long road to integration of children's services.

The officer working party was charged in 1987 with the responsibility of producing draft options on whether it was appropriate to integrate the management of some or all of:

- children's centres (which had been allocated to the education department)
- day nurseries (social services)
- registration and inspection of play groups (either education or recreation)
- beehive clubs (recreation)
- sponsored childminding schemes (social services)
- day fostering schemes (social services)
- nursery schools (education), and
- creche facilities (all departments).

In simple terms the options which were put forward in 1987 were: (a) create a separate department for under fives/children's services; (b) give the management of certain functions with immediate effect to the Chief Education Officer and ask him to bring formal proposals for staffing and management to bring about a new division of service within the education department: and (c) the same as (b) but bringing about a new service division within the social services department.

I have no doubt many local authorities have faced or are facing similar choices and the strategic thinking which makes up the decision making process is coloured by local as well as national issues and circumstances. In brief, the city council chose the second, the immediate transfer of some additional functions to the education department with the request to bring forward staffing proposals for the creation of a new division of service, new thinking and new practices. In particular, the reasons given for adopting this option were as follows:

1. The need to integrate and adopt a philosophy which saw the service as providing for people and with people rather than to them.
2. The ethos at that time of the two major departments considered.
3. The expense of setting up a new department at a time (subsequently reinforced) of cuts leading to reducing management and overhead expenses and the trend to decreasing the number of departments in the local authorities.
4. The legal difficulties surrounding the removal of certain functions from the education department/Chief Education Officer.

Establishment of children's services division

As a result, the authority appointed a Principal Officer, who subsequently became the head of Children's Services Division, to spearhead the project and formulate proposals for the integration of the services. The team of people who came together not only brought quality, they also brought leadership and much needed management skills to change the overall philosophy and create team work.

Of particular concern to members of the city council was not only the creation of an integrated administrative/management unit but the bringing together of people to have a common sense of purpose in providing a wide range of choice to parents.

The main aims of this approach, which led to a unified management structure, are set out below.

1. Break down barriers and distinctions between the types of service and look at the needs of children as a whole.
2. Have a more consistent approach which is understandable to both workers and parents, with the adoption of common goals and quality standards.
3. Have a system which allowed better transition between establishments and services, and served the all-round needs of parents and children.
4. Improve the opportunities for women for access to both education and training, and also employment.

The creation of the Children's Services Division has brought a number of major advantages:

1. The status of the work and its importance, and the status of the workers has improved, and children's services have been recognised as having a value in their own right.
2. A children's services committee of the city council has been created which has contributed enormously to the thrust and status of the work.
3. Various issues are now tackled with the involvement of Children's Services Division which brings a heightened awareness of the needs and aspirations of children and their parents.

4. A chief officers' group on children has been set up to bring about a corporate approach to the needs of children across the major departments of the council, including examining existing services and policies with the needs and aspirations of children in mind.

5. Budget provision has been separated out which directly relates to provision of children's services which means that elected members can make clearer decisions based on priorities at a time of competing claims for resources.

6. Much more accessible career progression has become available as a result of bringing together services plus enhancing both reputation and status. Some issues are, of course, national, but the introduction of new qualifications has increased the opportunities.

7. Integrated training with the exchange of best practice from the various sections of the division is now possible and happens on a regular basis.

8. The ability to provide better information and choice to parents has been created so there is now only one 'city council' rather than four or five parts.

9. The division has been able to forge new or better links with other parts of the education department as well as other departments.

10. The head of children's services is a key member of the education department's senior management team, not only able to contribute with respect to the department's particular areas of service, but bringing a different dimension to educational issues and problems and the running and management of the whole department.

11. Resource procurement has been made more possible leading to new and exciting developments, for example enabling childminders to achieve National Vocational Qualifications.

12. The establishment of common curriculum guidance for both daycare and education.

Team work is a very critical part of any success and the functioning of the senior management team is vital. Looking back, what were the main problems associated with this move?

1. The separation of various departmental budgets to create a new divisional budget was a nightmare and five years on everyone still thinks that they lost out on the deal. Whether that perception is real or imagined is another question but at times the debate was acrimonious.

2. Bringing together staff from a variety of backgrounds was neither easy nor without contention. There were professional jealousies, status issues, disparate loyalties, varying terms and conditions of service and some injustices—local, national and historical. Some, but not all, of these issues have been tackled successfully and in some cases only time will be the healer.

3. Training is now more integrated with a freer exchange of information and expertise, but there are still problems, particularly in relation to the ways in which training is funded and the rules governing that funding.

4. The service, like many others up and down the country, has suffered from the cuts which has not helped the process of managing change. Change at the same time as cuts arouses deep and lasting suspicion.

I believe the creation of an integrated Children's Services Division has been a great success and is a tribute to the vision shown by senior members of Manchester City Council and the head of Children's Services Division. One of the best ways of demonstrating that success was the work undertaken in reviewing children's services as part of the duty under the Children Act. The establishment of structures to co-ordinate the review, and terms of reference, assembling and analysis of data and the final publishing of the review gave us not only an excellent knowledge and information base but an insight into the quality and quantity of services, the range of provision, the shortfall, the social and economic factors which now form a major part of our thinking and planning.

There was a great deal of work to establish the Division, some pain and anguish but a great deal of success—if taken back to the 1986–7 period I would readily go down the same route with no doubt in my mind.

Looking forward

As far as the future is concerned, Manchester City Council is undertaking a collaborative review, with the National Children's Bureau, of services to children and their families across the full range of services within the fields of education (including children's services) and social services. The main features and terms of reference of the review are as follows:

- complete an audit of existing services, for example, services for children with emotional or behavioural problems, children in care
- evaluate the efficiency of current forms of service, taking into account statutory duties, and comparing relative returns, particularly in relation to value for money
- estimate unmet needs and project patterns for the future, and
- assess the parts played by the views of both parents and children in planning, providing and monitoring services.

As a result of this work it is planned to examine possible reformulations of both policy and practice within and between the departments, and also analyse potential changes in the distribution of resources to better meet needs. In particular the emphasis on this section of the work will be to switch the emphasis from crisis intervention to the provision of universal services and preventative work. This may well result in the creation of a new service for children and young people where a policy framework is laid down which guides professionals, irrespective of their discipline and allows common criteria to be used in assessing needs, thus avoiding the splits which can occur, for example in education versus care.

Some of the issues can only be tackled at national level—how much longer can we sustain a policy which does not have a unified education/training programme career structure and status for people working with under fives? It would be of great benefit to the nation if there were a cohesive national strategy for under fives which allowed not only parental choice but universal provision, status, adequate career structures and parental involvement in the processes of service provision.

Chapter 5

◆

COLLABORATION: SCANDINAVIA

5.1 SYNERGY OR FRAGMENTATION?

COLLABORATION BETWEEN SERVICES FOR CHILDREN AND YOUTH IN A SCANDINAVIAN CONTEXT

Terje Ogden
Research Director, Norwegian Institute of Child Welfare Research
Elisabeth Backe-Hansen
Associate Member, Norwegian Institute of Child Welfare Research

Introduction

Increased professionalisation of services to children and youth has been a common characteristic of the Scandinavian countries after World War II. The trend has been towards increased specialisation of professionals as well as services, and the number of professionals has multiplied. Correspondingly, a variety of services at different organisational levels has evolved, leading to a need for co-ordination and collaboration. At the same time, services for children and youth mainly form part of the general services offered to the inhabitants by the community, requiring accessibility to all who fulfil the criteria for acceptance into the services, irrespective of their ability to pay for such services.

In this contribution, we will discuss the issue of collaboration from three perspectives. The first question we address is how local government reorganisation has affected collaboration between services. Secondly, we will discuss structures and strategies that hinder or promote collaboration. This leads to our final perspective: implications for training. Initially we will, however, give a description of the Scandinavian system of services for children and youth, including recent important changes. Although the systems in the three Scandinavian countries are not identical, they are sufficiently similar to allow for a general presentation and discussion.

A compartmentalised and differentiated system of services

In today's Scandinavia, services for children and youth are characterised by a fairly high degree of compartmentalisation and differentiation. This has many reasons. For instance, laws regulating the various services have been made and revised at different points in time, and none of the Scandinavian countries has a single Act defining what such services are to be.

In addition, there has been a clear tendency to split up the problems that children and youth have into different areas, partly according to manifest symptoms, partly according to which developmental stages and social arenas these show themselves in and partly according to their supposed etiology. Services have evolved and separated out accordingly, in ways that are not always easily comprehended by the clients.

Thirdly, the professionals themselves have diversified and specialised, even if the types of professions have not increased to the same extent. Professionals like doctors, psychologists, and social workers may specialise in many different ways, to a greater or lesser degree narrowing the scope of problems they are able to address. This partly stems from changing perceptions of the complexity and diversity of the problems to be met, and partly from professional interests concerning status, specialisation, wages, turf conflicts, and so forth.

Up to now, responsibility for services to children and youth has been shared by national government, the counties and the municipalities. This sharing has partly taken place through financing, and partly through the actual provision of services. From this point of view, service delivery has also been organised according to the frequency and seriousness of the problems the various services are supposed to deal with. Most services are offered by the municipal and county levels, while the state (at the national level) has been responsible for services requiring special resourcing such as special educational schooling, and residential care for the developmentally retarded. Typically, counties have been responsible for other specialist services such as residential care or child psychiatric units, which are expensive as well as meeting relatively low-frequency needs, while the municipalities are responsible for services like child welfare and child protection, school psychology, and health control. When collaboration is to be discussed, it must be therefore kept in mind that it can be 'vertical'—between organisational levels—as well as 'horizontal'—between services at the same level. In this contribution, the main focus will be on the municipal level.

'Helping' services for children and young people have evolved into a diversified and fragmented system.[1,2] The ways of organising them reflect historical, legal, and professional concerns to a large degree, and the challenge has been and is to develop a better match between services and clients.[3] In the Scandinavia of the 1990s, this challenge is typically met by looking at the organisation of services as well as the collaboration between them, or making systems-oriented as well as service-oriented efforts.

'Everybody wants to co-ordinate but nobody wants to be co-ordinated'

The need for collaboration

Given the multitude of problems which face the typical client, and the narrowness of the boundaries of most child care services, it is inevitable that many clients and children and youth as well, will require services from a number of agencies. From the clients' perspective, the need is the opposite: for one-stop shopping centres rather than chains of stores.[4,5]

The need for collaboration is also a logical consequence of organisational autonomy and professional specialisation. Huntze[6] summarises some of the forces working towards collaboration, which may also apply to the Scandinavian countries. These originate at several levels. From the national or state level, there are recurring initiatives towards more collaboration. These initiatives may take the form of trial projects and government plans of action, and more directly, the use of economic pressure. Further, the realisation of unintended and negative effects of fragmented service delivery systems may in themselves create inter- and intra-professional pressures towards better collaboration. A similar effect may result from the development of new and improved treatment strategies, as these do not follow traditional divisions between professionals or services. Finally, the need for additional, comprehensive services and/or redistribution of existing services may work in the same direction, initiated by user groups or clients as well as professionals.

In Norway, as in the other Scandinavian countries, a number of projects have been carried out aimed at improving the co-ordination of resources and professional competence in order to attain more coherent as well as more differentiated services.[7] Evaluations have reported promising results and in general conveyed optimism about possibilities for developing better systems for service delivery. However, it has been difficult to substantiate enduring changes in the co-operative interface. Corresponding problems have been reported from Canada and the USA.[5]

Some of the main barriers to these efforts seem related to the question of organisation at the various political levels, leadership, decision making and economic responsibility. Two factors seem to be lacking. One is explicit models for the development of collaboration, the other is professional training to handle dynamic issues like communication, group dynamics, group behaviour, conflict resolution strategies, management of transitions, and commitment.[8] Amongst other things, the various studies show how difficult it is for each of the services to give up some of their autonomy and control over their own resources, an issue that may be formulated as 'everybody wants to co-ordinate, but nobody wants to be co-ordinated'.

Decentralisation and increased responsibilities

To understand the developmental trends in the organisation of services for children and youth, it is necessary to start out with the more fundamental change that has taken place on the state or national level, concerning the degree of freedom given to each municipality in organising services for their inhabitants.[9] The trend has been towards decentralisation from the national to the municipal level, giving each municipality more freedom in the organisation of services. The way the state allocates financial resources to the municipalities has changed accordingly, with general grants taking the place of grants that were earmarked for specific purposes. Increased freedom at the municipal level means that the political and administrative priorities may differ from area to area. Although some services are mandatory, like child welfare, health, and school psychology services, the quality and capacity of these services may vary considerably.

With greater freedom has also come heavier responsibilities. For example, formerly, the state had administrative and financial responsibility for psychiatric in-patients, residential care for the developmentally retarded, and residential special schools. Latterly, these have been closed and responsibility for their client groups has been shifted to the home municipalities. This puts a heavy strain on the economy, particularly of the small and relatively poor ones. In all the Scandinavian countries, there are a sizeable amount of municipalities with less than 10,000 and even less than 5000 inhabitants, and these still remain the primary administrative level. Thus, conditions for offering municipal services in general have changed, and developments within the service delivery field must be seen in relation to local conditions.

Reorganisation and collaboration?

It is important to see local government reorganisation as processes that have been and are still going on, and not as definite events. As discussed above, an important common characteristic of these processes over time is decentralisation and devolution of responsibility to the municipal (local) level. This leads to greater demands on collaboration, as a result amongst other factors, of reduced availability of resources. In general, increased responsibility at the municipal level will also be accompanied by an increased demand for inter-professional and inter-agency collaboration at the horizontal level. Decentralisation of responsibility for multi-problem, time-consuming, and competence-demanding clients to the municipal level increases this need even further.

Collaboration problems are well documented: some clients receive services that are not suited to their needs, some receive no services at all and some receive overlapping services. This is not only a problem for the clients, but also in relation to the effective total use of overall resources within municipalities.[10] In respect of services for children and youth, discussions have primarily concerned more united efforts in prevention, and the need to create sufficiently wide-ranging and long-term services for multi-problem children and adolescents. Up to now, service delivery has been too divided and unco-ordinated, with the effect that each single service carries too little weight.

Important issues in the ongoing discussions of collaboration

Several issues have emerged in the ongoing discussions about inter-professional and inter-agency collaboration, partly as a result of empirical studies, and partly as a result of theoretical and ideological discussions.

First, the user or client perspectives have been accorded greater significance during the last couple of decades, in Scandinavia as well as in the UK and the USA. One issue is whether the users or the professionals are best served by today's models of organisation and service delivery. It can be argued that the more diversified and complicated the services are, the more difficult it will be to match clients and appropriate services. This will partly be related to the needs for the various services to define themselves as different from the others, a rationality that may be far removed from the clients' way of defining their needs. It can be argued that different professional approaches to defining, understanding, and treating problems may be incomprehensible as well as confusing for the clients. If it is important to focus more on the clients' rights as consumers, organising the services according to knowledge of their needs is necessary. This will probably lead to a quite different way of looking at specialisation and integration. Further, one important aspect of the rights of clients in the sense of consumers, is to be able to choose between services if a particular service should prove unsatisfactory. However, this presupposes a real freedom of choice among similar or corresponding services, which is not the case. Rather, the existing plethora of services are more or less different from each other, and most of them have waiting lists.

Second, the question of what kinds of professional competence are necessary arises. One issue is whether the municipalities, and the clients, are best served by generalists or specialists. Seen from an administrative perspective, professionals with some kind of general competence should be preferred because they can provide several kinds of services from various kinds of positions, as well as reaching various groups of clients. Also, a more general competence might be preferable to the clients, as such an approach can lead to fewer changes because one service turns out to be insufficient after some time. On the other hand, it will never be possible to educate absolute generalists, able to cope with any and all problems whatever their complexity or severity. Even if the professions are well served by creating a system of status-giving specialisation, the need for specialisation seen from the perspective of the clients co-exists. How to select recipients of specialist services, and the criteria for offering them, are controversial issues that are likely to remain so.

Third, increased responsibility for services at the municipal level also raises the question of allocation of resources. The issue is whether changes in the types of services to be offered are to be achieved by increased resources, and/or reorganisation through formal or informal structures.

Fourth, there is the question of existing collaborative structures. The issue is whether the documented problems of inter-agency and inter-professional collaboration are such that the clients will be better served by a more radical reorganisation of services. The need for such collaboration has been recognised for decades.[11,12] Various ways of collaborating, both formal and more informal, have been tried out. The logical solution, when problems are greater than one service can solve, of course, is to bring services and specialisms together, but on the other hand, this in itself seems to create friction and disputes. Such friction may arise from different definitions of the clients' problems, different suggestions about how to solve them, disagreement about who is to take main responsibility, particularly for difficult and not very rewarding clients, and problems associated with the distribution of status and power.

Finally, the services are covered by different legislation, and there are specific regulations concerning professional confidentiality and the protection of individuals.[13] The issue is whether it is possible or even desirable to create collaborative structures that lead to greater pooling or interchange of sensitive information about clients. This issue becomes particularly pertinent if the child welfare service is to be an integral part of such structures.[14]

Structures and strategies promoting collaboration

It is not difficult to identify the array of problems confronting practitioners, managers, or policymakers when the goal is to achieve better integrated services. The challenge lies in identifying and agreeing upon the policies and implementation practices that will truly have a positive impact on service outcomes.[15] Crowson and Boyd[16] speak of the '*Noah Principle*': No more prizes for predicting rain; prizes only for building arks.

It is necessary to make a decision about the level of specialisation (vertical collaboration) of the services, and the types of clients that are to receive them. In Norway, the establishing of so-called 'service chains' has been an alternative for providing services to multi-problem youth ever since a trial project was established in one county in 1980.[11] A service chain consists of a working model and principles for a system of services on the municipal and county levels. The principles are based on thinking about the 'lowest effective intervention level', but in combination with available services at other levels. They include consideration of co-ordination between services and continuity in contacts for the adolescents. These service chains were introduced because of recognition that the problems of some children and youth are too complex and long-term to be adequately addressed by one kind of service at the municipal level. This kind of thinking presupposes agreement between the services concerning intake, responsibility, and financing.

Parallel to this, there has been a trend towards increased collaboration at the municipal level (horizontal collaboration). This has been tried out through a number of different models, ranging from *ad hoc*-organised 'responsibility teams', across more or less permanently organised teams, to collaboration within the context of entirely new organisational structures. More formalised collaboration implies common professional goals, platforms, and methods. Total integration presupposes one administrative structure and a common budget as well. This does not preclude differentiated services.

The latter model has been tried out in some Norwegian and Danish municipalities. The Norwegian city of Trondheim is one example (as described by Per Egil Toldnes in Chapter 5, p.126) In one part of Trondheim, Saupstad, a single service delivery system was established by merging the former child welfare and school psychology services, with one leader and one budget. In the Danish county of Fredriksborg, consisting of 19 municipalities, a trial project was launched aimed at localising more services at the municipal level, thus giving more comprehensive services to children and families. Taken as a whole, these aims were reached to a greater or lesser degree in most of the 19 municipalities, but the issue of balancing these services with services for multi-problem youth and families remained.[17]

Thus, the systems-oriented approach points in the direction of a more unified and co-ordinated way of working with, and professional thinking about, services to children and youth, vertically as well as horizontally. Whether this should imply integration of services or co-ordination between services, is an important and not easily solved issue.

When organisation and collaboration are discussed in a Scandinavian context, this will usually concern various public services. We do not have a large tradition of voluntary, and particularly not private services for children and youth. The exception has been residential care units for children in care under the auspices of the Salvation Army or various religious, non-profit organisations. In recent years, there has been an increase in private services for multi-problem youth, more or less profit-oriented. There are no statistics available about the relative proportion of such services, nor is there an official view that all such services should be public. There are worries, however, about how much such services cost in relation to the total cost of the services and the possibility of controlling them and monitoring their quality. On the other hand, the emergence of such services underlines the difficulties the public services have in coping with exactly this group of clients.

Further challenges and implications for training

> Whatever the organisational solutions chosen, there is a need to see service delivery from the clients' perspective, necessitating flexibility between services and professionals, as well as mutual openness and acceptance. It also necessitates collaboration skills, including clients as well as the service deliverers in the venture.

We summarise below a number of the issues and resulting implications for learning which arise from current studies and experiences, some of which we have briefly presented here.

Firstly, the service-oriented approach points to the need for direct collaboration rather than 'orders' and 'referrals'.[18] Increased focus on the users' or clients' perspectives underlines the need to extend this collaboration to them and their families in evolving and tailoring services, with focus on service delivery that is sufficiently comprehensive and varied to meet their needs.

Another central area is the selection of clients who are offered services. Important issues here are strategies for referring and sorting clients,[19] decision making,[20] and for seeing clients in a life-course perspective where timing and matching become important in the selection of services to be offered. This way of thinking presupposes that each service sees itself as part of a larger system of services for children and young people. It also presupposes generalised knowledge about children in general and children with problems in particular.[21] A logical consequence of this is reflection on the limits to professional help, and the need to include the children's own social networks when services are planned.

A third area is how service delivery in a municipality is organised; that is, the conditions for collaboration. If the municipalities are given more responsibility, they need access to professionals or volunteers with sufficient qualifications. From today's point of view, this will comprise quite a number of professionals with varied training and post-graduate specialisation. From the point of view of administrators it is far too expensive to develop and maintain services depending on a large number of specialists, if the municipalities are to bear the brunt of the costs. The consequences of this kind of thinking is a stronger focus on generalised training programmes, making it possible for professionals to switch between problem types as well as sectors. One line of thought in Norway is to do just that. This would lead to more generalised services at the 'horizontal' level, as well as more similar services owing to increased general and common knowledge and skills on the part of the professionals. In principle, this means trying to ameliorate collaboration problems originating in too incompatible professional approaches through reducing the number of such approaches.

On the other hand, the need for specialist services within, for example, the fields of medicine, psychiatry, child welfare, and family therapy will remain even if a greater degree of specialised training should reduce it. This might imply that the need for specialised services should be taken care of by buying them from professionals that are either privately employed or employed by the counties instead of the municipalities. This would lead to more diversification at the 'vertical' level. However, it can be argued that a certain amount of specialisation is necessary at the municipal level as well, owing to the fact that children's problems differ in complexity as well as severity and duration. Thus, increased generalisation will not take away the need for collaboration, and implies introducing collaboration skills and other necessary skills mentioned by McNulty and Soper[8] as part of the curriculum of all the relevant professions.

Whatever organisational solutions chosen, there is a need to see service delivery from the clients' perspective, necessitating flexibility between services and professionals, as well as mutual openness and acceptance. It also necessitates collaboration skills, including clients as well as the service deliverers in the venture.

Notes and References
1. Melaville, A. I., Blank, M. J. and Asayeh, G., *Together we can*. Report (US Department of Education, 1993).
2. Ogden, T., 'Samarbeid og samordning i kommunale hjelpetjenester', *Spesialpedagogikk,* 5, 6–13 (1993).
3. Backe-Hansen, E., 'Hjelpetjenestene og barna', *Report No. 3*. (Oslo: The Norwegian Institute of Child Welfare Research, 1995).
4. Arnkil, E., 'Social work in systems of boundary', Unpublished paper (1990).
5. Wharf, B., 'Organising and delivering child welfare services: the contributions of research', in *Child welfare in Canada: Research and Policy Implications,* B. Galaway and J. Hudson (eds), (Toronto: Thompson Educational Publishing Inc., 1995).
6. Huntze, S. L., 'Cooperative interface of schools and other child care systems for behaviorally disordered students', in *Mildly Handicapped Conditions. Handbook of Special Education: Research and Practice,* vol. 2. M. C. Wang, M. C. Reynolds, and H. J. Walberg, (eds), (New York: Pergamon Press, 1988).
7. Klefbeck, J. and Ogden, T., *Nettverk og økologi* (Oslo: TANO, 1995).
8. McNulty, B. and Soper, E., 'Critical elements of successful inter-agency practice', paper presented at the National Intervention Symposium of Inter-agency Collaboration, Denver, Colorado (ERIC document reproduction service no. 235 669), (June 1992).
9. In Norway, a new Municipal Act to this effect was sanctioned in 1991.
10. Achenbach, T. M. 'What is developmental about developmental psychopathology', in J. Rolf, *et al.* (eds), *Risk and Protective Factors in the Development of Psychopathology* (Cambridge: University of Cambridge Press,1990).
11. NOU 1985:3. *Tiltak for ungdom med atferdsvansker.* (Oslo: Ministry of Health and Social Security, 1985).
12. Sosialdepartementet. *Innstilling om verneskolenes funksjon og målsetting.* (1968).
13. All the Scandinavian countries have a State institution regulating the creation of data registers and the storing of information that is identifiable, and the protection of individuals is seen as extremely important.
14. Kjønstad, A., *Taushetsplikt. Kommunikasjon og samarbeid mellom helseetaten, skoleetaten og barnevernstjenesten* (Hamar: Kapère forlag, 1992).
15. Bloomberg, L., 'Interorganisational Development And Implementation: An Examination of the School-Human Services Redesign Initiative in Hennepin County, Minnesota', in B. Galaway and J. Hudson (eds). *Child Welfare in Canada: Research and Policy Implications* (Toronto: Thompson Educational Publishing Inc. 1995).
16. Crowson, R. L. and Boyd, W. L., 'Coordinated services for children: Designing arks for storms and seas unknown', *American Journal of Education,* 101, 140-79 (February 1993).
17. Spaten, O. M., Ertmann, B. and Scholz Jørgensen, P., Lokalisering. *En undersøgelse af omlægningen av indsatsen for børn, unge og familier i Fredriksborg Amt og kommunerne i amtet 1987–94.* (Fredriksborg Amt: Socialforvaltningen, 1995).
18. Killén, K., 'Barnevern, barne- og ungdomspsykiatri. Premisser for prosesser', in Christiansen, K. U. (ed.), *Forholdet mellom barnevernet og barne- og ungdomspsykiatrien.* Publication series no. 5 (Oslo: The Norwegian Institute of Child Welfare Research, 1993).
19. Backe-Hansen, E., Kristofersen, L., Ogden, T. and Sandbæk, M., 'Different approaches to the identification of children who receive help and evaluation from local helping services', *Social Work and Social Sciences Review* (1995).
20. Backe-Hansen, E., *Til barnets beste: Beslutninger og beslutningsprosesser i barnevernet.* (Oslo: TANO, 1995).
21. Parker, R., 'Theme and variations', in B. Kahan (ed.), *Child Care Research, Policy and Practice* (London: Hodder and Stoughton, 1989).

5.2 DEVELOPING CHILD-CENTRED SERVICES IN THE SAUPSTAD DISTRICT OF THE NORWEGIAN CITY OF TRONDHEIM

Per Egil Toldnes

Head Teacher, Huseby School/Growing Up Centre, Saupstad District, Norway.

Public service providers in Saupstad believe that *to make a change, you have to organise for change*. In 1992, the new District Administration in Saupstad adopted as a central aim that of providing an organisation and an environment which give the optimal possibilities for learning and growth for all children and young people. To achieve this involved looking at the range of services which meets their needs. It required asking, what do children in Saupstad need? The answers had consequences not only for the organisation of services, but also for their administration and management.

> In 1992, the city of Trondheim adopted a new organisational model, dividing its previously centralised administration into six districts, each with its own administration. The key concepts associated with the reorganisation have been decentralisation and delegation of political decision making and increased co-ordination, co-operation and effectiveness through closely defined goals.

Saupstad District is located on the outskirts of Trondheim city in the middle of Norway. Saupstad has a total of 13,000 people, one third of them younger than 19 years.

Until 1992 the administration in Trondheim relating to children, young people and families was organised in the following way:

- Department for churches, culture and leisure activities
- Department of education
- Department for health and social services

Working within this centralised administrative structure put limits on how much the services collaborated—although often concerned with the same child and family. It was necessary as well to look at where the responsibilities of some services fell short of what was required. For example, some children and parents required longer hours of day-care and a wider range of activities.

In 1992 the city of Trondheim adopted a new organisational model, dividing its previously centralised administration into six districts, each with its own administration. The key concepts associated with the reorganisation have been decentralisation and delegation of political decision making and increased co-ordination, co-operation and effectiveness through closely defined goals. The reorganisation was undertaken in the best interest of people living in the district, in particular children and young people.

In Saupstad district the department of children's services, known as the Division of Growing Up, was established. The Children's Services Management Team (comprising the district head and the six head teachers in the schools/growing up centres, Figure 5.1) administers education, leisure activities, social services, as well as all other public services. In addition the district is responsible for providing services to some groups of adults including mentally and physically disabled people, immigrants and the unemployed. Most services are located on the premises of six schools and seven kindergartens within Saupstad district (see Figure 5.1).

The administrative and organisational structure was designed to promote collaboration. First, it aimed to enable people to meet and get to know each other, as everyone is physically located in the same premises. This is based on the assumption that everyone collaborates much better with people they have seen and talked to. Secondly this structure means there is only one administrative leader for all the different groups of professionals working directly with the children.[1]

Within such a decentralised structure of relatively small districts, the leader is closer to his or her colleagues, making it much easier to establish one common strategy

TABLE 5.1 **Changes in roles and structures within children's services in Saupstad District.**

Service/post	Previous role/structure	New role/structure
Schools	Working with education only.	A centre for children's services—where one leader is responsible for education, spare time activities, club activities for all ages, pre school activities and—as admission of 6-year-olds into school is new in Norway—specially designed activities for children at this age.
Daycare centres	Taking care of the children who actually come to the daycare centre (because parents pay to have them there).	As resource centres for all children and families in the district where we aim to: • give a flexible service adjusted to the families' needs • give guidance to parents individually or in groups • offer organised club activities in afternoons and week-ends
Leaders	Responsible for institutions relating to separate aspects of the child's development, e.g. education or social services	Responsible for all activities and municipal funded services in the area
Special support services	Special services where the social workers work with child welfare, and school psychologists and child care workers are in separate divisions	The 'Helping Service', which is integrated, co-ordinated and decentralised

FIGURE 5.1 Organisational chart Saupstad District: Growing Up and Health Care Division.

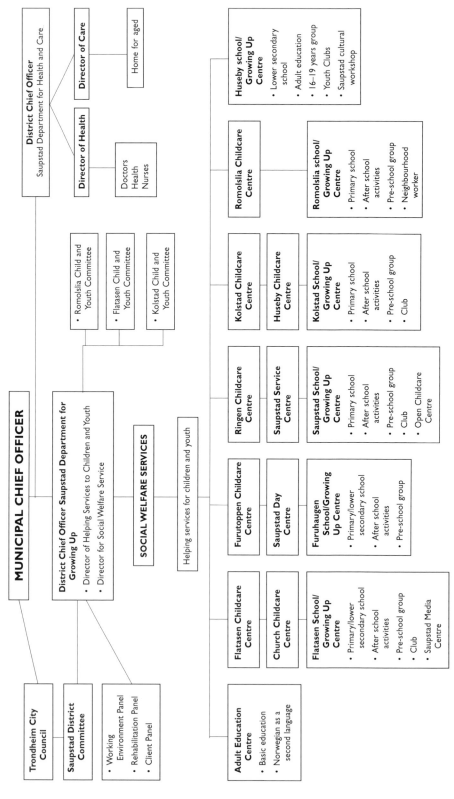

> It is an important principle for Saupstad that services are to be administered and managed near the *users*, defined in Saupstad as not only *children* and their *families* but also those working with them. Separately administrated services regulated by different legislation are now linked to one service institution.

for the work. This model becomes even more interesting as we move down to the institutional level; to each school, daycare centre and so forth. Table 5.1 shows the changes in the roles and structures of the services.

It is an important principle for Saupstad that services are to be administered and managed near the *users*, defined in Saupstad as not only *children* and their *families* but also those working with them. Separately administrated services regulated by different legislation are now linked to one service institution.[2] In other words, different services regulated by different sets of legislation are now under *one* administration managed by *one* leader—the head teacher of the school/growing up centre.

Strategies promoting collaboration

Children's services in Saupstad are organised at a district level, a zone level and at an institutional level, that is schools and daycare centres. Reorganising and adjusting the way services are administered and organised is not enough to promote collaboration. Changes are required in working methods for schools and daycare centres as well as for social services and leisure activities. This change in approach applies to parents as well as to professionals.

One strategy in addressing this has been the use of what is known as the home training programme *Marte Meo*.[3] This working method, which was developed in the Netherlands by Maria Aarts in the early 1980s, includes amongst other features a supervisor recording on video, parents or carers communicating with the child at home. The video is then analysed by the supervisor to establish what already exists of positive communicative patterns in that particular family, and the findings and the video are presented to the parents for further discussion. *Marte Meo* is based on the idea that by supporting parents in developing a positive communication with the child, the child will develop social skills which will help in preventing negative behaviours and attitudes. Such programmes are not only a method for working with children and their families,

> The head teacher's responsibilities do not stop at the school gate or at the end of the school day, but include questions concerning the situation in the homes and what the children are doing in the afternoon.

but may be seen as an ideology valid for all professionals working with and for children. The home training programme helps professionals and administrative departments to focus on their common understanding when they carry out their job.

The collaborative approach may be illustrated by the school where I work as a head teacher. The school has been renamed the School and Centre for Growing Up. The head teacher's responsibilities do not stop at the school gate or at the end of the school day, but include questions concerning the situation in the homes and what the children are doing in the afternoon. The responsibility has been extended to cover all children in our neighbourhood, not only the pupils of the school where I am a head teacher. In analysing the consequences of any incidents to the School and Centre for Growing Up, I attempt to adapt a broad approach, not only through the eyes of a traditional head teacher or my own service function as a teacher. The emphasis is on the perception that this is *our* job, not yours and mine.

Traditionally the head teacher's role was that of being 'the first among equals', serving as a guide to institutional learning and development. This status is often expressed in the view that the head teacher should do some teaching. The extended role of the head teacher now includes additional responsibilities within the school itself—such as budgeting, accounting and managing staff/personnel, including appointments. The head teacher has also been given full administrative responsibilities, managing numerous other activities, ensuring that the child is helped in all possible ways, for example through leisure activities, special services and parental programmes where this is needed. The head teacher is managing the budget as well as the staff in the Growing Up Centre which provides such services.

Today's head teachers in Saupstad are now area leaders of children's services rather than school leaders. Being a head teacher is a much more powerful position than it was before. In terms of collaboration the same argument applies as at the central administrative level: with only one leader to relate to, people work together, using the same strategy. It is clear that if after all available information is given and matters have been openly discussed, it is not possible to reach consensus due to professional disagreements or otherwise, the power to make decisions rests with the head teacher. The decision applies to all professions. As a consequence, existing teacher teams, which already have some autonomy concerning budgets, planning and choice of strategies, may be expanded to include others, for example social workers, special teachers, leisure workers and assistants. Teams with common goals and responsibilities work with the same group of children.[4]

Zone Groups are one example of such a team. These groups are organised in the school catchment area, and consist of a health nurse, psychologist, social worker and teachers with special training covering both the school and the daycare services in the area.

The main goal for the Zone Group, as well as for the School and Centre for Growing Up, is to help those children who are at risk. The work is based on a common plan that takes all aspects of the life of the child into consideration, and works together with the parents as a prerequisite.[5]

Summing up

Having adjusted the goals, reorganised and changed the methods of work, the question needs to be asked: has the intended collaboration become reality in Saupstad district? So far nothing indicates that children's services are on the wrong track, although there is still a long way to go. In relation to 'working together', it can be observed that different professions work together in teams on a daily basis. However, in the institutions there is a very strong feeling that the full effect is difficult to obtain. This is mainly due to the fact that nearly all the resources are attached to the area of teaching. My experience is that the teachers' organisations will not play along if current teacher resources have to be 'changed' into resources for other professions, as they naturally want to protect their own jobs as teachers.

It also has to be admitted that the training required within the institutions for collaboration has been neglected—training in knowing about each others' job functions, knowing about other professional views, being familiar with different Acts and regulations, obtaining a new common culture and developing *one* new profession. Despite this, the 'one leader—one strategy' seems to work quite well. However, the pace is slow mainly due to little time available to administrative tasks. This means that the establishment of an administrative team and delegation within the institutions is less effective than it should be. But it is only a matter of time before each institution reaches a level of collaboration quite close to what was planned.

The physical distance between administration and users has been shortened. The service manager and staff representing different professions are now working closer together organisationally on a daily basis, and are therefore able to develop common priorities for overall service provision. Nevertheless there is an identified need to build a management team at the institutional level—at the Growing Up Centre. It has become clear that the processes by which common priorities are decided have to be developed and made explicit. From the leader's perspective it has also become clear that a management team with a set of explicitly stated decision making routines must not undermine the importance of the leader's role as primarily concerned with one to one conversations with members of staff *as well as* giving priority to be with, and talk to, the children.

Notes and References
1. Alfred Oftedal Telhaug og Terje Veimo, *Rektorledet oppvekstmiljø* (Trondheim: Norsk senter for barneforskning, 1991).
2. Graham Clifford og Lisbeth Dalsnes, *Hjelpetjenesten—reform eller retrett?* (Trondheim: Norsk senter for barneforskning, 1992).
3. Meldheim, B., 'Marte Meo Metoden', *Barnevernpedagogen,* 1 pp. 6–13, 1993.
4. Berit Aanderaa og Gunnar Tveiten, *Kommuner for barn* (Oslo: Kommuneforlaget, 1994).
5. *Håndbok for grunnskolen* (Oslo: Pedlex norsk skoleinformasjon, 1992 pp. 84–99).

5.3   CHILDREN AT RISK

DEVELOPING STRUCTURES AND LOCAL COLLABORATION IN THE DANISH MUNICIPALITY OF SÆBY

Mogens Blæhr

Principal Psychologist, Guidance Department, Sæby Municipality, Denmark

The 1980s saw a number of key developments in the structures and role of Danish services for children and young people at risk. In the municipality of Sæby these changes have led to the strengthening of collaboration at a local level, as described here.

The need for reorganisation

Sæby municipality has 18,000 inhabitants of which 4000 are children and young people. At the beginning of reorganisation in the mid-1980s it had the same structures as most other municipalities in Denmark, with overall responsibility for developing and providing services to children and young people lying with two large administration departments: the school administration (education and culture) and the social administration (social welfare and health). The number of children and young people in need of special pedagogical arrangements in primary school was increasing as well as the number of children and young people taken into some form of care. The capacity of the schools and daycare centres to provide for children and young people with psycho-social difficulties was diminishing whilst at the same time the pressure on the specialised treatment system was increasing.

Looking back at the 1980s it is possible to identify three waves of changes contributing to the municipal reorganisation of public services. The first of these involved the shift away from providing services within centralised institutions—remote from the daily life of children and their families—to more local arrangements. The emphasis became that of co-operating with the child's daily environment.

The next, and most general development was the modernisation of the public sector. This involved the decentralisation of responsibilities to the municipalities and to services within the municipality. Public services were to be assessed according to the extent to which explicit goals were being achieved and services were to operate within framework legislation and guidance rather than through detailed regulations. As a result of the decentralisation the 275 Danish municipalities, varying in size, have organised their administration and services in different ways. The third change was initiated through a public debate about the large number of children and young people in residential care and the increasing number of children with special needs in schools.

The debate also focused on the respective responsibilities and rights of parents in relation to society and children and led, for example, to children in care of 15 and over, no longer being solely represented by their parents but having the right to be involved in decisions concerning them. Due to a perceived lack of documentation on children at risk, intensive research programmes were set up in Denmark as well as other Scandinavian countries. As the research results were made available, the Danish government initiated comprehensive development programmes supported by central pools within both social and educational services. The aim of the central pool policies was to give the municipalities incentives to take a more pro-active role in providing preventive services towards children and young people, rather than restricting their role to that of treatment.

The government also altered the legislation within special education (1990) and the field of social welfare. The Social Assistance Act (1993) included an extension of the rights of children, young people and their parents to information, counselling and support. A strengthening of the parents' right to co-operate was among the major changes. In 1994, the government announced an Action Plan which addressed children and young people most at risk. This decision was taken on the basis of research which showed that 12–15 per cent of Danish children are at risk of being marginalised, and that 4 per cent had an actual need for treatment. The Action Plan stressed the importance of developing cross-disciplinary and cross-sector links in service provision and in the methods applied. The main responsibility for implementing the Action Plan rests with each municipality—with its council, central and district administrations, and the public institutions providing services.

> Typically, the municipality had had knowledge of the children and their families for several years before the children were taken into care, but without succeeding in preventing this happening.

Sæby municipality and children at risk

In 1986 the principal psychologist in Sæby initiated an examination of the municipality's files on children at risk. The purpose was to look at ways of improving the quality of municipal services for children at risk. The majority of those in care were in the latter stages of their schooling. Typically, the municipality had had knowledge of the children and their families for several years before the children were taken into care, but without succeeding in preventing this happening. Reviewing the files of those in care the following was noted:

- The main objectives for the treatment of children taken into care were rarely made explicit.
- Progress reports were missing.
- Achievements were not registered.
- Results could not therefore be made subject to regular evaluation.

A conference was held for the members of staff from the schools and social administrations. Staff were asked to give their views and present their experiences of working with children and young people at risk, and present their ideas of how to improve the quality of the services. The conference showed that the staff were experiencing the following:

- extended decision making processes involving schools and services, administrative departments and various political committees in the town hall
- decisions concerning the individual child and the family made by the two main municipal departments were not coherent
- the work of the professionals was not co-ordinated, with duplication and professional conflicts common
- contact between professionals across administrations and departments, centrally and locally, indicated that the professionals did not understand each others' language.

Preventative work in the local area must be prioritised, and children, young people, parents and other citizens should be involved. The users of public services must take part in all discussions and their preferences and needs should be prioritised.

As a result of the conference five working parties were set up. During the winter of 1986–7 they worked on issues which the members of staff had themselves formulated. In the spring of 1987 the following goals and strategies were presented, based on the experience of staff and management:

- An earlier and more effective approach should be applied by identifying the children at risk at an earlier stage and developing better methods.
- Preventative work in the local area must be prioritised, and children, young people, parents and other citizens should be involved. The users of public services must take part in all discussions and their preferences and needs should be prioritised.
- A common language should be developed. Cross-disciplinary co-operation must be strengthened by encouraging good links and positive relationships. Further training should be provided including topic days, cross-disciplinary courses and arrangements of cross-disciplinary character.

The central idea behind this strategy was to initiate reorganisation of the present service structure and its strategies concerning children at risk. The main principles behind the new set of goals were to strengthen cross-disciplinary and cross-sector co-operation. The reorganisation of public services to children at risk was unexpectedly supported by additional finances, through the establishment by the government of a 'pool'[1] policy for children and young people at risk. Sæby municipality applied for and was given additional funding to take forward the reorganisation.

Reorganisation strategy

The reorganisation process in Sæby may be described as having begun with relatively small changes, moving towards increasingly greater changes as the new government strategy of *mal-ogrammestyring* or 'national goal and framework control' has developed. This provides for detailed objectives and targets to be set locally and overall aims nationally.

Supported by the central pool policies several small projects were started at schools, daycare centres and across the central departments at the town hall. Not all the projects had based their activities on main goals and principles articulated above. However, a certain degree of control was exercised through the project group, which was appointed to co-ordinate the projects. Consultancy assistance was offered to individuals and services, helping them to formulate their own ideas in the application for pool money. The project group made it conditional for their help that the projects outline a development plan which conformed with the previously mentioned goals and principles. The successful bids were supervised by the project group.

The project group ensured that information on the projects was disseminated through descriptions in the daily press. All members of staff in the school and social administration were informed through an internal newspaper and information leaflets were distributed to all parents in the municipality. During this period a closer co-operation between members of staff was developing, as they got to know each other much better professionally and personally. Through day-to-day work on issues concerning services to children at risk, closer co-operation and cross-disciplinary strategies have been developed.

Municipal reorganisation

At this point in time the municipal administration was still unchanged and was perceived as too slow and unco-ordinated in making decisions and following up initiatives from the services themselves. In 1989, however, Sæby carried out a thorough reorganisation of its administration. The school and social administration departments were merged, followed by development programmes for managers in the central administration, in schools and social service institutions. At the same time an extensive education programme for members of central administration staff was started, enabling staff to get out of their old habits of handling cases, which had been developed in a period of detailed regulation and control. Staff in the central administration were

---

The changes in the organisational structure and the new ways of working with children and young people have resulted in the services obtaining information at an earlier stage on those at risk, enabling them to undertake preventive work before the family's problems have become too great.

FIGURE 5.2 Cultural and social administration

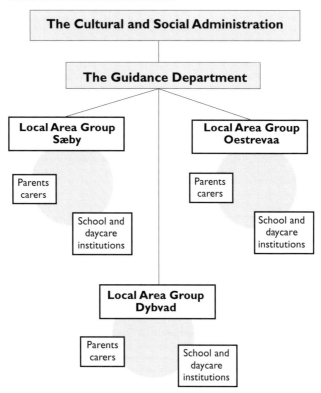

FIGURE 5.3 The guidance department

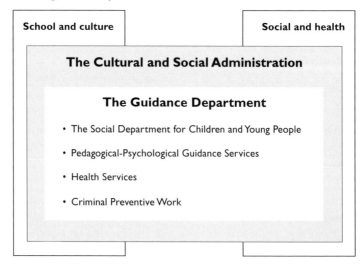

expected to learn and develop strategies more in line with the overall goals as they were initially phrased by members of staff in schools and institutions.

In connection with the reorganisation of the central municipal administration, the four departments (the social department for children and young people, health services, the pedagogical-psychological guidance services, and criminal preventive work) were merged into one department—the guidance department. This new department was given the following responsibilities:

- Provide guidance, information and services to families with children.
- Give guidance without formal registration.
- Attend monthly meetings with the service units for up-dating and guidance.
- Offer consultations to the local council and others.

Its main task is to secure that both a wide and a specific professional competence is developed and accessible, as well as to ensure a high degree of cross-disciplinary co-operation concerning child and family services. The staff in the guidance department were moved out of the town hall and divided into area groups, one in each of the three districts. Each group includes welfare officers, health staff, special needs teachers and psychologists.

During the same period a further decentralisation of the central municipality's responsibilities took place. This included some decision making relating to economy and service provision, now made within the districts.

The emergence of new forms of collaboration

Those primarily involved in implementing the new social policy and developing a new administrative culture are the parents, schools, institutions and the local area groups. In order to demonstrate the direction of future development of services to children and young people at risk, the cultural and social administration unit in Sæby is now expected to base its activity on the pedagogical goals developed locally in the guidance department. The reorganisation process is, in this way, moving from detailed central regulation towards goals formulated to meet local needs.

Schools and institutions are offered consultation and assistance throughout the process of reorganisation. At the same time the cultural and social administration in Sæby requires all institutions to develop activity plans. These include aims and budgeted activities and also involve reviewing the previous period's activities.

What has been achieved?

In 1992 the whole project was evaluated by the chief psychologist, in co-operation with the University Centre of Aalborg, focusing on the outcome in relation to the goals that were set out at the start of the project in early 1987.

The changes in the organisational structure and the new ways of working with children and young people have resulted in the services obtaining information at an earlier stage on those at risk, enabling them to undertake preventive work before the family's problems have become too great. This early intervention is a result of establishing local area groups in close co-operation with the local schools, residential centres and other social service institutions. Cross-disciplinary seminars and topic days which have been offered have contributed to this success. Through these the collaborating members of staff have been given the chance to deal with problem areas concerning children and young people in general and children at risk in particular. By updating and widening their knowledge of and insight in central problems within the area staff often find it easier to attack problems at an early stage.

> Many of the *professional and personal* barriers to collaboration previously to be found between and within public administration departments have been lessened ... Prevailing myths and prejudices have been diminished.

Many of the *professional and personal* barriers to collaboration previously to be found between and within public administration departments have been lessened. This change is mainly a result of spending time together in development and education activities. Prevailing myths and prejudices have been diminished. Each professional in the area groups has a solid knowledge of the 'children at risk' field. But the new services do not rely on single member of staff's knowledge and insight only. The welfare officers represent knowledge and insight based on the family point of view. The special need teachers and health staff represent knowledge and insight in the individual child's learning ability, health and social development. The psychologists contribute with theories and methods on the dynamics and the development, summarising the body of knowledge in each single case.

In order to enable further development and high quality of public service provision, it is necessary to secure resources offering in-service training, professional management development and supervision. Other possibilities include the introduction of standard administrative procedures and the use of new procedures.

The evaluation of the initial experience in Sæby indicates that the work with children at risk has increased its standing by being placed in a wider social and cultural context. The services are on better terms with the families, whose child is at risk or already in care. In addition to this parental 'good will', increased collaboration amongst providers and administrators has increased the possibilities for taking action earlier rather than later.

Note
1. 'Pools' have been established as part of the government policy of setting centrally determined strategies which municipalities are able to implement in their own way. See Annette Poulsen, Chapter 3.2, for more details.

PART III
PARTICIPATION

Chapter 6

◆

PARTICIPATION: UK

6.1 PROMOTING THE PARTICIPATION OF CHILDREN

OVERVIEW OF RECENT DEVELOPMENTS

Gerison Lansdown
Director, Children's Rights Office, London

Background

The welfare state introduced in the UK in the 1940s was rooted in a paternalism in which state intervention was viewed as essentially benign. In the event of inability to provide for oneself, the state would not only provide but would determine the nature of provision. Its philosophy embodied no recognition of conflict between the individual and the state, or the potential for user-participation in the design, development or monitoring of services. Thus health, housing, social security, education and social services were introduced in which the politicians, administrators and professionals who designed and delivered them gave scant regard to the experience of the individuals at their receiving end.

During the 1980s, the concept of paternalistic state provision came under increasing criticism. The political focus emphasised the importance of consumer rights, public accountability, competition and value for money. Legislation was introduced which gave parents, on paper at least, greater rights in respect of their children's education, schools more autonomy from local education authorities, GPs greater control over their budgets, and council tenants rights to buy their accommodation. The NHS and Community Care Act 1990 gave users more say in both the planning and kind of services offered. The concept of user participation and individual choice, together with the philosophy of the market, began to enter the language of welfare. These changes were designed to transfer control of services away from the state, particularly local authorities, and towards individual consumers. However, the creation of a 'market' in welfare provision rests on the presumption that the consumer is both able to choose whether or not they wish to use a service and also to exercise a choice in the nature of the service. For children neither of these choices exists. In reality the exercise of choice is highly constrained for many parents. Poverty, rural isolation or lack of appropriate minority ethnic provision will all serve to restrict real choices. For example, with the proposal from the Department for Education to issue vouchers for parents to buy nursery provision for 4-year-olds, choice is limited by both the availability of places at which it is possible to 'cash' the voucher, and the additional money to top up the amount given in the voucher. In other words, these developments which have dominated the political agenda in recent years have had no visible impact on the capacity of either children, or indeed many parents, to influence the nature of services they receive.

> It is no longer possible therefore for public policy to subsume children within the family, to be defined or hidden within it.

However, other changes have taken place in the relationship between children and the state. The family can no longer be considered without question as a secure, safe and stable environment for all children. The past 20 years have been characterised by growing recognition first that physical abuse and neglect and more recently sexual abuse of children exists within families. We have also been forced to confront the painful reality that children are equally vulnerable when removed into the supposedly protective arena of the child care system. A series of scandals has exposed the vulnerability to abuse and exploitation of children who live in local authority residential accommodation by adults with responsibility for caring for them.[1]

We have witnessed considerable changes in the nature of family life, which have increased the stresses on parents—more women in the labour market, higher male unemployment, geographical mobility, social isolation, and greater insecurity in relationships. The constant representation of successful and affluent families in the media places parents under growing pressure to achieve the lifestyles portrayed. These changes together with lower fertility rates, smaller households and fewer adults in the household have placed different demands on public services with increased demands for childcare services, babysitting, counselling, mediation, parent support and education, and appropriate provision for parents by employers. Children too have been affected, with many children likely to live through periods of marriage, divorce, single parenthood, cohabitation and possible remarriage. Over 150,000 children are affected by divorce each year. For these children the experience of family is neither static nor constant.

The cumulative impact of these developments has posed a challenge to the view that children 'belong' to their parents and that parents, within the privacy of the family, have unlimited rights to act and speak on their behalf. They have challenged the view that the state and indeed parents are invariably benign towards children. They have led to greater need for partnership between parents and the state in the task of providing for children. In the light of all these changes it is increasingly evident that the needs, interests and rights of children and their parents will not always coincide. It is no longer possible, therefore, for public policy to subsume children within the family, to be defined or hidden within it. These developments, arising as they have in the context of the broader debate around the rights of the individual within the welfare system, have lent some urgency to the need to ensure that children themselves are guaranteed avenues through which they can articulate their concerns both on matters affecting them within the family and indeed in the development and delivery of services provided on their behalf.

What does participation mean?

In order to consider the promotion of a more consultative relationship with children, it is first necessary to examine what participation really means. The idea of increasing children's involvement in decision making processes can provoke a number of responses:

- it will impose burdens on children at too young an age
- young children lack the capacity to be involved in decision making
- children cannot be given rights until they are capable of accepting responsibility
- giving children rights undermines the authority of the family.

These concerns reveal a number of fundamental misconceptions about the nature of participation. It is important firstly to distinguish between self-determination and participation. The principle of *participation* is clearly defined in Article 12 of the UN Convention on the Rights of the Child, ratified by the UK Government in December 1991, which states that governments must 'assure to the child who is capable of forming his or her own views the right to express those views freely in all matters affecting the child, the views of the child being given due weight in accordance with the age and maturity of the child'. In other words, the right of a child to participation is the right to be involved in matters affecting them, to articulate views and have them respected but not necessarily to be able to determine the outcome of that process. The process of participation is not contingent on a judgement of the child's competence, nor is it restricted by adult perceptions of the best interests of the child. It is a right of all children capable of expressing a view and extends not only to individual decisions affecting a child's life but broader issues affecting children and young people as a body.

Meaningful participation for children both within personal relationships at home and at school as well as in the wider field of public services, requires recognition of the need for:

- encouragement of the child to express views and a willingness to take those views seriously
- provision of sufficient information to enable the child to express informed views
- an explanation of all decisions, including in particular decisions that go against the expressed wishes of the child

- an indication of the decisions that the child can make for him- or herself, from the earliest age.

Participation, however, does not imply an automatic right to *self-determination* in which the exercise of choices and decision making is transferred on to the shoulders of children. The transfer to children of responsibility for decision making must be bounded by judgements by adults of both competence on the part of the child and their need for protection. The UN Convention on the Rights of the Child acknowledges this responsibility in Article 5 which states that governments must 'respect the responsibilities, rights and duties of parents ... to provide ... appropriate direction and guidance in the exercise by the child of the rights [in the Convention]'. It also recognises the potential conflict in the exercise of those responsibilities by asserting that they must be carried out 'in a manner consistent with the child's evolving capacity'. In other words, adults do not have unfettered rights to act on children's behalf. They must have regard to the growing competence of the child to take responsibility for those decisions themselves as they mature.

> Respecting children and providing them with opportunities to participate in matters of concern to them is one of the most effective ways of encouraging them to believe in themselves, gain confidence and learn to negotiate decision making with other people.

Participation, then, is a process of involving children in decisions that affect their lives. Respecting children and providing them with opportunities to participate in matters of concern to them is one of the most effective ways of encouraging them to believe in themselves, gain confidence and learn to negotiate decision making with other people. It is through participation that children can develop understanding of the consequences of their actions and their responsibilities to others. The UN Committee on the Rights of the Child in its recent examination of the government on the implementation of the Convention in the UK expressed concern that there appeared to be greater emphasis placed on the rights of parents to the detriment of the views and best interests of children[2] and specifically recommended that

> 'greater priority be given to incorporating the general principles of the Convention especially the provisions of ... Article 12 concerning the child's right to make their views known and have those views given due weight, in legislative and administrative measures and in policies undertaken to implement the rights of the child.'[3]

Is participation for children a reality?

The 1980s gave birth to the Children Act 1989 in England and Wales (and comparable legislation being introduced in Northern Ireland and Scotland) which embodies a number of key principles which demonstrate respect for the voice of children. It requires that local authorities and courts consider the wishes and feelings of children when making decisions concerning their welfare, and in public, although not in private law proceedings, children are automatically entitled to legal representation. Children can apply to the court for leave to apply for an order, for example, in respect of their residence or contact with other adults. Children who are subject to a child assessment order and who are competent to make informed choices can refuse to be assessed or examined. Local authorities are required to establish complaints procedures for children in need.

Certainly the Children Act has begun to inform practice within social services departments. A number have appointed children's rights officers to advocate on behalf of children looked after by local authorities. Children are increasingly enabled to participate in reviews and child protection conferences. Some authorities are exploring methods of encouraging children and young people to contribute to the development of policy in the child care field as well as participating in decision making in relation to their individual lives. Recent research into the views of young people in care, however, indicates that developments in this direction have not yet had a great deal of impact on many young people affected. Real participation in decision making processes is not a reality for substantial numbers of young people in care. For example, of 600 young people taking part in a recent survey into the experiences of care, as many as two in five felt that they were not listened to in case conferences and reviews.[4] One of the messages arising from the public inquiries established to investigate the series of scandals relating to abuse of children in care has been that those children had no opportunities to make their concerns heard and no avenues of complaint or access to independent advocacy.

> Real movement beyond the rhetoric of participation will not happen until there is both a legal responsibility and cultural expectation on adults to consult with children on matters of concern to them in the normal day-to-day living of their lives—within the family, at school, in the wider public arena and not only at a point of conflict necessitating state intervention.

It is also important to acknowledge that the scope of the Children Act is extremely limited. It only has application once conflict arises within a family, or between parents and the local authority, over the child's care. It contains no duty on parents to take account of their children's wishes and feelings (although the Children (Scotland) Act 1995 has introduced this provision), and no general right for children to participate in broader matters of concern to them. What this means is that there is no general presumption in legislation that children have a right to participate in decision making or that they should be encouraged to articulate their views. Such a presumption only comes into play once the child is in a situation of conflict. It therefore provides a much more limited right than that contained in Article 12 which insists that children in every sphere of their lives have the right to express their views and have them taken seriously. Real movement beyond the rhetoric of participation will not happen until there is both a legal responsibility and cultural expectation on adults to consult with children on matters of concern to them in the normal day-to-day living of their lives—within the family, at school, in the wider public arena and not only at a point of conflict necessitating state intervention. Without this, how can we expect children who are not used to being listened to, suddenly acquire the skills and the confidence to articulate their experiences at a point of crisis in their lives? At the point of parental separation or divorce for example? Or when seriously ill and needing to make decisions about treatment? How can we expect adults to listen effectively when to do so is not part of the normal expectation of relationships with children?

There is also little evidence that medical practitioners have moved very far in the direction of involving children in decisions concerning their health care and treatment. Whilst there are developments seeking to promote children's participation, such as the work of the Great Ormond Street Hospital in allowing very young children to take responsibility for their own pain relief, many practitioners remain unclear about what rights children have to consent to treatment. There is often inadequate information given to children, and there is little or no training for practitioners on the legislation or practice of children's participation. A recent initiative by the Royal College of Nursing, funded by the Gulbenkian Foundation, to provide awards for innovative developments in promoting children's participation in their own health care was motivated by concern at the lack of priority given to respecting children's views within the health service.

Apart from the limited requirements under the Children Act, local authorities are under no obligation to consult with children and young people when developing services for them; for example, when developing recreational or leisure facilities, children are rarely asked about what is needed; problems with existing provision; who uses what services; difficulties of access for disabled children; or transport. Young people are rarely even consulted over the development of youth services, or crime prevention strategies. Some authorities are now beginning to explore possible structures for building in the views of young people to the development, monitoring and evaluation of services but these approaches are far from being the norm and have no statutory base.[5]

Children have no formal rights to participation in matters concerning their education. The focus of politicians in addressing rights of access to information or choice of school has been exclusively on the parents. Children neither have the right to participate in individual matters such as school choice, curriculum or appeals over exclusions nor in school policy or administration. There is no requirement to involve children in decisions on, for example, school uniforms, arrangements for school meals, supervision in the playground, tackling bullying or discipline. Schools are not required to introduce complaints procedures and comparatively few have school councils which provide a structure within which to consult children and ensure that their views are reflected in the development of policy. Pupils under 18 are precluded from representation on school governing bodies. There are a number of innovative and highly effective examples of schools councils, peer counselling projects to tackle bullying and consultation exercises with school pupils to explore strategies for reducing truancy, but these exist in a tiny minority of schools and are dependent on the goodwill and imagination of individual teachers.

Conclusion

The introduction of the Children Act together with the ratification in 1991 by the UK government of the UN Convention on the Rights of the Child has given the lie to the belief that children's rights in the field of participation have been significantly enhanced. These developments have provoked considerable discussion around the concept of participation in ways that were unthinkable in the early days of the welfare state, but the reality of those developments has been to create, as yet, only minimal change.

> Children lack the autonomy and independence to benefit from the recent evaluation of consumer rights. Without either political or socio-economic power, the forces of the market will not serve them.

In fact, we do not have a culture in this country of listening to children. There is some evidence from children that they do not have confidence that adults value and respect their opinions. During a consultation exercise undertaken by the Children's Rights Development Unit in 1993, 45 groups of children aged between 5–18 years were approached to discuss their perceptions of how their rights were respected.[6] The children came from a wide variety of life experiences but common to all groups was a powerful sense of frustration that their views and experiences were not taken seriously at home, at school, by politicians, by policymakers and the media. Research into bullying being undertaken by Sheffield University reveals that as many as 50 per cent of children fail to report experiences of bullying because they have no confidence that teachers will listen sufficiently seriously to take action on their behalf.[7] These perceptions of powerlessness also extend into the broader political arena. Research published in 1992 on attitudes of children to power and politics reveals an overwhelming sense of impotence.

> 'All the children suggested that even if a law were unfair, there was little anyone could do....They all accept that some laws are unfair, and some decisions are imposed against the wish of the majority. They have an almost cynical belief that the authorities can do what they want, and that citizens are there to put up with the consequences.'[8]

We have achieved limited legislative change to promote the rights of children and young people to participate in decisions that affect their lives. But this is not enough without attitudinal change. Children lack the autonomy and independence to benefit from the recent evaluation of consumer rights. Without either political or socio-economic power, the forces of the market will not serve them. The views and interests of planners, administrators, carers and service providers will not always coincide with those of children, and their knowledge of what children want and need is unlikely to be adequate unless they ask them. Local and health authorities need to explore the creation of structures which build in a presumption that the views of children are solicited both at a micro and macro level of service development. There is no blueprint for achieving this goal. Some authorities are developing close links with local youth councils; others are creating committees of young people through whom policy papers are passed before going to members; others are seeking to promote universal and genuinely participative school councils; others are finding ways of institutionalising dialogue with young people who are looked after in order that all policy is informed by their perspective. In the field of health, initiatives have been taken to work with young people to identify how to create a more healthy local environment, to involve children more in their own health care and to seek the views of young people on the development of health education services. Children have unique knowledge, understanding and experience from which to draw in the development of services. These initiatives need to be evaluated, disseminated and developed throughout the country. Without respect for the voices of children, the paternalism that has for so long dominated the welfare state will be perpetuated for children, and with it children's continued vulnerability to both intentional and unintentional abuse and neglect by adults in positions of power over them.

However, it is important to recognise both in the private sphere of the family and in the public service arena that giving children greater rights to participate in their own lives does involve adults relinquishing some power. It means not only listening but also taking account of what has been heard. It means allowing children to take some risks and to make mistakes. It means acknowledging that children have a valuable contribution to make. If we can achieve this, then the outcome will be greater respect for children as people in their own right, better informed and improved services for both parents and children, and a generation of young people growing up believing that they are able and have a responsibility to influence the society they belong to. It is a goal well worth the sacrifice of some power.

References
1. Levy, A. and Kahan, B., *The Pindown Experience and the Protection of Children: The Report of the Staffordshire Child Care Enquiry* (Staffordshire County Council, 1991) and Kirkwood, A., *The Leicestershire Inquiry 1992* (Leicestershire County Council, 1993).
2. Consideration of reports of States parties: UK of Great Britain and Northern Ireland CRC/C/SR.205 (30 January 1995).
3. Concluding observation of the Committee on the Rights of the Child: UK of Great Britain and Northern Ireland CRC/C/15/Add.34 (15 February 1995).
4. *Not just a Name: The Views of Young People in Foster and Residential Care* (Who Cares Trust and NCC, 1993).

5. See *Checklist for Children: Implementing the UN Convention on the Rights of the Child – Developing Local Authority Policy and Practice* (AMA/CRO, 1995).
6. Lansdown, G. and Newell, P., *UK Agenda for Children* (Children's Rights Development Unit, 1994).
7. Sharp, S. and Smith, P. K., 'Bullying in Schools: the DES Sheffield Bullying Project' in *Early Child Development and Care*, vol. 77 pp. 47–55, 1991).
8. Cullingford, C., *Children and Society: Children's Attitudes to Politics and Power* (London: Cassell, 1992).

6.2 PARTICIPATION AND THE CHILDREN'S HEARING SYSTEM

Deirdre Watson
Director, Scottish Child Law Centre

In 1961 the government commissioned a committee known as the Kilbrandon Committee to

> 'consider the provisions of the law of Scotland relating to the treatment of delinquents and juveniles in need of care or protection or beyond parental control and, in particular, the constitution, powers and procedure of the courts dealing with such juveniles.'[1]

The Social Work (Scotland) Act 1968[2] saw the establishment of the children's hearing system in Scotland following upon the deliberations of the Kilbrandon Committee. The 1968 Act created children's panels, social work departments to service their decisions, and an official known as the Reporter to the Children's Panel who is responsible for making referrals to hearings where panel members make their decisions. Hearings consist of three panel members who are lay members of the community specially trained in child welfare issues. The idea behind the creation of this new system was to remove children who were having difficulties from the jurisdiction of a court and bring them into the less formal, more sensitive environment of a children's hearing. One leading commentator on the children's hearing system, Andrew Lockyear, has put it thus:

> 'What is called the Kilbrandon philosophy is not only embodied in the existing legislation, it is the inherited ethos, or shared credo of those who work in the system. It provides a foundation of principle against which institutional arrangements are to be understood and practice is to be evaluated.'[3]

The hearings deal with children no matter what the nature of their problem, whether offence-related or a matter of care and protection. Most other jurisdictions separate child care issues such as care and protection, from issues of offending. The system was undoubtedly ahead of its time in many respects and is still much admired as a system of juvenile justice by other jurisdictions. Certain principles contained within the system—the recognition of the child as an individual, the principle that all children with problems are treated in the same way, and the recognition of participation as a core-function—are particularly admirable. Children's hearings decide whether compulsory measures of supervision are necessary. Within this system supervision means protection, control, guidance and treatment. If a hearing decides that formal help is needed it makes what is known as a supervision requirement in respect of the child.

Children's hearing system and the Children (Scotland) Act 1995

The principles which underlie the children's hearing system are preserved, for the most part, within the Children (Scotland) Act 1995 although it does introduce some

> There are clear indications that the terms of the United Nations Convention on the Rights of the Child have been addressed by the legislators: listening to the child is an integral part of the legislation. However, what the 1995 Act fails to adequately address within the primary legislation is the creation of mechanisms conducive to the more effective participation of young people in hearings.

significant procedural changes. There are clear indications that the terms of the United Nations Convention[4] on the Rights of the Child have been addressed by the legislators: listening to the child is an integral part of the legislation. However, what the 1995 Act fails to adequately address within the primary legislation is the creation of mechanisms conducive to the more effective participation of young people in hearings. Section 16 of the Act talks about giving the child an opportunity to indicate whether he wishes to express a view and giving that opportunity. We know from experience that some young people are very vulnerable and reticent at hearings. Is simply providing an opportunity sufficient? Do we not need to be pro-active in our encouragement to participate? If so, what is needed?

Children's hearing system and the United Nations Convention on the Rights of the Child

It is interesting to look at how the theory of participation as it is contained within the Convention equates with practice as it exists within the hearing system. The United Nations Convention on the Rights of the Child is quite clear on the importance of the principle of children's participation. It states:

Article 12

12 (1) States parties shall assure to the child who is capable of forming his or her own views the right to express those views freely in all matters affecting the child, the views of the child being given due weight in accordance with the age and maturity of the child.

12 (2) For this purpose, the child shall in particular be provided the opportunity to be heard in any judicial and administrative proceedings affecting the child, either directly, or through a representative or an appropriate body, in a manner consistent with the procedural rules of national law.

Although the Convention does not explicitly state that every effort should be made to encourage and facilitate participation by young people, this is surely implicit within its terms. Although children's rights are being recognised more widely, that recognition and the procedural implications thereof have a long way to go. In order to clearly identify the gap between theory and practice we need to ask the question: 'What is effective participation?'

> Research does show that children, even the very young, are able to make decisions if provided with information, support and most of all, encouragement to do so. Why then, even within our hearing system which is built upon principles of co-operation, non-adversarial conciliation and respect for the child as an individual, do we not take every possible step to ensure that their thoughts are heard?

'What is effective participation?'

In my view, to achieve meaningful participation of children and young people in any system requires:

- provision of sufficient information to enable a child or young person to form a view and provision of that information in a way which is readily understandable to them
- provision of a mechanism for eliciting any view which the child may wish to express
- listening to that view
- respecting that view and attaching due weight thereto
- explaining all decisions and implications clearly to the child or young person, and providing a right to challenge.

Children in the hearings system

Research[5] does show that children, even the very young, are able to make decisions if provided with information, support and most of all, encouragement to do so.[6] Why then, even within our hearing system which is built upon principles of co-operation, non-adversarial conciliation and respect for the child as an individual, do we not take every possible step to ensure that their thoughts are heard? There is evidence that the existing mechanisms do not. It is very sad when children contact the Scottish Child Law Centre's advice line having attended hearings and not having understood why they were there, or perhaps what their rights were when present, or the consequences of the decisions made about them. Often they are not aware that they could have taken a representative with them to the hearing, or even that it would have been advisable to consult a solicitor upon receipt of the paperwork relative to the hearing. Grounds for referral to a hearing are often couched in technical, legalistic terms and adults also find the terminology problematic.

Whilst without doubt sincere efforts are made to communicate procedures and the implication of decisions to young people, our hearing system would appear to be failing on a number of occasions to communicate effectively. It would appear that we need to do more to encourage responses from the people the system was designed to serve.

Representing children

How can we improve this situation? Children can take a representative with them to a hearing but solicitors cannot get legal aid for attending hearings, and the reality for a number of families who attend hearings is a very limited budget. If we accept that representation for the child at the hearing is an obvious step in the right direction, what form should it take?

Within the children's hearing system there is provision for the appointment of a person known as a *safeguarder*[5] although such appointments are not mandatory. The safeguarder's role at a hearing, or in court proceedings in connection with it, is to make recommendations as to the child's welfare, based on what he considers are the child's best interests. The safeguarder is not acting as the child's representative. Whilst, on the face of it, the very existence of a safeguarder would appear to be advantageous and should ensure that at the very least the child's views are communicated to the hearing or sheriff, it must be noted that at present there are many problems of definition and practice which surround the role. First, safeguarders tend to go about their task in significantly different ways. For example, some spend a considerable amount of time with young people, others do not. Some, where they recognise that their interpretation of what constitutes the child's best interests differs from that of the child, may steer the older child towards a legal representative. Others may not see this as part of their role. The fact is that the role remains confused, with a dearth of unified comprehensive training for safeguarders in Scotland and low remuneration rates contributing to a low usage rate by hearings and courts.

Where does this leave our young people? Where we fall down in our efforts to ensure the effective participation of young people in decisions which affect their future is fairly obvious. We must make greater efforts to do the following:

1. Explain procedures to young people in a child-friendly way—if young people know and understand what is happening round about them, they are more likely to participate.
2. Children need encouragement and pro-active assistance to speak out. They need an effective right to representation and that representation must be knowledgeable not only about the particular person, but also about the arena in which the young person is appearing.
3. Young people need realistic access to a complaints procedure. Children often feel overpowered, not only by their position, but by the plethora of officials and paperwork which surrounds them.

Other jurisdictions

We must recognise that not all children are able to respond within the albeit less threatening forum of the Scottish juvenile justice system. Other jurisdictions have recognised the problems of effecting meaningful participation in differing ways. In England and Wales in juvenile courts experienced social workers are appointed as

Guardians ad Litem[7] to young people in all cases unless it is felt not to be necessary in their best interests. The *Guardian ad Litem* can also arrange for the appointment of a solicitor to represent the young person. Where the *Guardian ad Litem's* interpretation of a decision in the best interests of the child differs from the wishes of a child or young person whom a solicitor has deemed to be mature and intelligent enough to form his or her own view, then the solicitor will take his instructions directly from that young person and not the *Guardian ad Litem*. Certainly, enhancement and clarification of the role of the safeguarder within the Scottish children's hearing system would be of assistance. In the USA some jurisdictions use non-lawyer volunteers who have ready access to legal services and there is in fact a growing trend in the use of Court Appointed Special Advocates who are an amalgam of specially trained lawyers, volunteers and/or social workers. The USA has a number of other models of child representation ranging from *Guardians ad Litem* in the same mould as in England and Wales, to children's attorneys and counsel for the child. In Australia children have separate representation available to them in family law cases and in New Zealand the Counsel for the Child represents the child's interests in matters of family law.[8]

It is clear that what movement there is towards more effective participation internationally is progressing through the development of various forms of representation. There is a tendency towards a recognition that the child should be separately represented in any proceedings, but the form of that representation varies greatly from one jurisdiction to another. It is perhaps a little ironic that there is no provision within our hearing system for automatic representation of children at hearings given the system's evident foresight in other areas. One interesting model which we could look to for some inspiration is that put forward by Donald Duquette.[9] He suggests that young people should be independently represented in children's hearings by the introduction of a person to be known as the child advocate, responsible for looking at both the interests and wishes of the young person. He suggests that this person would need training in co-operative and non-adversarial problem-solving techniques but feels that this model would be particularly appropriate to the children's hearing system: 'Because of the unique non-adversarial traditions of the Scottish system, Scotland has an opportunity to establish a child advocate role without importing some of the unwelcome characteristics of an adversarial due process model.'[9]

Conclusion

In conclusion, whatever model we choose to adopt the provisions within the Children (Scotland) Act 1995 will not necessarily by themselves advance the cause of effective participation of children and young people. Whilst there are some very welcome signs within the terms of the Act which show that the principles of the UN Convention have at least played a part in the formation of this legislation, the provisions relating to the safeguarder's role have not gone as far as one would have hoped, and the question of representation for children and adults at hearings has not received any significant attention. One would have hoped perhaps that consideration could have been given to the question of providing legal aid for lawyers to attend hearings. As stated, they are not covered by legal aid to attend, although some do so without payment. An ideal solution would perhaps have been to consider the sanctioning of legal aid for attendance at hearings to accredited child law specialists thereby encompassing the positive emphasis on specialised training contained in Duquette's model with a healthy respect for due process and the very special and essentially non-adversarial nature of the children's hearing system.

References

1. Kilbrandon Committee Report (1961).
2. Social Work (Scotland) Act 1968 (1968 c.49).
3. Lockyear, A., Chapter 8 in Asquith, S. and Hill, M. (eds), *Justice for Children* (Dordrecht: Martinus Nijhjoff, 1994).
4. United Nations Convention on the Rights of the Child.
5. Section 34A of Social Work (Scotland) Act 1968.
6. Alderson, P., *Children's Consent to Surgery* (Buckingham: Open University Press, 1993) and Salzberg, A., 'Negotiating childhood' in James, A. and Prout, A. (eds), *Constructing and Reconstructing Childhood: New Directions in Sociological Study of Childhood* (Basingstoke: Falmer Press, 1990).
7. Section 27 Children Act 1989.
8. Cleland, A., 'Models of participations—New Zealand, America, Australia and England', Scottish Child Law Centre (unpublished paper).
9. Duquette, D., 'Scottish Children's Hearings and Representation For the Child', in *Justice for Children*, Asquith, S. and Hill, M. (eds), (Dordrecht: Martinus Nijhkoff. 1994).

6.3 WORKING TOWARDS THE PARTICIPATION OF CHILDREN IN DECISION MAKING

A DEVON CASE STUDY

Mary John

Professor of Education and Dean of the Faculty of Education at the University of Exeter, England

Penny Townsend

Co-ordinator of Devon Youth Council, England

Setting the scene: the local context

The county of Devon is the third largest shire county in England with a population of just over a million. It is a largely rural county with an economy dependent on fishing, farming and tourism. As an institution of local government the county council ensures that national legislation is followed and manages a decentralised budget which allows for a distribution of resources within the county in response to perceived local needs.

Young people are disproportionately represented in the county's unemployment statistics. Twenty-six per cent of the Devon total unemployed persons are aged between 16 and 25 whilst this young group form only 16 per cent of the Devon population and are therefore fairly marginalised in service provision. Even if young people as a group were to be pro-active there are not enough of them elected[1] as members of the county council to make any significant impact which is why the Devon youth council is so important and forms the bridge between young people and the county council. The youth council works in a similar way to the county council in terms of its democratic function. It is there to influence the distribution of resources, representing the 'purchaser' rather than the 'provider'.

Emergence of the Devon Youth Council

The initial setting up of this council was at a relatively low level of participation if judged by academic models of children's participation, such as Hart's.[2] The initial young people were consulted and shaped an idea that originated with and was facilitated by adults but which rapidly moved to the full participation of young people initiating shared decisions with adults and directing activities. The young people eagerly grasped an opportunity that was offered by adults and have used this as a catalyst for developing a large number of activities of their own and consolidating as a force to be reckoned with within the county council.

The council presently has a membership of about 150; 40–50 of that membership is made up of individual members and the remainder is made up of affiliated organisations, ranging from small youth clubs to the Devon Guides. It answered a need in that the Devon youth service, social services, Devon and Cornwall constabulary and so forth, were all anxious to work with and be advised by a representative body of young people. A measure of the success of the council has been that its members are much in demand up and down the country. This has been seen as a triumph for the way they have overcome the traditional cynicism of young people and have involved them effectively in the political processes with traditional agencies within their local authority and the ways in which not only have members been transformed in their belief in the system but also the way that they have transformed that system itself.

The emergence of Devon Youth Council as an independent organisation has its roots in the Devon Year for Youth (in 1992) and the Youth Awareness Day, which was held on a school day. Young people from schools and youth clubs aged between 13 – 19 were invited to attend to find out how their local authority worked. During the day young people began to appreciate:

- the *significance* of the local authority to their lives and
- how *remote* from their lives the county council appeared.

The concern of young people about these was evident. A group of youth workers put forward the proposal for a junior county council which was enthusiastically received so the investigation of this possibility was agreed. The education committee provided modest funding to underwrite the costs of a youth working party which was facilitated by a youth worker. Eighteen months later, March 1993 saw the official press launch of the constituted Devon Youth Council although indeed there was nothing more than an agreed structure to launch. At that point there were no affiliated organisations and no electorate, only a working party. On the day of the launch a long list of things that the council should address was drawn up including bullying and youth crime— two areas in which the youth council has now done a substantial amount of work.

Participation

The 'vision' of young people's participation in the decision making processes in matters that concern them is framed by the UN Convention on the Rights of the Child— particularly Articles 12 and 13. To what extent are the rights of the child to be actively involved in the development of services that directly impact on their lives a practical reality in Devon or a vain hope?

> Through direct consultation Devon Youth Council has identified a degree of rejection of the traditional political system by young people in favour of issue-based 'pressure group' politics. As the percentage of young people in the population decreases so does their sense of value within political processes.

Through direct consultation Devon Youth Council has identified a degree of rejection of the traditional political system by young people in favour of issue-based 'pressure group' politics. As the percentage of young people in the population decreases so does their sense of value within political processes. Young people are sceptical of agencies which claim to be committed to involving young people in service provision and developments within the new purchaser-provider models. At an individual level young people do not trust politicians and feel cynical about traditional three party politics. Where young people are notably involved and committed is in pressure group politics as, for example, Greenpeace, the veal trade protests and so forth. Here they feel they can join with belief and conviction as they do not sense the same dishonesty as within political parties. The work of the Devon Youth Council has responded to the two positions they have identified by engaging in and influencing the decision making of a local authority and at the same time acting in a similar way to a pressure group to win support among young people.

Operational aspects of Devon Youth Council

In September 1993 a co-ordinator was appointed on a 3-month honorarium which was later extended and there is now a commitment to regularly fund such a post which must be held by a young person (namely a person under 25 years of age) who is an active member of the youth council. The way in which this post has been set up, the conditions of service, remuneration, an office in county hall, the car and a mobile phone (all very important given that the nature of the job has been to involve rural as well as urban youth) have made a clear statement of how the post is seen and valued within the local authority. The budget for running the youth council is about £20,000 which covers the basic operation, that is it:

- pays the salary of the co-ordinator
- covers the running costs
- provides a budget for conferences and publications.

Additionally, small grants are given to the youth council for specific projects for projects they might wish to run and occasionally they are commissioned to do specific things as, for example, the development of a successful £20,000 funding bid from the Department of Health (Drugs Grants Programme) for a 'Young People at Risk' project.

In establishing young people's participation in a realistic and effective way the support and resourcing by the key decision makers in the county has been sensitive,

> Adults created the space for this organisation to develop and young people have capitalised upon the opportunity to grow and develop.

insightful and crucial. A youth worker as facilitator has been provided to support the recruitment and outreach work; time from the personnel department has been allocated to the council to assist them in getting everyone to work together; the council has been given a budget for which it is entirely responsible but in managing it they are given appropriate expert help. Youth councillors' own perceived needs for training have been responded to by sending them on courses on how to chair meetings, IT training and so forth. They have therefore been given power, resources and, most importantly, trust.

Adults created the space for this organisation to develop and young people have capitalised upon the opportunity to grow and develop. The paradox of the council growing out of an adult-initiated activity rather than as the culmination of intensive grass roots activity has been resolved around the work that they have put into analysing young people's resistances and activating them to become involved in their community as powerful agents for change. The particular challenges experienced of achieving a fully inclusive, representative group of active young people which thoroughly embodies equal opportunities and is able to deliver specialist services to and about young people are being met. The process has involved the highest degree of control and direction over its own activities by Devon Youth Council and this has certainly paid off in what has been achieved to date.

Opposition from different and surprising sectors of the community has been encountered. This has come from teachers and youth workers claiming that young people do not want to have a say in how things are run. The council's position is that unless young people realise that they have choices, power and support they will not ask to participate. Much of the outreach work of the council has involved making young people feel confident about this. For the youth councillors opposition has acted as a catalyst to raise the consciousness of young people about their democratic rights. The council's paradoxical role in being accountable to and representative of young people has created some tensions, dilemmas and internal debates which have been growth points.

Devon Youth Council—an example of good practice?

Since its establishment the Council has had considerable impact both within Devon and on the national and international scene. A significant amount of time has been spent with the Council by Swindon and District Young People's Forum, the Welsh Youth Crime Reduction Forum and the National Association for the Care and Resettlement of Offenders. Advice has been given to a variety of other organisations within the UK. An invited paper was given to ANACEJ (the French National Association of Youth Councils) in Paris last year and Devon's Youth Council were invited to make an input into the European Community Education Association.

The youth council has undertaken a number of activities and published a pack of advice and information.[3] The work has been important in ensuring that other organisations in the county take young people seriously and treat them with respect. Two examples of good practice of work that has been undertaken have been the 'Rural Challenge' submission and the bullying leaflet.

The first example indicates how the youth council has animated and motivated a number of organisations to work with them around a matter of common concern particularly to young people and future generations. The youth council sponsored, organised and wrote the submission to Rural Challenge last year, coming a close seventh in the national competition for funds in which six projects were to be selected. The work that the youth council did in the preparations for this bid has meant that they are held in high esteem for the highly professional way in which they operated, by the 52 organisations who were all happy to be chaired and organised by the youth council co-ordinator. The bid aimed at the economic regeneration of the county and the terms of the submission meant that these organisations' appreciation of the role of young people in sustainability and regeneration was considerably enhanced by this collaboration. The internal success of this venture has partly been a function of the way the council is imaginatively resourced and supported.

The second example of the council's work on bullying picks up on present concerns of young people and the way they have worked positively together. The leaflet was written from the victims' point of view in consultation with experts. The leaflet is aimed at middle-school children and makes clear to them possible ways of dealing with bullying, what the school's responsibilities are and the wider social context. Young people themselves were commissioned to provide the graphics for the leaflet which was then produced and distributed by the youth council.

A member of the youth council chairs the county council working party for the implementation in Devon of the UN Convention on the Rights of the Child. This is seen as vital work as the Convention provides a clear indication of young people's rights and a useful starting point for work with decision makers in Devon. The council is increasing its level and diversity of influence, its membership and links with the national and international movement. Further work is being undertaken in imaginative new partnerships with the local authority. Currently, the youth council's 'The Next Generation' project aims to define young people's 'Agenda 21' for Devon in the context of environment, citizenship and international responsibility.

Looking forward, the broad implications of the new European funding opportunities now available to youth councils are an added stimulus to growth. The work has in a sense come full circle with the youth council now setting up an adult advisory panel. The youth council has worked hard and successfully to fully involve Devon young people themselves in exploiting the opportunities for participation and in claiming their rights to a full partnership in the lives of their communities into the next millennium.

References
1. Eligibility for election to the county council is 21 years of age.

2. Hart, R., *Children's Participation: From Tokenism to Citizenship,* (*Innocenti Essays*, No. 4. Florence (UNICEF, International Child Development Centre, 1992, p. 44).

3. Devon Youth Council, *Publication Pack,* (1993). Available from Devon Youth Council, Crossmeads, Barley Lane, Exeter EX4 1TF, Devon UK.

6.4 A 'NAMED PERSON'S' VIEW OF EMPOWERMENT

Carole Moore
Special Needs Development Officer, Children in Scotland

The 'Named Person' in legislation

This case study examines how empowerment of children with special needs and their families can work in practice by eliciting the views and actions of a 'Named Person' operating in Scotland. A Named Person is someone who supports the parent(s) of a child with special educational needs in a voluntary capacity, to enable them to contribute effectively to assessments of their child relating to special educational needs and subsequent appropriate provision.[1]

Formally, their role is to provide 'information and advice' to parents. Their position is formalised at the time a Record of Needs[2] (referred to as a Statement of Needs in England and Wales) is drafted, and they can operate in this capacity until the Record is terminated, they are no longer required by the parents or they choose to stop.[3] If a Record is not opened then their jurisdiction is not valid once this decision has been taken. Both the Record of Needs and the concept of the Named Person were introduced in the Education (Scotland) Act 1980[4] (amended by 1981 Act[5]).

This Act—drawing upon recommendations made by the Committee of Enquiry into the Education of Handicapped Children and Young People in the Warnock Report 1978[6]—outlined the provisions for a new system of special educational provision in the UK. For instance, it recognised the value of involving parents as partners, so that now parents, as well as professionals, can instigate and take part in assessments and reviews. However, the Act only partially implemented Warnock's recommendations for the Named Person. Warnock believed that the role of a Named Person was to: 'Provide a point of contact for the parents of every child who has been discovered to have a disability or is showing signs of special needs or problems ... to provide them with a single point of contact with the local educational service and expert counsel in following their child's progress through school'.[6]

The remit of the Named Person described in the Act was far more limited, requiring him or her to focus on supporting parents with children with pronounced, specific or complex needs requiring ongoing review to address their educational needs (only those children who have a Record of Needs, or where one is being considered).

The requirement for a Named Person to give 'expert counsel' was also not introduced, so that neighbours/friends as well as professionals can now become a Named Person.[7] In Scotland, frequently, Named Persons tend to be professionals working directly with parents. However, some are also parents who may have been empowered to take on this role through having their own Named Person previously. In one study of 40 cases, five families had chosen to have a friend or relative as a Named Person whilst 27 chose professionals. One chose a minister and seven chose not to have a Named Person.[8]

'They have to know what to ask for in order to get it. They need to be able to gain the confidence to say they don't understand, to say 'it's all too much for me', that they can't make the meeting and want to reschedule it. You have to help them understand the complexities of understanding the assessment processes and tools that professionals use, breaking down the language they use and what they mean.' (Named Person)

The case study

The case study presented here involves a nurse working in a child development centre who has operated for many years as a Named Person. For the purpose of this case study we will call her Mrs Mack (all details are given in such a way as to retain confidentiality). In this case, the self-perceived role of the Named Person is aligned more to Warnock's model than that suggested by the Act. Currently, the Named Person here operates as a Named Person for six families. This case study will focus on one of these, to explore some of the issues surrounding effective empowerment of families who have a child with special needs.

When Mrs Mack began working with children with special needs at a child development centre, she perceived part of her remit to include enabling and advising roles to support parents and help them access services and understand professional actions, that is a key worker role. This was the main reason why being formally named as a Named Person was, as she saw it, a natural extension of her advocacy work.

> I felt that one of my jobs was to be a key worker and these families required to be enabled and supported to use services across all sectors, and part of that was looking at how to enable families to use services and how to make choices about services by informing them. They have to know what to ask for in order to get it. They need to be able to gain the confidence to say they don't understand, to say 'it's all too much for me', that they can't make the meeting and want to reschedule it. You have to help them understand the complexities of understanding the assessment processes and tools that professionals use, breaking down the language they use and what they mean. (Named Person)

Working with families—partnership in action

In her capacity as a professional about five years previously, Mrs Mack met the mother of a child with mild learning difficulties and physical disabilities. She worked with the family to link them into services, exploring service options and changing the attitudes of the family to enable them to make use of services. She then encouraged them to become more aware of the importance and relevance of their contact with professionals, by advising them to keep a diary updating their child's progress, to prepare questions and a checklist of items to discuss, and so forth.

After the child had an accident on public transport, she advised the parents to contact an educational psychologist, to see if they would consider providing transport to the child's nursery. This resulted in the child being assessed for a Record of Needs. At this time, the parents were informed about the option to choose a Named Person:

> 'I chose her because she was a key worker closely involved with the family. She was aware of the family situation. She was also able to liaise with professionals and cross the boundaries that some professionals have difficulty doing. I chose her as I felt she was not only a professional working with the family but also a valued friend.' (Mother)

Conversely, the reason Mrs Mack chose to act as Named Person for this family was because: '… they didn't have too many problems. This meant we could go through the process quicker. The issues and timescale were different, which made it easier'. As a result of assuming a key worker role, Mrs Mack found that when the time came to involve a Named Person, the parents had already become empowered to the extent that her advocacy role was not as extensive as it might otherwise have been. She attended the initial meeting, where the draft Record of Needs was discussed, so that people would know who she was. She also briefed and debriefed the parents and informed them of their rights. More recently, she has been less involved, being available for the family if they require her assistance, but otherwise simply adopting a monitoring role and staying informed of decisions taken at reviews, for instance.

Limitations and advantages of the 'Named Person' role

The ability of Named Persons to empower families is restricted by two main factors: the time available to commit to the task, and the prescriptive role laid down in legislation.

Additionally, Mrs Mack is concerned that her contact with the child has been limited recently and feels this affects her ability to know what actions would be in his best interest. Although the Named Person is formally present to support parents, Mrs Mack would rather this role was child-centred, and feels that tension between the parent's needs and those of the child can place the Named Person in an awkward situation.

By law, a Named Person can only become involved fairly late on in the recording process—limiting potential input and impact. Given that the role only extends to education, it is restrictive in that it precludes support in other professional spheres.

> A major problem for many people operating as a Named Person is the amount of work and time that is required to empower parents effectively.

A major problem for many people operating as a Named Person is the amount of work and time that is required to empower parents effectively. Mrs Mack feels strongly that if professionals are to be used as Named Persons this should be a recognised aspect of their work, and time allocated to allow them to take on the role. As the mother remarked when asked what else she would have liked the Named Person to do:

> I would have liked [the Named Person] to be available for meetings but her workload did not always allow for this. However, she always made time to liaise with me either before or after the event – whichever was necessary. (Mother)

As a result of the constraints upon professionals who cannot justify such advocacy work within their remit, increasingly, the active Named Person—such as the one described here—is asked by parents to take on the role. Such Named Persons are therefore able to select which families to work with, but Mrs Mack is concerned that other families may see this as differential treatment if they are not chosen.

Mrs Mack is philosophical about the current application of the Named Person. At present there is no national system of training for Named Persons in Scotland—or indeed any structures allowing Named Persons to network. Recognising the fundamental importance of support for families, she declares that:

> We are devaluing the role by not having a structure for recruitment and training such as that which exists for panel members of the children's hearing system. It is a total delusion that parents can have a Named Person if they want one. There aren't nearly enough, and there is nowhere to go to get one. I think we should scrap the Named Person if it is not developed further, and begin promoting advocacy generally instead. (Named Person)

She adds another reason for feeling this way, and that is professional defensiveness where families have a Named Person. The mother agrees:

> Sometimes other professionals think that the Named Person is a threat to them, and the things the parents request are actually the wishes of the Named Person, not what the family wants. Other professionals think the parents behave like puppets for the Named Person. (Mother)

However, the benefits of empowering families should not be underestimated. Since Mrs Mack met the family, the mother has set up a self-help group for other parents and runs a health advice club. Both parents have been involved in the training of professionals, have spearheaded a campaign against closure of the child development centre and have attended further education courses. Their child is now about to begin a process of part-time attendance at a mainstream school—a long-term aim of the parents.

> The parents clearly took on the role of the Named Person themselves, based on what I had been doing, and very quickly. (Named Person)

The self-perceived benefits of having support such as a Named Person can be considerable for families:

> Through having the experience of meetings with professionals my self-esteem and confidence were given a boost, we therefore now feel capable of advocating for ourselves and our son. We were informed of all the relevant services, even ones Mrs Mack knew we wouldn't use. My level of knowledge was considerably improved due to Mrs Mack and other parents taking time to explain the procedures. (Father)

Conclusion

The use of Named Persons in Scotland at present is extremely *ad hoc*. It is dependent on parents being informed that Named Persons can work on their behalf, and also on people willing to become Named Persons. At present there is no available information on how many persons operate in this way in Scotland, or on the roles they adopt. There is an urgent need for research in this area to elicit such details. It has been suggested that if the existing system is not strengthened—and the commitment of professionals enhanced—the Named Person should be abolished, with the emphasis changed to empowering parents in other ways.[9]

The need for a system whereby practical advice and information can be offered in a way that empowers and enables parents is now particularly acute, given the increased responsibility on parents to become involved in the educational provision of their children. In order for partnerships to be effective between parents and professionals, a bridge is sometimes required to enable the smooth transfer of information, facilitate joint decision making and to exchange viewpoints. The Named Person can act as this bridge (at least initially—until parents feel able to assume the role).

In England and Wales, the role of the Named Person has recently been strengthened through the Education Act 1993[10] and associated guidance. Local authorities must identify potential Named Persons and provide training for them. Central funding has also been allocated for Parent Partnership Schemes to be developed locally. However, these initiatives are not extended to Scotland, and given the constraints under which Named Persons currently operate here, it is likely that the lack of training opportunities and professional support for Named Persons act to mitigate against the expansion of this potentially highly valuable service for parents.

References

1. Kerr, L., Sutherland L. and Wilson, J., *A Special Partnership* (Edinburgh: Children in Scotland HMSO, 1994, p. 13).
2. A Record of Needs is a an individualised statement of special educational needs, and indicates specific provision required as a result.
3. Scottish Society for the Mentally Handicapped, *Information for the Named Person* (Glasgow: SSMH, 1987 p. 5).
4. Scottish Education Department, *Education (Scotland) Act 1980* (London: HMSO, 1980).

5. Scottish Education Department, *Education (Scotland) Act 1981* (London: HMSO, 1981).
6. Department of Education and Science, *Special Educational Needs (The Warnock Report)* (London: HMSO, 1978) and para. 9.26–9.27, p. 157.
7. Kerr, L., Sutherland, L. and Wilson, J., *A Special Partnership* (Edinburgh: Children in Scotland HMSO, 1994, p. 13).
8. Dyer, S. and Thomson, G., 'Legislating for Partnership with Parents—An Effective Strategy', Interim Report 3: Children with Special Educational Needs: Policy and Provision, November 1988, University of Edinburgh.
9. Achamore Centre Parents' Group. 'We want reality, not rhetoric or lip service'. *Newslink*. ENABLE Newsletter. Spring 1995.
10. Department for Education, *Education Act 1993* (London: HMSO, 1993).

Chapter 7

◆

PARTICIPATION: SCANDINAVIA

7.1 THE ROLE OF PARENT ORGANISATIONS IN NEGOTIATING QUALITY DAYCARE SERVICES

Henrik H. Jessen

Convener, Danish Daycare Institution, Aabenraa, Denmark

This chapter describes two examples of parental participation in the management and development of *daginstitution* (daycare services) for children between 6 months and 12 years of age in Denmark. The first part focuses on the role of the Association of Danish Daycare Institutions for Children (FDDB[1]) in facilitating parental involvement in daycare in Aabenraa municipality. The second part describes FDDB's involvement in developing a municipal daycare plan in Aabenraa. The latter is used as an illustration of the type of problems which arise when the wishes and needs of the parents are weighed against the political demands of municipalities and national government.

Aabenraa is an old market town on the east coast of Southern Jutland, with a population of about 21,000. The birth rate has been rising during the last five years and in the mid-1990s it is approximately 40 per cent above its lowest point at the end of the 1980s. The town is the administrative centre of the county council. The seats in Aabenraa's municipal council are divided equally between the liberal parties on the one side and the social democrats and socialists on the other.

FDDB was founded by Danish nationalists in the national struggle between Denmark and Germany at the end of the 1930s. At that time Southern Jutland had been reunited with Denmark for less than 20 years, and a minority group wanted the region reunited with Germany. This local conflict has now been replaced by a peaceful co-existence.[2]

Parental influence through a voluntary daycare association

Everyone living in the municipality can take out membership of the FDDB which is run by a board of 30 and an executive committee of 7. Today the FDDB runs 20 of the 25 daycare institutions in the municipality, with a total of about 1000 children. Each of the 20 FDDB institutions is led by a board of parents, who occupy one seat on the board of the FDDB. Of the remaining 10 seats, nine are elected among the members of the association and the last seat is occupied by a central FDDB staff member. This structure guarantees a parental majority. The FDDB has its own Secretariat and administrative unit with a total of five employees. The head of staff is also the secretary of the board and the executive committee. The Secretariat is responsible for administering wages, collecting parents' fees and preparing accounts for the daycare centres. It also assists the parents with questions concerning their role as employers. One third of the revenue comes from parents' fees, the rest from municipal grants. A seat on the FDDB's board is in general voluntary and unpaid.

A structure similar to the one described above is seen elsewhere in Denmark, particularly in the big cities, where private and religious organisations run up to 1000 daycare institutions. All private and publicly owned daycare institutions in Denmark are established and run according to the Social Assistance Act, which is a comprehensive Act regulating social services. However, unlike the FDDB and its daycare centres, most of these services are not based on co-operation nor on a dominant influence by parents sitting on governing boards. Unique to FDDB is the fact that the majority of daycare institutions in Aabenraa have decided that it is beneficial to be part of and run by an association, rather than operating individually. The daycare centres run by the FDDB are divided into three basic types, as shown in Table 7.1. A fourth type, 'age integrated' institution, provides for children aged from 3 to 10.

All the institutions share a number of common features. For example, in all of them 80 per cent of the staff have attended three and a half years at a teacher training college, there is a minimum of 2 square meters[3] floor space per child, and parental payment cannot exceed 30 per cent of the total running costs. Due to its size, the FDDB runs an attractive summer camp for its institutions, and it is planning to purchase a shared bus and establish a large common playground.

Table 7.1   Types of daycare centres run by the FDDB.

Type	Age	Number of institutions	Opening hours	Staff: child ratio	Monthly parental payment in DKR[a]
1	6 months – 2 years	2	7–17	1:6	1980
2	3–5	9	7–17	1:12	1040
3[b]	6–10	5	7–8, 12–17	1:16	790
2+3	3–5 (6–10)	4	7–17	1:12 (1:16)	1040 (790)

NOTES
    a.   100 DKR = c. £10.
    b.   Fritidshjem.

A strategy for developing quality daycare services

Due to the relative strength of the FDDB it plays a significant role in the planning of new daycare institutions. Aabenraa municipality has decided, after many years of parental pressure, to establish a new age-integrated institution based on type 1 and 2. Its influence is also seen clearly in the relatively large number of places of type 1 and 3. In the neighbouring municipalities such places are completely replaced by family daycare and *skolefritidsordninger* (school daycare services) which are less expensive to establish and run. Family daycare involves a person, normally without any special training, obtaining a contract with the municipality to care for four children at home. School daycare is established according to the Primary Education Act, and not as daycare institutions, by the Social Assistance Act. As a result of this the school daycare is established on school premises, often in classrooms and without direct parental influence on staff recruitment and pedagogical principles. Such services often have a large number of children in each group, and the parental payment is not necessarily limited to 30 per cent of the running costs.

> The FDDB secretariat, with all its resources, is vital to the association's strength and the building of solidarity between institutions. In addition it ensures that parents have direct and broad access to all important information.

The co-operation between institution leaders and institution boards ensures that information and experiences are exchanged for the benefit of all. The FDDB secretariat, with all its resources, is vital to the association's strength and the building of solidarity between institutions. In addition it ensures that parents have direct and broad access to all important information. This is derived from the knowledge of FDDB staff, from co-operation with other daycare associations and through the well-established contact with trade unions, municipal authorities and the national Ministry of Social Affairs. The organisation's influence is assisted by the broad composition of the board, which is helpful for lobbying. The FDDB can rely on personal contacts with the political system and the municipal authorities. Voluntary members of the board bring their professional experience to the task of ensuring the quality and efficiency of children's services in their local community. The FDDB has been able to take advantage of its political strength to arrange open election meetings to discuss children's services and puts forward its views at local and national conferences.

As the millennium approaches, the FDDB's principal task is that of fighting for the quality of children's services. During periods of relative calmness, there is a real risk of losing parental interest and involvement in the organisation, which can threaten its existence. Parental interest is highest when political decisions are seen as threatening the interests of parents. However, maintaining a level of conflict is obviously not a sound and lasting basis for a trustworthy strategy. But it is important for the future influence of the FDDB to maintain a steady recruitment of new parents. This is not easy. The number of years when daycare is needed by the family are relatively few compared with the numbers of years when the children go to school, and the pre-school years are often when a job makes the most demands on parents. Therefore the FDDB has realised that, in order to recruit enough new parents, it must extend its information to new parents about its existence and purpose. Currently, an information leaflet is sent out once a child is enrolled in any of the 20 services run by the FDDB, and short presentations are made in each of the meetings held during the year.

It has also proved difficult for some of the daycare institutions to participate actively in the political work of the association. Typically it is stated that such work seems less relevant than working directly for the institutions where your own children are, and that it may be difficult for parents to take a strong interest in the fight for better daycare services in another part of the municipality.

Municipal daycare plan: conflicting interests

Since the early 1990s there has been an effort in Aabenraa to prepare and agree on a daycare plan for the whole municipality. A comprehensive plan, covering all the five districts of the municipality, describes the development and necessary adjustments of daycare services over the next years. The work was initiated by the town council in December 1991, as an indirect result of promises made at an election meeting held by the FDDB a few months earlier. The FDDB had worked out its objectives the previous year and therefore welcomed the decision of the town council. By the end of 1995 the work is still not finished, and the course of events illustrates the difficulties.

The work in Aabenraa has been affected by radical external political, demographic and economic changes. First, the Parliament decision introducing reduced payment for parents with more than one child in a daycare centre along with the introduction of parental leave. Secondly the significant increase in the local birth-rate and finally the government's decision from 1993, *(pladsgaranti)* demanding that municipal daycare services should ensure that full parental demand be met before the end of 1995.

Consequently the municipal daycare plan has been subjected to no less than three rounds of public debate. Each round includes a report from the municipal administration, followed by a hearing among parents and daycare institutions, and ending with an inconclusive discussion in the Town Council's sub-committee on daycare services.

After the latest discussion the politicians have decided to ask the municipal administration for yet another report on the possibilities of replacing the institutions of type three, children aged 6 to 10, with the previously described school daycare. This procedure results partly from the conflict of interests between parental demands for both quality and freedom of choice and political pressure to reduce public spending. The politicians want a redistribution of the existing level of public resources in daycare services, arguing that these resources should contribute to financing the required expansion of childcare places. The FDDB's board, and probably the politicians too, are convinced that the FDDB has contributed to postponing the intended financial cuts by its active participation in the hearing procedures. It is the conviction of the FDDB that the town council do not want to enforce a daycare plan which is likely to meet sharp and broadly stated criticism by parents. However, frequent and inconclusive hearing rounds may possibly wear down the parents' belief that a consensus can be reached.

Organising parents: some conclusions

The following conclusions may be drawn from the experience of the FDDB.

- Historically it has been possible to establish, expand and maintain an active, voluntary, cross-sectional and influential parents' organisation in Aabenraa. However, it is a demanding task to maintain parental interest in this and the existence of separate legislation for children's daycare services and primary education limits the possibilities for co-operation.
- Parental influence has contributed to Aabenraa municipality, as distinct from some of its neighbours, offering a daycare service of considerable quality which is in great demand by parents both in and outside the municipality.
- Whilst politicians value the contribution of parents' voluntary work in children's services, the political strength of parents is seen as limiting their own freedom of action and removing influence from the municipal authorities to the parents. As a result the FDDB has met with some opposition from the political system.

Aabenraa's experience demonstrates the benefits of organised co-operation between parents in different daycare institutions. This model of organised parental participation attracts only limited interest from politicians and the municipal administration because it may be seen as threatening their control. However, parent organisations of this kind may be a means of strengthening community interest in the political process. A recent study revealed a remarkably weak interest and lack of respect among young citizens[4] for the work of the town councils. More attention needs to be paid at both local and national political levels to strengthening the possibilities for parental co-operation across different daycare institutions. One way forward is to make legislative changes at a national level. Currently, children's daycare services are regulated by the Social Assistance Act which also regulates many other aspects of child welfare. FDDB would prefer regulation of daycare services to be through a separate Act—a Daycare Act in much the same way as education is regulated through the Basic School Act.

Notes and References
1. Foreningen De Danske Børneinstitutioner i Aabenraa.
2. Witte, J., *Fra nasjonalkamp til kvalitetskamp* (Aabenraa: FDDB, 1990, p. 16).
3. About 20 square feet.
4. Torpe, L., *Landsdækkende borgeranalyse 1995—Borgerne og kommunestyret* (Aalborg: Kommunedata, 1995, pp. 33 and 36).

7.2 PARENT-STAFF INTERACTION IN EARLY YEARS SERVICES

FINDINGS OF A NORWEGIAN SURVEY

Tove L. Mordal

Senior Researcher, National Institute for Consumer Research, Norway

In Norway, the main responsibility for developing and expanding early years services rests with the municipalities. The structure and content of both public and private institutions is regulated by national legislation, the most recent of which is the Day Care Act (1995) which came into effect on 1 January 1996. Since 1975 legislation has determined the minimum requirements for management, staff training, available space per child, health and hygiene. Pre-school teacher training involves a 4-year higher education training, and is a requirement for daycare managers. Only 3 per cent of managers in municipal services, and 7–8 per cent in the privately owned services, do not have such training. There are two main categories of privately owned institutions. Semi-private services receive public funding, and access is often regulated and managed centrally by the municipality. In fully-private services the costs are met in full by parents or private funds, and access is decided by a Board of Governors.

In 1993, Norwegian municipalities owned slightly more than half of all daycare institutions, including the provision of pre-school programmes for 6 year olds. Available public statistics do not make a distinction between semi-private and private but, according to data from our 1990 survey[1], 109 of 112 municipalities owned daycare services, 66 of them had semi-private and 61 had private institutions. A 1994 survey[2] found that, in households with children aged 0–6 years, 41 per cent reported having children in public services, whilst 24 per cent made use of private services.

Staff-parent communication: 1990 study[3]

The new Norwegian Day Care Act seeks to promote close co-operation between parents and their children's services. The Act states that the child's opportunities for development and activity must be considered in close co-operation with the child's family. Our study was carried out in 1990 and involved two postal surveys, one of staff (managers) and one of parents, in a total of 163 municipal and privately owned daycare institutions in 15 municipalities. In sampling the 15 municipalities, emphasis was placed on the presence of both municipal and private daycare services, with and without municipal subsidies. The municipalities were spread across the country, including urban and rural, and central and peripheral areas. The study examined the following questions.

- Do staff show understanding of parents' demands and wishes?
- Do parents respect and show interest in staff and their work?
- What reactions and behaviour do the parents show in relation to any dissatisfaction they feel?

- Are parents' experiences of staff co-operation positive or negative?
- What measures are likely to increase the perceived relationship between the two groups' expectations and demands?

Staff perspectives

Table 7.2 outlines characteristics and views relating to the perspectives of daycare managers on the staff-parent interaction.

The survey also found that the majority of services had explored parents' views in relation to their services in some form. This was more likely to be the case with municipal-owned institutions than semi-private and private institutions. More than 7 out of 10 managers of municipal-owned institutions reported that they had asked for parents' views in some form. In semi-private and private institutions, the numbers were 68 and 60 per cent respectively. However, the survey does not reveal whether initiatives were taken by the staff themselves or initiated by some external body.

TABLE 7.2 Managers of daycare institutions expressing certain characteristics or views (percentage).

Characteristics, view or understanding	Municipal	Semi-private	Private
	Type of daycare Institution[a]		
More than half of the parents participate in parent meetings	60	79	77
Most parents are very understanding of the staff's work	30	40	44
Parental interest in the professional skills of the staff is high	16	16	33
Parental interest in the children's need for care is high	39	31	31
Parental interest in the use of unorganised play is high	7	6	14
Parent meetings, very important to parents' expectations	80	81	64
Parent talks, very important to parents' expectations	62	55	47
Written information, very important to parents' expectations	60	73	43
Agreements, very important to parents' expectations	39	32	23
Parent-staff co-operation is affected by time constraints	42	46	47
No children with adjustment problems in the institution	12	37	61
The admission criteria created few/no problems last year	40	68	91
Most/quite a lot of parents channel their dissatisfaction directly to the staff	48	54	56
Most/quite a lot of parents channel their dissatisfaction through parents' representatives	17	9	14
Most/quite a lot of parents channel their dissatisfaction by asking for an individual parent talk	62	51	61
Most/quite a lot of parents channel their dissatisfaction directly to the administrator	26	40	47

NOTE
a. Municipal N=70, Semi-private N=57, Private N=36. There may be some variations in the Ns according to missing observations.

> About two thirds of the staff also thought that one-to-one discussions with parents are important in clarifying parental expectations over what staff may do for them and their children.

More staff in the municipal services than those in private services thought that parents' meetings were very important in clarifying what parents can expect from the staff. Staff in these services emphasised the importance of parent meetings, discussions with parents and agreements. Staff in municipal services and semi-private services also thought written information for parents was more important than those in private services. Between half and a third of staff thought that most, or quite a lot of, parents asked for individual meetings too readily as a means of expressing their dissatisfaction. About two thirds of the staff also thought that one-to-one discussions with parents are important in clarifying parental expectations over what staff may do for them and their children.

Parents' perspectives

Table 7.3 outlines parents' views on staff-parent interaction. Only a small proportion (less than 10 per cent) of parents thought that parents know too little about what happens in their child's service. Most of the parents (88–90 per cent) reported satisfaction with the way in which their children were taken care of by staff and approximately the same proportion (87–91 per cent) were pleased with the information they received about their child and the child's activities. Eight out of 10 parents had participated in regular parent meetings or theme discussions in the past year. The parent meetings raise particular questions related to the activities whilst the theme discussions look at more general issues related to the upbringing of the child, for example, traffic and children, setting the right boundaries, media violence and children, children with disabilities. Parents said they were not afraid that reporting dissatisfaction directly to a member of staff would affect the staff's relationship with their child. One third of the parents had expressed dissatisfaction occasionally—these tended to be parents who were more concerned about the effect on their child. However the survey also found that parents did not manage to communicate their interests and views to staff on some central issues such as possible conflicts or perceived problems.

Parents' views suggested the significance of informal communication with services. The survey suggested that parents in private services had a more limited need for formal interaction and that the private services seemed to be more informal and flexible in their attitude to parents' wishes. The smaller size of the private services and the lower instance of children with special needs may promote a greater use of informal communication between parents and staff in these services. Parents' perceptions on the importance of informal discussion appears to partially extend to parent meetings.

TABLE 7.3 **Parents in daycare institutions expressing certain characteristics and views (percentage).**

Characteristics, view or understanding	Type of daycare institution[a]		
	Municipal	Semi-private	Private
Taken part in parent/theme meetings last year (in 1990)[b]	83	83	83
Staff shows great/fairly great understanding in child care	90	90	92
Only good experiences concerning how their children are taken care of	89	88	90
Parents should be involved to a great degree in deciding how child care should be given	56	57	57
Parents should be involved to a great degree in deciding the professional framework for the daycare centre's activity	19	14	17
Completely agree that it is important that the daycare centre provides time and room for children to play	73	69	69
Is very/fairly pleased with the information given about the children and the activity in the daycare centre	87	87	91
It is very important to get written notes about what happens to the parent's own child	51	42	38
It is very important to have verbal information if anything happens that one should know about	98	94	96
Now and then channelled dissatisfaction directly to the staff	33	34	31
Not afraid that channelling dissatisfaction directly to the staff should influence the staff's relation to one's child	93	91	97
Now and then channelled dissatisfaction at parent meetings	19	27	19
Now and then channelled dissatisfaction by parent talks	10	10	7
Now and then channelled dissatisfaction to the management	12	17	14
Altogether very pleased with the daycare centre	63	67	70

NOTES
a. Municipal N-367, Semi-private N=306, Private N =206. There may be some variations in the Ns according to missing observations.
b. Missing is here coded as no meetings last year. If missings are excluded we will have the following figures for municipal, semi-private and private kindergartens respectively: 99 per cent, 98 per cent and 98 per cent.

Most parents prefer to be given information orally rather than in writing and therefore the service's ability and willingness to arrange meaningful meetings with parents is important. Equally the willingness and ability of parents to participate in such meetings was seen as important by staff.

Summing up

Our study did not come up with clear answers to all the questions we asked but the findings presented here demonstrate what we see as important aspects of existing patterns of parent-staff interaction. The data indicate that parents' opportunities to influence and co-operate with their child's service is particularly linked to questions concerning the following:

- Informal communication between parents and staff.
- Parents' feelings of being understood.
- To what extent parent meetings are user-orientated.
- Parents' fear of expressing dissatisfaction.

Without doubt the parents want the staff to tell them more about what happens in the services. An open and informal dialogue between staff and parents can increase understanding on both sides and strengthen mutual confidence. This form of communication may be crucial in determining the willingness of parents to speak up about problems. The degree to which this happens relates to the prevailing staff culture and whether this is primarily internally focused on staff themselves and mostly preoccupied with professional skills, or supporting staff interacting with the parents.

The new Daycare Act is intended to reinforce the authority and participation of parents in daycare activities. The new Act follows earlier legislation which required day care staff to work closely with parents. The new Act is likely to have the effect of increasing parents' authority through clarification of their role on the parents' council and the establishment of a liaison committee at each daycare institution. However, the study described here suggests that such factors as staff culture and levels of understanding and willingness to co-operate are likely to be the decisive factors in producing effective partnership between services and families.

References
1. Mordal, T. L. and Sander, K., *Kommunenes barnehageadministrasjon. Foreløpige tall fra en delundersøkelse*, Working Report No. 2 (Lysaker: The National Institute for Consumer Research, 1991).
2. Mordal, T. L. and Bjørnjaard, J. H., *Forbrukerperspektiv på utviklingen i barnehagesektoren*, Working Report No. 1 (Lysaker): The National Institute for Consumer Research, 1996).
3. Mordal, T. L. and Sander, K., *Offentlige og private barnehager i foreldreperspektiv*, Working report No. 1 (Lysaker: The National Institute for Consumer Research, 1992).

7.3 DISABILITY AND CHILDREN'S SERVICES

THE PARTICIPATING PARENT

Helga Skeidsvoll

Parent and Member of the Swedish Association for Mentally Disabled Children and their Families (FBU[1])

The moment we become a parent we are faced with demands and expectations, reflecting the society and culture in which we live, and the social class to which we belong. Normally those demands are not difficult to fulfil because becoming a parent is usually such a happy event. This is why parents normally fulfil the expectations which are laid upon them. It is another matter if the child is disabled. Then the parents must learn to accept their child, at the same time as they are entering an unknown world of services with which they are, in general, not familiar.

I have two children, the youngest of whom has several 'illnesses': Down's syndrome, autism, reduced eyesight and orthopaedic problems. There were good reasons to be grateful. The first child was healthy, giving me confidence in my abilities as a parent. I had two professions: as teacher and social worker, and therefore knew a little about pedagogy and social rights. At the time I was also politically active and used to speaking up for what I believed in.

Even though it was important to have first-hand experience and an appropriate education, I was a mother, and not a professional. It is always more difficult to fight for your own child. Luckily, I had no difficulties in recognising the child as the person it was, in addition to all the good feelings that go with being a mother.

Parental participation for me takes place on many different levels.

- Participation in my child's treatment and exercise: co-operation with doctors, physiotherapists and pedagogues.
- Participation in parent organisations and groups: co-operation with other parents by being together socially; deriving strength and knowledge from other parents.
- Being a leading force in making sure my child obtains what he is entitled to: daycare with extra resources, adapted education, suitable spare time activities and financial compensation.
- Participation in developing a society for everyone: collaboration, dissemination of knowledge and discussion with politicians on how to ensure a better society.

Those levels are inter-linked. During some periods one level becomes more prominent than the others. It depends on the child's age, what is important at the time, how much energy one has, and where one lives. Looking back I can see that my own move from Norway to Sweden has been a significant factor. In Norway we first lived in a relatively large municipality and then moved to a smaller one when my second child was four years old. To provide a perspective on my parental participation during my son's life I have therefore chosen to give a relatively chronological account.

Eirik was born in 1977. His sister was two years old. I was married and working as a teacher in a psychological treatment centre for young people. My background was relatively uncomplicated. I was educated as a teacher and social worker and had working experience as a teacher, a teacher's aide in the USA and a social secretary in a prison. I was politically active on the Left and very interested in women's issues. During the 1970s the category of women I belonged to did not consider giving up their professional career, still less their political involvement, because of having children. So I continued. After working and remaining politically active for some time I decided to exchange my more general political activities for those around issues I was facing as a parent.

Eirik was often ill as a young child. I had to learn about illnesses, health care, hospitals, medical staff and so forth. Dealing with the public health system as a parent was not easy. At the same time as worrying about one's own child, one has to know what to ask for, when to ask and how to ask. I felt I had to find an acceptable way of participating in Eirik's health care.

As parents we participated from the very beginning in the National Association for Mentally Disabled Children (NFPU[2]). It was interesting to meet different people with a common focus; their child—or siblings—with a mental disability. We took courses and went to family gatherings where we met other children and saw how other parents tackled life and at the same time we received practical advice on the community and our legal rights. What could we expect from the local educational authority? What sort of claims could we file? How should we make our claims known? What common claims were there? The NFPU worked throughout the country, at the county and municipal levels, with overall questions. I was active both at the local municipal and county levels. Relatively early I became involved with the group whose main task was developing parental support for new parents. When staying with Eirik at the hospital, I talked to the staff about the importance of parents meeting other parents shortly after their baby was born. At the local level I gave courses for other parents and undertook administrative work for the organisation.

> To ensure that things went our way—that people with disabilities should be given a chance to participate in society—we as parents had to take part and influence as much as we could.

In the early 1980s, Norway went through a period of decentralisation. Municipalities were given the right to decide their own spending policies. The previous system of earmarked financial grants from the central government was to be abandoned. This could mean that different groups in a municipality had to compete for a much reduced financial pot, fearing that the strongest would win. The parents of mentally disabled children saw this as a threat because we defined ourselves as a weak group. At the same time the increased local autonomy could have some positive effects—we would be closer to where the decisions were actually taken. To ensure that things went our way—that people with disabilities are given more opportunities to participate in society—we as parents had to become involved and influence policies as much as we could.

I think it is also an obligation on parents to teach the politicians about our situation. My perception is that we were listened to and that we were a group to be reckoned with. The politicians also invited us to discuss and debate the issues with them.

> In a small municipality the individual became visible to a much higher degree, and an expense visible on the social budget.

When my family and I moved to the small municipality I continued to be involved at a county level. I became a member of another municipal group with a different type of activity. Eirik had been in a nursery where we lived before. This small municipality had not given priority to building daycare centres. A private nursery, which received grants from the municipality, existed and we applied for places for both our children. Eirik required an assistant, but this was not easy to obtain. In a small municipality the individual became visible to a much higher degree, and an expense visible on the social budget.

During this period Eirik started school. It was not obvious that he could attend the local school. During the 1970s and 1980s the norm was to integrate—children with disabilities of different kinds were to attend their local school in an ordinary class. The progress has come as a result of active parents fighting the central and local authorities. Our main claim has been that children with disabilities should be entitled to the same rights and possibilities as other children.

In our case this was too big a task for the local municipality and its administration, and as parents we accepted an offer in a special class in a neighbouring municipality. I was now working at the inter municipal office for pedagogical-psychological services so I had the influence to ensure that Eirik attended one day a week at his local school. This was met with scepticism from the teachers and the local school authority, but at the same time it was seen as a challenge. When it was seen to work well, several other children secured the same educational arrangement. I see it as an aim to ensure that all children are give the chance to attend the school which is best for them, and that they are entitled to sufficient resources, economic and others, to make sure they receive a good education. Parents have the right to decide which school their child attends, but advice from school authorities is required. It is difficult for parents to have a different view from the authorities. At the same time it is important to take into consideration that it is not only the formal teaching which is important in the school, but also the social life.

In 1987, my children and I moved to an academic city in Sweden and we had to get to know a new system that was similar but also different from the one we were used to. The Swedish system is built around legislation that has been added to the Social Act and the Education Act. The services were managed at that time by the county council, (and have since been transferred to the municipality). Special schools had and still have their own administration and teachers. The special classes are located in the normal schools throughout the municipality, but the children are divided into groups according to age and level of ability, not according to where they live. People with disabilities have the right to certain services from the county (municipal) council, regulated by law. In the beginning it looked like paradise to me, sliding into a system without having to put forward any claims first. At the same time I had to familiarise myself with the bureaucracy, and that was not always easy. It was natural to sign up as a member of the Swedish sister organisation for the mentally disabled and their families (FBU[1]). It was interesting to see what they were concerned with when they already appeared to have a lot.

I soon realised that the system was so well organised that it was difficult to come up with individual programmes. The pupils are placed in previously defined and established groups. The result for Eirik was that he had to change groups almost every year. Many teachers and still more assistants have passed through his life. He experienced a lot of different teaching methods. I found that attachment could be a problem in the Swedish system.

From 1 January 1995 Swedish municipalities have assumed the main responsibility for disability services. The new Act states that we all are entitled to individualised services. The special school is now also run by the municipality. After the local elections in 1995, the municipalities' new Social Democrat administration has shown some enthusiasm for taking over from the county council. This may be an advantage for parents and other interest groups. The local politicians in the social committee wanted to establish a dialogue with the parents. At a meeting which was organised by the FBU, one of the politicians taking part suggested setting up a parental reference group—a possible think tank—for the social committee. I was anxious to become one of the members, but I do not have great hopes for it. It has not yet been decided what sorts of problems to discuss, what tasks it will be given and how long we will be sitting. What is important now is that the politicians take it seriously and start building up local centres of competence.

> My private conclusion is that whatever services we are offered we will never be fully content. The pain and frustration we feel towards our children make it necessary to find somewhere to unload.

To look at the differences in parental participation between Norway and Sweden requires a deeper analysis of the different social systems and the popular culture than is possible to do here. My experience suggests that the different experiences of decentralisation in Norway and Sweden have led to some differences in the approach of parents in the two countries. At the time I moved to Sweden, disability services were the responsibility of county councils and I found Swedish parents more willing to accept centrally-made decisions. In Norway a more individualistic approach has meant that it is sometimes difficult to agree on general improvements but, at the time I was living there, this opened up more possibilities for creating good individual and local solutions. This, however, requires a great deal of individual activity and it is an effort. Such individual activity can be good for many parents with disabled children in that it provides a form of 'therapy'. My private conclusion is that whatever services we are offered we will never be fully content. The pain and frustration we feel towards our children make it necessary to find somewhere to unload. We will nevertheless always fight for our children because progress has come through parental struggle. We are dependent on the government's money and legislation, and we have to protect what we have achieved.

Notes
1. Föreningen för utvecklingstörda barn, unga och vuxna (FBU).
2. Norsk Forbund for Psykisk Utviklingshemmede (NPFU).

7.4 THE ROLE OF THE NATIONAL PARENTS' ASSOCIATION FOR CHILD AND YOUTH SUPPORT (FBU) IN HELPING THE PARENTS OF CHILDREN AND YOUNG PEOPLE AT RISK IN DENMARK

Birte Nielsen

Convener, National Parents Association for Child and Youth Support, (FBU[1]), Denmark

As a parent whose child was taken into care for 10 years, I have learnt to appreciate the help and advice other parents can offer. Having to deal with the Danish social welfare system over an extended period made me realise the importance and value of parental support and participation. I signed up as a member of a parental association where other more experienced parents offered their advice and support. In this contribution I describe the organisation and work of two such organisations, one a national organisation and the other a local advice centre. Both promote participation amongst parents whose children are or have been taken into care by the child welfare service. I include, from my work as an active participating parent, a few examples of other parents' reactions. My intention is to illustrate how important this type of organised support is for parents in a vulnerable situation.

A national network of supporters

The National Parents Association for Child and Youth Support (FBU[1]) was founded in Denmark in 1969 by a group of parents of children and young people at risk. Some parents were highly displeased with the extended period they had to wait before their child was given treatment in a residential institution or by foster parents. Others felt they had been treated badly by members of staff in the public administration.

FBU is made up of county associations with a central administrative body. Individuals as well as organisations may take out membership by paying a moderate annual fee. They then become members of their local county branch. The FBU is a member of the Common Board on Children's Issues[2] enabling it to influence legislation on children and youth. The organisation also has representatives on county and municipal boards for users of social welfare services,[3] in addition to being a member of the Nordic Child Protection Union.[4] FBU has formalised its collaboration with social pedagogues in Denmark.

The majority of the FBU members have or have had a child who has been in care, residential or otherwise. Today there are approximately 250 members, of which 20-25 are active in supporting other parents and disseminate relevant information to parents, carers and the wider public. All work is done by unpaid volunteers. The FBU provides assistance and guidance to parents who feel they need support in handling their child, co-operating with professionals and service providers. The FBU volunteers offer help in different ways: by acting as 'neutral' observers when parents feel they need it; by organising support groups where parents can meet and talk to others in similar circumstances; and by offering courses to parents on topics relevant in enabling parents to face what for most is new territory in the upbringing and care of their children. Active members of the FBU also offer lectures and classes on topics where they as parents of children at risk have acquired first hand experience.

The tasks that the FBU is expected to do have become increasingly complex and being an FBU volunteer has therefore become more difficult than in the earlier days. Many of our members have children who are placed outside their home without parental consent. And in some cases parents feel they are pushed into agreeing that their child has to be placed outside the home—often for the rest of his or her childhood. During recent years the FBU has also been contacted by an increasing number of parents who themselves have serious problems such as severe learning difficulties, suffering abuse or mental illnesses. These parents have often been neglected during childhood and youth themselves, and they contact the FBU in order to get help and advice.

> 'It is so nice to come here. Here I don't first have to explain how I feel inside. Here you immediately understand my grief and my chaotic feelings.' (Parent at an FBU weekend course for its members).

As parents' supporters and advisers the FBU volunteers must be able to provide help and guidance without becoming too emotionally involved. By attending the FBU's weekend courses the active members are given a chance to develop interpersonal skills as well as knowledge. Such courses are managed by the FBU's chairperson and professionals from the services are invited to teach. Through role play the volunteers learn conversational techniques and other skills necessary for acting as parental supporters. The course participants' background and experience varies and many of them have had traumatic experiences from their own encounter with the service system. In undertaking the task of supporting other parents, it is important to avoid expressing negative experiences. The active members keep in close contact locally and nationally. They give each other support regarding the 'counselling' job, and as important, when problems occur in their own families. Without this social network it would be impossible to work as a volunteer

Once a year the FBU offers a weekend course for all its members. Professionals, social welfare officers and public administrators are invited to present their views on a previously agreed subject, followed by a plenary discussion. By meeting and discussing with other parents with similar problems and people from the social welfare services, the assumption is that parents are likely to gain confidence and thereby more insight into their own problems. As one parent said during one of the annual weekend courses: 'It is so nice to come here. Here I don't first have to explain how I feel inside. Here you immediately understand my grief and my chaotic feelings'.

Copenhagen local advice centre

In May 1994, the City of Copenhagen, in close co-operation with the FBU, established a local support and advice centre for parents with children and young people in care.[5] The advice centre is run according to the FBU's ideas, and is the only one of its kind in Denmark. A psychologist, family counsellor and volunteer parents are attached to the centre. In addition the centre co-operates with nurses, daycare centres, residential homes, foster families, child and youth consultants, home counsellors and social welfare officers. The advice centre offers parents the following services: personal advice, participation in parent groups, emergency psychology services, a social meeting place, evening discussions and lectures.

The work, as in the FBU, is based on the idea that the entire family, not only the child in care, should be given help. Parents have to get through the emotional grief following the 'loss' of a child in addition to facing up to other social as well as practical challenges. It is important for the whole family that the parents are given adequate support as soon as possible, in order to keep going. It is in this respect that active participation by experienced parents, through the advice centre and the FBU, can make a difference. By providing other parents access to, not only professionals, but a social peer network, the whole family will benefit. All the volunteers have been through this themselves, having had to face the upheaval and shortcomings of having a child taken into care by the child welfare officer, or having had to ask for the child to be taken into care. The fact that the volunteers are not party to the case enables them to reach out to parents, helping them to reassess their own situation. In cases where there are communication problems between case workers and parents, active advice centre members may be able to help them bridge the gap in understanding. In this respect they can also be of help to the case workers, and in the end add to the quality and the effectiveness of the child welfare services.

> 'Our starting point is that *all* parents have something positive to give their children.'

Working as a volunteer: being open and non-judgemental

Parents and professionals working for the FBU and the advice centre do not express a view on whether or not it is necessary to take a child into care. The leading assumption is that all parents, within their abilities and resources, do their best. Our starting point is that *all* parents have something positive to give their children.

As a parent with the experience of having my son placed in care I have for many years worked as a volunteer for FBU and the advice centre. Being in the position of an adviser it is of great importance to be honest with the parents, talking openly with the parents about the reason why their child is taken into care, and helping them to understand that they themselves are also responsible for changing the situation. What

I experienced working with Annie is an instructive one. She is a mother with serious alcohol problems. At Annie's request I sat in on several meetings she had with the public social welfare administration regarding her daughter. In order for Annie to be allowed to take her daughter with her to an independent boarding school for young people *(folkehøgskole)* for a holiday, the social welfare officer demanded not only that Annie had to take her medication, but that she had to agree to be supervised by one of the teachers at the school. In a follow-up talk I had with Annie, where I felt I had to be straightforward, my main intention was to help her to come to an understanding of what was expected of her, and that she, by accepting the terms, could show that she was serious about controlling her alcohol abuse.

Or as Bente, one of the mothers seeking help and advice at the advice centre, said when she came back the following day: 'I felt like dancing down the street when I left the centre. For the first time in many months someone cared to listen to my experiences. Here I was allowed to cry without anyone immediately starting to talk about something else'.

Notes
1. Forældrelandsforeningen for Børne-og Ungdomsarbeid (FBU).
2. Børnesagens Fællesråd.
3. 'Sociale Brugerråd' and 'Sociale Forbrukerråd' respectively.
4. Nordisk Sammenslutning til værn for Børn og Unge.
5. Støtte-og rådgivningscenteret for anbragte børn og unge's forældre.

PART IV
ACCOUNTABILITY

Chapter 8

ACCOUNTABILITY: UK

8.1. CHILDREN'S SERVICES IN ENGLAND AND WALES

IMPROVING ACCOUNTABILITY TO CHILDREN, YOUNG PEOPLE AND THEIR FAMILIES

Keith Bilton

Self-Employed Child Care Consultant, England

In all public services in the UK, there are traditional structures of accountability. These structures and the ways in which they work are being affected by changes in the way the services are organised and delivered and in the nature and roles of public service organisations. There has also been a significant development in expectations about the directions in which accountability is owed. It is not sufficient to consider accountability up the line to managers and elected representatives. Accountability is also owed to service users and to a range of local representative organisations. Professional accountability is also at issue. This contribution will consider the implications for traditional accountability structures and processes of recent developments and changes in the organisation of children's services in England and Wales. It will also consider how these changes may affect the prospects for improved accountability to children, young people and families. The main focus is on the personal social services, with some reference to education and health services for purposes of comparison and contrast.

Traditional accountability structures

Traditional accountability arrangements are hierarchical. Within a social services department, staff are accountable to managers who are accountable to a chief officer, who in turn is accountable to elected councillors. Councillors can be held to account by local people at periodic elections, when they may vote either for serving councillors or for alternative candidates. This is a fairly minimal form of accountability, and young people under 18 have no vote. Councils are also accountable at law. The local democratic process outlined above is circumscribed by councils' duties to provide services prescribed by law and to avoid doing things which are outside their statutory powers. It is further circumscribed by accountability to government ministers. In carrying out their personal social services functions, local authorities may be both guided and directed by the Secretary of State. The processes of accountability and control which subordinate local authorities to central decision making are often considerably stronger than those which subject them to local democratic influence.

Within the work organisation, the processes by which upward accountability is maintained may be accompanied by considerable delegation of discretion to exercise judgement and make decisions, or they may, at the other extreme, be based on ensuring that an unvarying set of detailed instructions is consistently applied to all cases. Traditional accountability is, therefore, consistent both with a flexible, professionalised and individualised service and with one which is bureaucratised and strictly equitable.

Schools have been subject to a similar but not identical form of traditional accountability which in recent years has undergone many changes. Although part of the local authority structure, schools have been somewhat distanced from the full force of its accountability arrangements by the existence of statutory governing bodies, so that the accountability of a school's teachers to its head has been clearer than the head's accountability to the education authority. Governing bodies have typically acted as support groups for head teachers, thus reducing the perceived need for close supervision of heads by their employing organisations, and as champions of their schools in differences with the education authority, thus perhaps inclining the authorities to favour a light touch in holding heads to account. The need for local authorities to embrace within the system of state education schools provided by voluntary bodies has probably also contributed to the relatively greater degree of independence enjoyed by schools compared with social services departments' children's homes.

Professional accountability

> Whereas for doctors and nurses there are national regulatory bodies which can debar them from practising on grounds of professional misconduct, there is no such body for social workers and other social services staff, and, although there is pressure to set one up, it is by no means certain that government will respond to it.

There are variations in how the arrangements in health, education and social work services take account of professional accountability. In the National Health Service (NHS), there has traditionally been a clear separation between the professional accountability of doctors and accountability for the administration of the service. In the 1974 reorganisation of the NHS, an interesting attempt was made to bring the different accountability systems together in a collegiate structure, in which a multi-disciplinary management team brought together doctors representing their colleagues with the heads of managed hierarchies of nurses and administrators. The subsequent change to general management, and the creation of NHS trusts headed by chief executives, has subjected doctors to an unprecedented level of accountability, and has narrowed down the area within which they exercise clinical freedom subject only to regulation by their own professional bodies and free from managerial oversight. The local authority system, by contrast, provides no guarantee of professional freedom and does not require the existence of a separate and independent system for handling complaints against professionals. The formal position is that councils are advised by professional officers but are free to reject the advice. In practice, this applies mainly to policy matters where professional and political considerations are both relevant. The great majority of decisions about individuals are taken by staff, and the extent to which discretion is delegated is determined largely within the staff hierarchy. The important fact remains that almost any decision made within a social services department can be, and sometimes is, reviewed and changed at any higher level.

Whereas for doctors and nurses there are national regulatory bodies which can debar them from practising on grounds of professional misconduct, there is no such body for social workers and other social services staff, and, although there is pressure to set one up, it is by no means certain that government will respond to it. Therefore, although there are professional associations, and professional hierarchies within social services departments, and although many staff personally acknowledge professional responsibilities, it would be correct to say that no national system of professional accountability exists.

Outward accountability

The types of accountability discussed above (which might be called upward accountability) make no provision for accountability to the people for whom the services are provided. (This we might call outward accountability.) The elements which may protect their interests are in the legislation governing the services, which generally reflects benevolent purposes, in an assumed public service ethos and in similar assumptions about professional ethos and commitment. It is clear that upward accountability on its own is not sufficient to ensure that the interests of service users are properly served, and that mechanisms for outward accountability are also needed. Equally it is clear that upward accountability cannot be dispensed with, and that the two must be able to live together. By governing the response to need from above, rather than by negotiation with service users or by simply placing services at their disposal, the system does in theory provide a means of bringing into balance decisions about the amount and quality of service to be provided and the amount of public money to be spent, although numerous uncertainties make this a difficult task in practice. The introduction of more explicit managerial systems into the NHS has made the interaction between financial and clinical decisions more obvious, and has shown that clinicians need more than just professional accountability if they are to take or share responsibility for expenditure decisions. More fundamentally, without upward accountability there is no service structure. Many organisations may, for a large part of the time, function without much explicit regard for their formal accountability systems, and may give the appearance of working very well through informal co-operation. Nevertheless, the system of upward accountability will be there in the background, providing a fall-back means of settling disagreements when informal co-operation fails to resolve problems.

Changes affecting accountability

Recent developments and changes have had and will continue to have significant implications for public service accountability, and these will be considered in the following paragraphs.

The government's community care policies, although introduced for services to adults, have in many local authorities also been applied to children's services. They include the promotion of a mixed economy of welfare, to be pursued by separating purchasing from providing responsibilities, so that purchasers may promote competition for contracts to provide public services. They also emphasise collaboration between health and personal social services with the objective of providing seamless services. Other features of these policies are the introduction of care management and the promotion of needs-led or user-led services. These are accompanied by value statements which affirm equal rights of citizenship for all service users and carers; respect for their independence and right to self-determination; regard for their privacy; understanding of their dignity and individuality; a responsibility to maximise individual choice in the type of services on offer and the way in which those services are delivered; and a duty to promote realisation of an individual's aspirations and abilities in all aspects of daily life.

These value statements clearly call for a service in which responsiveness and accountability to service users are predominant features. Among attempts made to meet these requirements are complaints procedures and forms on which to record users' and carers' statements of their needs and acceptance of the organisation's proposals for meeting them. Requirements to record need not met are also important in promoting responsiveness to consumers, but local authorities have been to some extent deterred from this by the fear that they will by ordered by a court to provide services which they cannot finance. Complaints procedures, which are also required by the Children Act 1989, have come in for considerable criticism and are seen by many consumer organisations as deterrent rather than facilitative, over-formalised, slow and defensive. A weakness in government community care policies as vehicles for outward accountability is their individualisation of the clientele. They contain no recognition of the benefits to clients of acting collectively, and place no duty on local

> It may be suggested that the client who receives services from a private sector organisation will instead benefit from the market-oriented organisation's greater sensitivity to customers' needs. To refer to the client as a customer does not, however, change the basic relationship. The service recipient is not really a customer, does not buy the service with her or his own money, and remains merely the beneficiary of a contract between the purchasing public sector organisation and the providing private business.

authorities to promote the collective as opposed to individual interests of service users.

The promotion of a mixed economy of welfare through the development of a contract culture has implications for both upward and outward accountability. A contract between a local authority and a service provider creates a point in the chain of upward accountability at which it divides into two separate chains linked by the contract, through which the accountability moves from one organisation to another. Since it is difficult or impossible to define in advance and write into a contract all the service user's future requirements, situations can easily arise in which the person receiving a service deserves redress, but the contract is being properly fulfilled. It is important, therefore, that the local authority conducts its care management function in such a way as to promote a direct contract between the service user and the service provider, which is underwritten financially by the authority and monitored by the care manager on behalf of and in co-operation with the service user. If the right set of relationships and mutual obligations can be set up and maintained, this system can have some advantages for the client over the traditional hierarchical model governing direct service provision by the local authority. There are drawbacks, however. The client may have to use two complaints procedures, exhausting the provider's procedure before setting in motion the local authority's. The role of the elected member in taking up issues on behalf of constituents is limited by the difficulty of intervening in the business of an independent organisation. The service is moved further away from the local authority's exercise of democratic accountability.

It may be suggested that the client who receives services from a private sector organisation will instead benefit from the market-oriented organisation's greater sensitivity to customers' needs. To refer to the client as a customer does not change the basic relationship. The service recipient is not really a customer, does not buy the service with his or her own money, and remains merely the beneficiary of a contract between the purchasing public sector organisation and the providing private business. He or she does not acquire the real market power which comes from purchasing with one's own money.

Both community care policies and the Children Act 1989 call for collaboration between services. Community care guidance focuses on the relationship between social services and health, and calls on them to deliver seamless services. The Children

Act requires co-operation among social services, health, housing and education authorities. 'Working Together'[1], which gives guidance on inter-agency child protection work, similarly requires close co-operation between agencies including, in this case, the police. There is a problem here in relation to accountability in that the legislation does not provide a sufficiently clear basis for allocating responsibility among the authorities which are required to co-operate. The NHS Reorganisation Act of 1973 established a principle that the authority responsible for providing and paying for a service is the one which employs the professional group primarily involved in delivering it. This principle was never extended to education, and is now breaking down in the face of the increase in cross-charging for services which has inevitably accompanied the creation of markets. It is unclear, for example, who is responsible for paying for speech therapy to meet educational need. Difficult as it is for a young person or a family to call a single public service to account, it is even more difficult if they cannot establish which service has the responsibility. Collaboration is essential to the delivery of useful services. The needs of children and families are not neatly parcelled up in conformity with the boundaries of services' individual responsibilities. There are, however, few effective mechanisms for enforcing co-operation, although government funding is sometimes made dependent on evidence of it. There is, therefore, no apparatus of accountability to ensure it. If one partner in, for example, a child and family consultation centre, withdraws its staff, there is not much the others can do.

The Children Act requires local authorities to take account of the wishes and feelings of children whom they are looking after. The Act and its accompanying guidance also emphasise the importance of working in partnership with parents. There are other expectations that authorities will encourage participation by children and parents, for example through parental attendance at child protection case conferences and young people's participation in decisions about the running of the residential homes they live in. These arrangements for participation can clearly be helpful in providing opportunities for accountability to children and families, but they operate very much on the agency's terms and within its world, in accordance with its policies and in response to government guidance. They do not generally offer opportunities to service users to come together to set the style of and arrangements for their participation. If participation is to provide a vehicle for the exercise of real accountability to children, young people and their parents, it needs to develop in this direction. Among developments which may help to promote types of participation in which children and young people set the style and content are the appointment by social services departments of children's rights officers and support for the formation of user groups, including local and national associations for young people looked after by local authorities. These developments, providing, on the one hand people on the inside of organisations whose brief is to be on the children's side, and on the other representative structures independent of those organisations, may have some impact.

In the education field, legislation is characterised by an extreme reluctance to accord any rights to pupils, and the partnership is seen as one between schools and parents. Pupils have no right of representation on governing bodies, no right to form a consultative body within the school, and no right to a formal hearing in respect of a proposal to exclude them from school. Schools are not seen as being accountable to their pupils. Pupils are, however, not entirely without power, because no school can function without at least the tacit consent of a substantial majority of its pupils, and to function well it needs their active and willing participation. All the more reason, therefore, to promote at least a formal consultative role for pupils.

The move to local management of schools, with the option of grant-maintained status, means that schools are no longer effectively accountable to local education authorities, and that the role of governing bodies in holding them to account has been substantially increased. Viewed from the standpoint of traditional democratic accountability, an important link has been broken. This has been replaced by a market pressure brought to bear on schools by their need to compete for pupils on the basis of results. Problems arise from the narrow view of results as success in academic examinations, and from the pressure on schools to offload unrewarding and particularly demanding pupils in order to provide a better service to the majority. This provides a good example of a form of accountability which provides only a crude measure against which to make judgements and in consequence discriminates against minority needs.

Children's services throughout Wales (and also in Scotland) and in some parts of England will soon be experiencing the consequences of local government reorganisation, which will fragment existing education services and social services departments among several authorities serving smaller areas and populations. In Wales there are possibilities of yet further fragmentation, as the Welsh Local Government Act allows 10 or more elected members in an area to apply to the Secretary of State for decentralisation. There will be several consequences for traditional democratic accountability. The move to a single tier of local government will reduce the total number of local councillors: fewer representatives of the people. Individual authorities, being smaller, will be able to provide fewer services on their own, and will instead have to buy them in or provide them jointly with neighbouring councils. More services will therefore be more remote from democratic control. On the other hand, each individual councillor in a unitary authority will serve fewer people than his or her predecessor on the county council previously providing social services and education, and may therefore be closer to them.

It is argued that placing responsibility for services on smaller areas and therefore more local councils is a decentralising measure which will bring the services themselves closer to the public and thereby promote greater accountability to that public. This is a somewhat simplistic view. Many larger authorities practise extensive administrative decentralisation of service provision, and it is by no means evident that the smaller authorities replacing them will set up more local service delivery points than currently exist. The argument therefore turns on whether the more local focus of the elected council itself will promote or hinder the exercise of power and influence by the service's local clientele. The statutory provision for further decentralisation in Wales opens up the possibility of an even more local political focus. Personal social services for children and families are frequently provided for unpopular people: parents whose care of their children is found wanting, and young people in trouble with the law. Respect for their views and wishes at the political level is often over-ridden by attention to the views of the majority, and by definitions of the public interest which prioritise the cost of public services over their benefits.

Improving accountability

Taken as a whole, the changes brought about by community care competition policies, by compulsory competitive tendering and market testing, by the creation of NHS Trusts and the promotion of fund-holding by GPs, by the local management of schools and the reintroduction of a grant-maintained (direct grant last time round) sector, and finally by a reorganisation of local government which produces less self-sufficient authorities, are producing a fragmentation of publicly-funded services among a welter of self-governing and independent units, and a relatively fluid and unstable system in which responsibility for delivering services is likely to move between different enterprises from year to year, creating uncertainty about the ownership, interests and accountability of these enterprises. The machinery through which the state will hold these enterprises accountable for the spending of public money and for the discharge of public functions becomes less clear. There may be scope here for provider organisations to develop their own partnerships with service users, and to build mutually protective alliances with them. Organisations representing children and families may be able to have a greater impact on individual service-providing enterprises which are not part of, or are relatively separate within, a larger and more bureaucratic public organisation. This would certainly be in accordance with the view that the rolling back of the frontiers of the state will empower the people. Possibly, self-help, user and local community groups could compete for contracts to provide publicly-funded services to themselves. It may be that certain barriers are being broken down. Within a market-oriented approach, however, it is difficult to see how the possession of a need, and the business opportunity which this creates if the state is willing to pay for the meeting of it, can of itself empower the possessor. In some areas local government reorganisation may, however, prove to be a check on the general tendency to reduce the role of the state. The more local political focus created by the setting up of new, smaller authorities, and in particular the possibility of further decentralisation in Wales, may increase local awareness of the significance of local government services, and may offer families and young people new opportunities to engage with politicians to demand services which respond to local needs and promote local community development.

There are various different ways of seeking to increase accountability to service users. One is to channel public funds direct to the users, and not to the services. This

In view of the low economic and political status of children, accountability systems based on their legal rights may serve them best.

logical extension of community care principles meets however with misgivings when advocated for adults, let alone children. Another is to take the legislative route of giving the service user enforceable rights against the agencies charged by the state with meeting need. The state's concern with controlling public expenditure generally ensures, however, that any such rights are merely procedural, for example, the right to an assessment of need, or to formal consideration of a complaint. A third approach is to seek to get the right attitudes into the service organisation—responsiveness, consultation, listening, flexibility, an inclination to say yes. This generally requires more delegation of discretion and hence more professionalisation (and, of course, professional accountability, which hardly exists in the personal social services), and it can be difficult to reconcile with a more traditional view of what is due to service users in terms of demonstrable fairness ensured by the bureaucratic application of rules. More adventurously, organisations may agree to set up power-sharing arrangements with local communities or their representatives, by delegating functions and agreeing to exercise them in partnership. This last course does not guarantee that power shared with local adults will be shared with local children. Stripped of its mechanisms and procedures, accountability is about power, and none of the changes discussed in this paper reflects a significant change in the balance of power between the funders and providers of the personal social services and their clientele. It would be unreasonable, therefore, to expect these changes and reorganisations to lead to a dramatic increase of empowerment of children and young people, but there are modest improvements here and there, and the Children Act 1989, with its emphasis on the paramountcy of the child's welfare (though only in matters of upbringing), the child's right to be heard and the state's duty to support families, provides a sound basis for an approach based on developing legal rights. In view of the low economic and political status of children, accountability systems based on their legal rights may serve them best.

Reference

1. Home Office: *Working Together Under the Children Act 1989: A Guide to Arrangements for Inter-agency Co-operation for the Protection of Children from Abuse* (London: HMSO 1991).

8.2 LOTHIAN CHILDREN'S FAMILY CHARTER AND THE ROLE OF ITS ADJUDICATOR

Alan F. Finlayson

Adjudicator, Lothian Children's Family Charter, Scotland

The UK ratified the UN Convention on the Rights of the Child in 1991, and the Convention's impact on legislation, policy and practice has been significant. Prior to its ratification, the Convention influenced the enactment of new children's legislation in England and Wales. More recent legislation in Scotland similarly reflects its influence, incorporating for example (in specific areas) rights relating to due regard being given to children's views, making the welfare of a child of paramount concern and giving due regard to a child's religious persuasion and racial origin and linguistic background. Unlike the White Paper which preceded it, the new Children (Scotland) Act 1995 does not however set out at the beginning a set of basic principles relating to children's rights to underpin all its provisions.

In some areas the UK seemed a less than enthusiastic subscriber to parts of the Convention. In Scotland in particular old habits die hard and, legislation notwithstanding, many children continued to be viewed as the property of the parent; 'Father knows best'; 'Children should be seen and not heard'. Legislative changes which had included the abolition of juvenile courts and establishment of the children's hearings system had increased the involvement of local authority elected members and their staffs in service departments.

Lothian Regional Council was sufficiently concerned to advance the principles underpinning the UN Charter to introduce their own 'Children's Family Charter'. The Charter developed out of discussion engendered by the Convention and provides at a local authority level a rights framework embodying the philosophy of the Convention, and, incorporated into the Charter, the right to adjudication of complaints over entitlements it provides. Here I describe the Charter and my own experience as Adjudicator over the 3-year period since the post was established.

Until reorganised in April 1996, Lothian Region was one of nine Scottish mainland regions servicing a population of some 750,000. The Charter was launched in 1992 using the seven initial letters of the word CHARTER to set out statements of entitlement for children. These are:

- **C**hoice and challenge
- **H**ealth safety and security
- **A**ccess and assistance in understanding
- **R**esponsibility, recognition and representation
- **T**houghtfulness, respect and consideration
- **E**ncouragement, praise and appreciation, and
- **R**ecreation and creative play.

The subscribers are the large service departments of education and social work of the regional council and the health board which covers the region. Lothian Regional

Council comprised the city of Edinburgh and the adjoining districts of Midlothian, West Lothian and East Lothian. For many years the Region had already promoted and operated an inter-agency Youth Strategy approach by service departments to the issues of children who present special needs or particular problems.

The principles, aims and practice issues relating to the Charter are clearly set out in a detailed publication, available in every social work establishment that has any responsibility for children, all education establishments (and in particular every nursery, primary and secondary school) and all hospital and health board departments dealing with children.

These documents and a smaller cartoon version more easily read by, and comprehensible to, younger children, expands on some 56 entitlements, under the various 7 Charter principles. For example:

C *Choice and challenge* includes development of challenging educational curricula geared to individual children's potential and achievement in which the child's choice must be considered

H *Health, safety and security* includes health and safety for children in care

A *Access and assistance in understanding* includes access for children to information held on them

R *Responsibility, recognition and representation* reinforces recognition of the right of children or young adults to make representations on all issues and decisions affecting them and their responsibilities in that regard

T *Thoughtfulness, respect and consideration* includes being listened to and having account taken of wishes and feelings

E *Encouragement, praise and appreciation* includes encouragement and support to continuing education after age 16

R *Recreation and creative play* includes access to recreation and play in education whilst in hospital suited to age

Each school child in the region was issued with his or her own Charter membership card.

All relevant regional council staff were expected to practice the principles set out in the Charter. The Charter and its operation were included in in-service staff training and internal staff bulletins. Staff were expected to ensure that children in respect of whom they had responsibilities were aware of the potential of the Charter as a medium whereby they can have entitlements met. To that end children, particularly in the primary school sector, have been involved in school and inter-school seminars on the subject which have been marked by the pupils' comprehension, participation and enthusiasm.

The Charter requires the three participating agencies to establish and operate a complaints procedure to address the complaints of any child who believes an entitlement is being denied. The Charter document details how children may complain and how departments must respond. It recognised however that internal complaints procedures may not suffice and that credibility and effectiveness might require an external outlet. To meet that need the post of Adjudicator was established, open to a complainant who has exhausted the departmental complaints procedure but still feels that the complaint has not been satisfactorily resolved.

The author, formerly an employee of the regional council for some 20 years as their Reporter to the children's panel under the children's hearings system, was appointed Adjudicator on the launch of the Charter and acted in that role on a voluntary basis for the first three years of its existence.

Although appointed by the council as Adjudicator and provided with an operational base in, and secretarial support from, one of the service departments, the Adjudicator worked independently of the council. I had the right to investigate complaints referred by the child without first obtaining the consent of the person or organisation against whom the complaint was made and could obtain all information relevant to the pursuit of a complaint. I had the discretion to make visits and arrange appropriate meetings and could appoint the venues for such meetings in regional premises though these may also be held in a neutral location.

Once a complaint was referred, it was expected that the Adjudicator would discuss the complaint with the child who may elect to see him alone or be accompanied by his or her parent or a friend. On completion of the investigations a report of the Adjudicator's findings was compiled and sent to the complainant and the person or organisation against whom the complaint was made. Where appropriate, parents also received a copy of the findings. Though it was envisaged that in the majority of cases any complainant would have exhausted the internal complaints procedure prior to referral, the Adjudicator could receive direct referrals and decide to refer it back to an earlier stage of the complaints procedure or deal with it personally immediately.

As far as the Adjudicator's powers are concerned the Charter stipulates that:

1. The adjudicator's findings are not legally binding on any party to a complaint.
2. There is no appeal against the Adjudicator's findings.
3. The essence of the Adjudicator's authority is 'persuasive'.

While these caveats may seem to diminish the potential effectiveness of the role it was anticipated (and in the event has become a reality) that departments and their staff, in the knowledge that the Adjudicator acted under the aegis of their employers to whom he would submit an annual report, would feel obliged to respond positively to such interventions and findings as the Adjudicator might make. Over the period of my office I have in fact received unfailing co-operation and openness from all personnel in the enquiries with which I was involved.

The writer entered two further personal caveats before accepting the appointment. The first was that I would operate on the basis that complaints to the Adjudicator would be dealt with, as is included in the original Charter document, not solely from the perspective of the child's complaint against another without the child taking on board his or her own responsibility in regard to the issue in dispute. The legal maxim in which I was trained that 'every right has a correlative duty' appeared, in my view, to be particularly apposite to child development.

The second was that, if the Charter resulted in large numbers of referrals, and necessary enquiries, I would be unable to continue in office. Part of that arose from selfish considerations that I would not have the time to deal with the work. More importantly, an abundance of referrals would indicate that departments were not committing themselves to the aims and objects of the Charter and that if they did not do so the Charter would amount to no more than a meaningless piece of paper and high-flown window dressing.

In the event, neither caveat has produced any problem. Indeed as the Adjudicator's two annual reports and demands for the third year exemplify, referrals to the Adjudicator have been very few and months can elapse between them. It is not possible to say with any certainty whether the dearth of referrals indicates that the Charter is operating so effectively that involvement to the Adjudicator is unnecessary or that in reality it is irrelevant.

Such referrals as there have been do suggest that for at least some children establishment of the Charter has constituted a positive advance in relation to the issue of children's rights. One matter which has not yet been satisfactorily resolved is the particularly low referral rate by children themselves. In most instances referrals have been by their parents claiming to be acting as guardians, and that the children through age or lack of understanding do not possess the capacity to advance their own rights. Preliminary decisions are made by the Adjudicator on an *ad hoc* basis after enquiry in respect of such referrals. Where the Adjudicator believes that the parent is genuinely acting in a guardian role the referral is accepted. Where it can be concluded that parents are attempting to use the Charter as an additional avenue for their own, until then unsuccessful, complaint, the referral will be declined and parents advised on how to prosecute their own complaint under the complaints procedures open to them.

The role of the Adjudicator and indeed the council can be faced with difficulties in relation to the area of provision of services and availability of resources. The Charter includes a clear aim to provide appropriately for children but this can be defeated through limitation of funding the optimum, whether in educational, social work or health terms. The Charter's statement of principles specifically includes the phrase 'within limits of appropriate resources'. The Adjudicator has felt obliged to interpret 'appropriate' as 'available' while reserving the right and actually commenting on such unavailability in his annual reports.

Some examples of actual referrals taken from the Annual Reports may demonstrate the benefits and limitations of the Charter and the issues raised.

Three examples demonstrate the communication difficulties which can exist between and within departments.

In the first case, a 14-year-old boy had been assessed as needing a special residential care and educational resource. All parties and especially the boy and his parents were anxious to take advantage of such a place. It was available within the region but the particular place had staffing difficulties which had prevented admission. Despite the region's advanced youth strategy procedures the number of people involved from the two main service departments had resulted in the directorate being unaware of the urgent need. Completion of the Adjudicator's report appeared to expedite the individual child's admission and more lastingly help establish a procedure to address future like cases.

In the second case, an 8-year-old girl had been assessed as one who would benefit from additional support teaching within her local primary school. The referral was made by her parents. The Adjudicator was satisfied after investigation that the particular school had received a marginally better than average share of the disposable regional budget allocated to support teaching. More general overall needs in this area are considered in the annual report but the Adjudicator concluded that the child's needs had been fairly dealt with within available resources and so advised the parent who expressed appreciation for the efforts which had gone into examining the issue. The individual report drew attention to the need for the administration to advise school heads of the basis of allocation so that they in turn could advise, and possibly satisfy, parents earlier.

In the third case, an 11-year-old ethnic minority child was distressed at the inability of the region to place her in the secondary school of her choice for the new session. Though her parents may have been the prime movers in the referral the Adjudicator had no doubt that the child was advancing her own rights. Though the Adjudicator's enquiries were about to disclose that the education department had dealt with the child's application on the same criteria as they had applied to many other applicants, happily the situation was resolved to the child's satisfaction by additional places becoming available and her placement in her school of choice. Again the Adjudicator's report made comment on communication issues and the ways in which families can be better advised in future cases of this kind. Subsequent information from the department indicates that they are now acting on these recommendations.

Two further examples illustrate that a child's views can be different from those of the parents.

In the fourth case, a 13-year-old boy had been excluded from school as a result of his aggressive behaviour. The parents believed their child had been treated unfairly; they wished him to be readmitted; they were particularly concerned as to what effects the exclusion might have on the boy in the future and that it might adversely affect his career prospects. The child did not want to return to that school. He was more than happy with the transfer arrangements which had been made. The Adjudicator made no finding.

In case five, the mother of a 13-year-old girl referred her to the Adjudicator. The child was in the care of the local authority. The mother made various bitter allegations against her carers. The child did not want to go back home. She had no complaints to make and wanted to stay in her placement. The Adjudicator declined to take up the referral.

These examples illustrate that the system of adjudication has provided an avenue for children and parents to enable decisions taken about them to be more closely examined. No sweeping conclusions can be drawn from such a limited number of cases. In three years there have been no more than 20, but those complaints which have been referred suggest that the system has had some value in the following areas.

The cases have highlighted communication difficulties within and between departments. It is perhaps arguable whether a department should need the intervention of an Adjudicator to resolve some of these, but the intervention has, in these limited number of cases, been effective in resolving the problem, not only for the individual child but in some cases through addressing the more general failure in the system.

Adjudication does also appear to have clarified problems resulting from different points of view which can exist between a child and his or her parents.

Individual cases can also highlight the resource issues. A recurring dilemma for the Adjudicator has been the fear that some children or parents, or indeed departments, might make use of referral to the Adjudicator as one way of advancing a child's claim to limited resources ahead of the claim of others who had not been aware of or made use of the Adjudicator. The system of Adjudicator cannot resolve resource issues as such but can draw attention to them and can at least ensure that access to available resources is seen to be fair.

The cases which have been referred to me may well be seen as useful pointers to more general issues. Awareness of the position of Adjudicator is low. A survey carried out for the region's own evaluation of the Charter found that only 30 per cent of children and young people knew of the post of Adjudicator and only 4 per cent knew how to get in touch, although over 70 per cent had heard of the Charter.[1] There are probably many more similar cases which are not referred because of lack of knowledge of the system.

I have no doubt however that Lothian Region has taken very positive advances in the field of children's rights by their actions and that their Charter amounts to much more than a paper exercise. Children have been helped to recognise their rights and responsibilities. Parents have received much relevant information about them and contrary to some expectations have welcomed the initiative and not expressed fears about 'child power'. Staff have become more aware of their responsibilities to children and the necessary requisite that children do have rights. In many instances it is clear that staff have actively adopted and practised the reality of the UN Convention on the Rights of the Child. Elected members, who control the purse strings, may find themselves unable to meet all the needs as they might wish but by having established their Charter they may not now ignore their responsibilities in that regard.

Reference
1. Buist, MacPherson, Asquith, 'Lothian Region Children's Family Charter' Centre for Study of Child in Society.

8.3 ACCOUNTABILITY IN ACTION
HEARING THE YOUNG PERSON'S VOICE
Cathy Jamieson
Principal Officer, Who Cares? Scotland

Who Cares? has helped me to have my say. When I first got involved, I wasn't really sure about it. I didn't have the confidence to speak up, but Who Cares? helped my confidence. They believed that I could do it, and gave me the support I needed. Now I want to help other young people who are going through the same thing.

You can't really understand what being in care feels like unless you've been there. The staff try to do their best for you, but at the end of the day they go home—we don't. We have to live with it all the time. To some people it's 'procedures,' and we can't do this or do that, but it's our lives. They need to listen to us, because if they don't then it won't get any better.

Young people in care need to speak out if they're not happy. There's no point in just sitting back and letting things happen, or taking it out on other people. A lot of young people end up taking it out on themselves. Sometimes you don't do anything about it when you're in care, but when you leave the problems are still there, and then you've got nobody to turn to.[1]

Who Cares? Scotland is recognised today as the representative voice of young people with experience of 'public care' in Scotland. The organisation was set up in 1978, after a group of young people from Scotland attended a conference organised by the National Children's Bureau . From these early beginnings, Who Cares? has developed against a background of growing political and public concern about standards and quality of life for young people in public care in Scotland.

Feelings of powerlessness, anger and frustration about not being consulted about decisions made and a desire to improve day-to-day life for all young people in care were the main reasons for young people and sympathetic adults coming together originally and choosing to try and work together to put across the views of the consumers of care.

Who Cares? wanted people to listen to the young people themselves, and to take their views into account when planning and providing care services. From its early beginnings, and with the support of many committed individuals in the statutory and voluntary sectors, Who Cares? has rapidly expanded in the last three years to the point where 11 members of staff are employed across Scotland.

A 'partnership approach' has been developed, as people recognised that change would be brought about by young people, adults supportive of the organisation's aims, and those who provided care services all working together.

Another Kind of Home—a Review of Residential Child Care in Scotland[2] made it absolutely clear that the voice of young people should play a major role in shaping residential child care services. *Scotland's Children*, the government White Paper on the future of children's services in Scotland backed this up, as do the principles of the Children (Scotland) Act 1995.

Ensuring accountability of services

> Going into the Reviews was the worst. Sometimes there were all these people sitting round, and you'd never seen them before. Everybody had all these reports with everything about you written down—sometimes there was a whole list of things you had done and they all got talked about over and over again. Everybody would be asking me why things had happened and going on about them. I never really knew what to say.

> Sometimes its the wee things that really get to you, like one day you'll come in and somebody's been through all the stuff in your room again. So you get really angry and crack up at the staff. Then you get hassle for your attitude, and you forget why you got angry in the first place, you just want to hit out, to make somebody listen to you, to know that you're there.

So how has Who Cares? gone about ensuring accountability of services provided for young people in public care? *Accountability* in this context means several things. Service providers, policymakers and practitioners have a view of the world based on their own life experiences, on theoretical perspectives and on knowledge and practical skills based on their work experience. This can give them very useful ideas about how to plan and organise services in an efficient way, but what it rarely provides is a real understanding of what it is like to live in 'public care'; for your whole life to become 'public property' open to question, challenge and scrutiny 24 hours a day, 7 days a week. Young people living in public care know also what it feels like to be constantly made accountable—having to explain their actions, talk about their feelings—often in relation to situations which would largely pass by unnoticed or not remarked upon in other living situations.

What Who Cares? has been able to do is provide a focus for the strength of these feelings in young people, and to turn the anger and frustration experienced by individual young people into a collective voice advocating very strongly and powerfully on behalf of young people with experience of care. This has been done at an individual level, by supporting young people in, for example child care reviews and children's hearings, and by helping young people write their own reports for such meetings.

Young people have also been helped to make use of the complaints procedures available to them—this can often be a daunting process, and they have benefited from assistance in understanding the procedures, making the complaint, and being supported through the process. Access to an independent voice can make a very real difference for young persons, who may be lacking in confidence, and give them a real sense of having a right to their say.

Collective advocacy has been one of the major elements of our work, particularly through the production of a Charter of Rights. The original Charter of Rights was drawn up in 1988, at a conference involving young people from across Scotland. This early Charter was very much a 'wish list' of the things young people wanted to see as the standards in good quality residential care—things like the right to privacy, the right to attend reviews, the right to a clothing allowance and pocket money.

Who Cares? Scotland asked local authorities to adopt this Charter, and to implement it in their services to young people in their care. Although the early Charter was adopted by most authorities, and did assist in ensuring some changes were made to basic practice, perhaps the most significant factor was that for the first time, young people felt the value of working collectively. Here was something they had drawn up themselves, now being acted upon, which gave them a baseline to work from if they wanted to complain about the quality of their lives in care, or if they felt they were being denied their rights. Staff in residential units could also use the Charter as a way of improving the service and policymakers could ensure that it was considered in a much broader way, when planning new services, by ensuring young people's views were taken into account at all stages.

> Accountability is also important in the formal Inspections of residential establishments, and the increased role for former users of services has meant that young people have actively assisted the inspection process.

The limitations of the original Charter became apparent in the next few years as policy and practice changed, and Who Cares? Scotland began a process of updating the Charter. What was assumed was going to be a simple exercise in fact turned into a major operation, as the principles of the UN Convention on the Rights of the Child, existing child care legislation and agreed policy and recommendations from the key reports regarding residential child care were brought together into a new Charter . This Charter clearly spelled out for young people exactly what rights they do have, rather than the original 'wish list'. For the first time, the Charter also made reference to the *responsibilities* of young people in care as well as their rights, and extended its scope to include care settings other than children's homes.

Some local authorities have now chosen to produce their own local Charters, as suggested in *Another Kind of Home*, and young people from care have again been involved in drawing these up.

Accountability is also important in the formal inspections of residential establishments, and the increased role for former users of services has meant that young people have actively assisted the inspection process. The value of this approach has been shown in the way that those with experience of living in residential care often pick up on slightly different aspects of a home's culture, or the way things are organised, which others might not consider. For example, in one home, the positioning of an office next to the girls' bathroom had never been seen as an issue until the young people were asked directly by someone who had been in care, and remembered how it seemed that there was little personal privacy anywhere—even in the bath.

In other situations, individual young people have felt more comfortable raising their concerns to someone they feel will understand the whole culture of residential living, and why certain aspects take on such importance.

Significant improvements have also been made in the way young people are consulted about major policy initiatives—young people from the organisation were involved in making submissions to the major reviews of residential child care, as well as numerous local authority policy forums. Conferences, training events and seminars have provided further opportunities for young people to put forward their views, and also to question the service providers in a very direct way. Young people from Who Cares? Scotland spoke directly to Members of Parliament during the consultation on the Children (Scotland) Act, and put forward examples of how legislation affected their day-to-day lives, and how particular changes would benefit them.

Looking to the future

Young people get more of a chance to have a say now, with meetings in the home, and there's more choices about things like your clothes and stuff. But everything's not perfect—more needs to be done for young people when they've left care.

It was really good talking to the MPs. I think they really did listen to us, and they asked a lot of questions about how things could be changed. I just hope that they do change. There's not much point in listening if you don't go away and do something.

Changes have been made, but more needs to happen—particularly regarding the planning of services for children and young people, and ensuring that every strand of the process is woven together in a way that stops young people falling through the gaps in the net.

Ensuring that services are accountable to users means that users must have ways of putting their individual and collective, views across to those who provide services. Changing trends in the use of residential care, with more teenagers in children's homes, but for shorter periods of time, will in future mean that young people need ways of getting their views heard quickly and easily, and that the phase of moving on from residential living to 'independent' life is not forgotten in the accountability stakes.

> Listening to young people means asking the right questions in the first place, being open to hearing the answers, and being prepared to act on the views expressed.

A network of local Who Cares? Scotland groups is seen as the key to making real changes, giving an opportunity for young people to meet with those who make decisions affecting them, in their areas, as well as feeding in to a wider Scottish organisation which can influence policy, practice and legislation.

Making services accountable to users is an ongoing process, not something that happens every now and again. When involving young people in the process, it is important that everyone is open to hear what is being said. If the same points are being raised time and time again, maybe it's the system that needs changing. Listening to young people means asking the right questions in the first place, being open to hear the answers, and being prepared to act on the views expressed. By doing this as an integral part of the process of caring for young people in residential care, the service will genuinely become more accountable to those using it.

Notes and Reference

1. This and other quotations in the paper are the voices of young people who have experienced public care in Scotland, as expressed to *Who Cares? Scotland*.
2. The Social Work Service Inspectorate for Scotland. *Another Kind of Home: A Review of Residential Child Care* (Edinburgh: HMSO, 1992).

8.4 LOCAL PLANNING OF SERVICES FOR YOUNG CHILDREN

THE ROLE OF THE SECTION 19 DAYCARE REVIEWS IN WALES

Dr June Statham

Member of the Thomas Coram Research Unit, London University Institute of Education

Introduction

The Children Act 1989[1] imposed a new duty on local authorities in England, Scotland and Wales to carry out a review (often known as the 'Section 19' or 'Daycare' review) of pre-school education and daycare services for children under the age of eight. This review has to be undertaken at least once every three years, and provides a mechanism for involving a wide range of interested parties in planning services for young children. This chapter examines the experience of the first reviews in Wales, from the perspective of both statutory officers and local childcare organisations.

Background

In the UK, there is a great diversity of services providing care, education and play for young children, offered by a variety of agencies including government departments (education, welfare and leisure), voluntary organisations and private individuals. The main forms of provision are nursery education, public and private day nurseries, family centres, childminders, playgroups, holiday play schemes and out of school clubs. These services have different philosophies, different hours, different training and working conditions for staff and different funding levels. They generally aim to meet particular needs, for instance daycare for working parents, education for children about to start school, opportunities for children to play with their peers, or support for children and families experiencing difficulty. There is substantial geographical variation in the level and pattern of services, with rural areas often having lower levels of provision, especially of publicly funded services.[2,3] Across the UK as a whole, there is a low level of early years services and little public funding compared to most other European countries.[4]

At a national level, central government is responsible for the overall policy on children's services in the UK. The current policy on nursery education is that it is provided at the discretion of each local authority, rather than as a statutory duty; and the policy on daycare is that public responsibility is limited to welfare circumstances where the child or family is regarded as being 'in need'. Central government sets this framework of general policy and principles through legislation, which is then interpreted and applied by each local authority in the light of local circumstances and priorities. In England and Wales, the main legislative framework for children's services is the Children Act 1989. This brings together in one Act public and private law affecting children up to the age of 18. Only a small part of the Act concerns daycare and pre-school services, but these sections give local authorities three main duties: to *provide* services for children in need; to *regulate* private and voluntary daycare services for children under eight; and to *co-ordinate* the services that are offered to young children by different agencies.

A key aspect of the co-ordination duty under the Children Act is the requirement to carry out a review of daycare and related services at least once every three years. This review has to be done jointly by the social services and education departments, and should involve a wide range of other agencies including the voluntary and private sectors. The aim is to provide an overview of existing provision, identify gaps and begin to plan a more co-ordinated service. The guidance issued with the Act makes it clear that an important purpose of the review is to emphasise local accountability for the level, pattern and range of daycare and related services for young children.

> The review process needs to be seen as an active procedure which encourages development of good quality services planned and delivered in the light of local wishes and expectations.[5]

So has the review had an impact on how services are planned for young children, and made them more responsive to local needs? Has it given local communities more say in the development of services for the under-eights? The rest of this contribution draws on information collected as part of a research project evaluating the implementation of the Children Act as it affects daycare and related services in England and Wales. The methodology and wider results of the first stage of the project have been described elsewhere.[6,7] This chapter focuses on the work in Wales, but similar results have been found in the linked project in England and also in research on the reviews carried out by the National Children's Bureau[8] and by Children in Scotland.[9]

Participation: who was involved in the reviews?

The first review had to be produced by local authorities by October 1992, within a year of the Children Act coming into force, and in most cases few extra resources or staff had been allocated to the task. It was added to existing workloads, at a time when many social services departments were reorganising in response to new policies on community care, and when both education and health services were also undergoing substantial changes which affected their ability to work together with other agencies. In these circumstances, it is perhaps not surprising that education departments rarely participated as equal partners in the joint review duty, and that difficulties were often reported in involving other statutory agencies such as health authorities.

All eight local authorities in Wales had made some attempt to involve non-statutory organisations in the review process. In some cases this meant little more than requesting information and offering the opportunity to comment on a draft document. In other cases it was a much more participatory process, with a variety of multi-agency task groups set up to work together on the review. Most authorities had taken on board the requirement that they 'seek views from all interested parties and individuals',[10] but had not always found it possible to involve the wide range of community groups recommended in the guidance. In practice, some groups were more frequently consulted than others. Playgroup and childminding organisations and local branches of national children's charities were involved in most cases; private day nurseries, smaller charities and organisations representing children with disabilities (except for children with learning difficulties) had been included less often. There was also little involvement of minority ethnic groups. In Wales, with a very low minority ethnic population (less than 2 per cent in all counties), there were few associations or groups that local authorities could identify to ask for their views. But it was not just a problem of low numbers and lack of a representative voice. In England, local authorities with significant minority ethnic populations also felt that they had failed to consult adequately with minority ethnic families, and that they needed to develop more sensitive ways of trying to involve them in the review process.[11,12]

> Political involvement and commitment is necessary if the reviews are to be a mechanism for local accountability and if their recommendations are to be taken forward, since it is elected members who ultimately take the decisions on policies and spending.

Elected members had played a significant role in the review in only a quarter of Welsh local authorities, again reflecting findings in England. In the remaining local authorities, officers reported that elected members had taken little part, had not been involved in setting the terms of reference for the review nor taken an active interest in its progress. Political involvement and commitment is necessary if the reviews are to be a mechanism for local accountability and if their recommendations are to be taken forward, since it is elected members who ultimately take the decisions on policies and spending.

Most local authorities had found it difficult to include parents in the review process, although they had tried. A minority had undertaken surveys and included the results in their review reports. Most had attempted to use the draft review document as the basis for consultation with parents and interested members of the public, either through public meetings or by attaching a questionnaire asking for feedback. They reported that the response had generally been poor. The best results were obtained by going out to talk to parents in their own environments, for instance using 'Fun Days' or mobile toy libraries, rather than expecting them to attend public meetings or send back questionnaires.

Young children themselves are obviously stakeholders in early childhood services, although their views are rarely heard. One or two local authorities were beginning to develop ways of involving older children and young people in planning the kind of services they would like, but had not specifically addressed this for younger children. However, one Welsh authority was investigating the possibility of using the annual inspections of independent daycare services under the Children Act, as a way of ascertaining for the next review what children themselves wanted from a good quality service.

The success of the reviews as a planning tool

So far the difficulties local authorities reported with the first reviews and the lack of involvement by certain key groups have been highlighted. Despite this, it was widely agreed that the review had been a worthwhile exercise. It had brought together many different agencies, increased dialogue between them, and raised awareness of the importance of early years services. It had produced an overview of the services available for young children, often for the first time, and highlighted the differing needs and levels of provision of local areas. What it often had not produced, yet, were tangible outcomes in terms of service developments. The first reviews were mostly descriptive audits of existing provision, rather than detailed planning tools. The situation in Wales was further complicated by the impending reorganisation of local government (from 8 counties into 22 new unitary authorities by April 1996), which had taken precedence over work on the second review.

From the perspective of local organisations concerned with provision for young children, there were mixed views on the effectiveness of the review as a mechanism for involving them in planning local services. Representatives of these organisations generally agreed with the statutory sector that the review had led to better liaison and consultation, and that there was now more interest in obtaining their views.

> We're working together much more since the Children Act. There's more interlinking and people sharing information.
>
> (Representative of childminding organisation)

Most local interest groups felt that this increased consultation had not yet given them a real voice in the planning and development of services. They commonly felt that they were not involved in determining the issues and agenda, but instead were responding to local authority concerns.

> We were asked to contribute to the review, but we feel very much on the sidelines as far as planning goes. Plans are made and we are allowed to comment on them ... we would rather be involved at the beginning.
>
> (Representative of Welsh-language playgroup association)

> When the Review came out, social services had made up their minds what was going to be their priorities. We weren't asked, just given a document to comment on.
>
> (Representative of English-language playgroup association)

This reflects the fact that the first review was for many authorities a learning exercise, undertaken in a short time and often without the structures and networks in place that would have facilitated joint working. One of the concrete achievements of the first reviews in Wales was to establish better contacts between all those involved with young children, and to encourage the development of local early years fora which local authorities hoped to use to involve a wider range of groups at an earlier stage in the next review process.

Local childcare organisations, especially small organisations without paid development workers, pointed to a number of obstacles hindering their effective participation in multi-agency children's planning groups. These included the lack of expenses for unpaid volunteers to attend meetings; their lack of confidence in the face of meetings dominated by the local authority's agenda and language; difficulties in finding a representative voice who could speak for a wide range of voluntary organisations; and little recognition of the need for such representatives to have time to consult with their membership before taking decisions.

Despite this, the published review reports often did address issues which community organisations in Wales saw as particularly important. Areas of unmet need, which were identified by voluntary organisations and included in at least some review reports, included an expansion of Welsh-language early years provision, inspection procedures available through the medium of Welsh, an awareness of the particular needs of childcare services in rural areas, and increased availability of training for childcare workers. One issue which the voluntary and private sector saw as important but which was rarely mentioned in the reviews was the need for increased resources to meet new inspection standards and to subsidise training. Local authorities, perhaps understandably, were reluctant to raise expectations which they felt they had little chance of meeting.

Accountability: some lessons from the reviews

> Effective participation requires attention to be paid to the process as well as the structures for involvement ... Attention needs to be paid to the language and conduct of meetings, to issues of representation, and to the inequality of power inherent in the local authority's relationship with community groups who may depend on it for their funding. More flexible ways need to be found to make sure that the views of some interest groups, such as parents and minority ethnic families, are taken into account.

The experience of local authorities in undertaking the first daycare reviews raises a number of issues for accountability in planning services for young children. First, for the review to provide a genuine mechanism for joint planning, it needs to be clearly linked into the decision making structure of the local authority and part of an ongoing process of working with local childcare groups, rather than an exercise carried out once every three years. The review recommendations need to be incorporated into a children's service plan, and this needs the commitment and backing of senior officers and elected members if it is to be translated into practice. Whilst local childcare organisations appreciated the increased dialogue and liaison over early years which had resulted from the first review, they are unlikely to maintain their involvement or feel that services are becoming more accountable if there are no practical outcomes as a result of the review, and if the structures it sets up are no more than talking shops.

Secondly, the participation in planning of other agencies and local community groups depends on building up effective networks and developing trust. Consultation is not something that can be switched on and off at will to suit the local authority's needs or the requirements of the Children Act. It takes time and skill, and some commitment of resources. The authorities that had managed the most extensive consultation with a wide range of voluntary and community bodies were generally those who had appointed an officer with specific responsibility for early years services and the review. The least consultation generally happened when the review was added to the duties of an officer already responsible for a wide range of children's services.

Effective participation requires attention to be paid to the process as well as the structures for involvement. It is not enough to just invite the main childcare organisations to send a representative to a multi-agency group. Attention needs to be paid to the language and conduct of meetings, to issues of representation, and to the inequality of power inherent in the local authority's relationship with community groups who may depend on it for their funding. More flexible ways need to be found to make sure that the views of some interest groups, such as parents and minority ethnic families, are taken into account.

Finally, a balance needs to be struck between local accountability with the flexibility to respond to local circumstances, and the need for a clear framework of agreed policies and principles for an early years service. There needs to be a debate about what should be non-negotiable (for instance anti-racism or equal access to services) and what can be decided locally (which might include models of provision, type of curriculum, and the balance between statutory and voluntary services). In recent years there have been increasing calls for a national childcare policy for the UK which would acknowledge the importance of good quality services for all children and parents, and provide the infrastructure and resources to make this possible.[13,14,15] The Section 19 review creates an important opportunity for planning and developing services for young children in a way that responds to the needs of local communities. There needs to be a commitment to early years services, from both central and local government, if this potential is to be realised.

Notes and References

1. *The Children Act 1989* (London: HMSO).
2. Statham, J. and Cameron, C., 'Young children in rural areas: implementing the Children Act', *Children and Society*, Vol. 8, No.1 (1994, pp. 17-30).

3. Cohen, B., *Childcare Services for Rural Families: Improving Provision in the European Union* (Brussels: Council of European Communities, 1995).

4. Moss, P., *Childcare in the European Communities 1985–1990* (Brussels: CEC, 1990).

5. Department of Health, *Guidance and Regulations (Vol. 2): Family Support, Daycare and Educational Provision for Young Children* (London: HMSO, 1991, para 9.18).

6. Bull, J., Cameron, C., Candappa, M., Moss, P., Owen, C. and Statham, J., *Implementing the Children Act for Children under 8* (London: HMSO, 1994).

7. Statham, J., *The Children Act and Under 8s in Wales* (London: Thomas Coram Research Unit, 1993).

8. Elfer, P. and McQuail, S., *Local Wishes and Expectations* (London: National Children's Bureau, 1996).

9. Martin, C. (ed), *Children Act Review: A Scottish Experience* (Edinburgh: Children in Scotland/HMSO, 1994).

10. Department of Health, 1991, para 9.7.

11. Candappa, M., 'Equal opportunities and ethnicity in the early years: Implementing the Children Act', *Children and Society* vol. 8 no. 3, pp. 218–31 1994.

12. Elfer, P. and McQuail, S., *Local Wishes and Expectations* (London: National Children's Bureau, 1996).

13. National Children's Bureau, *A Policy for Young Children: a Framework for Action* (London: Under Fives Unit NCB, 1990).

14. Equal Opportunities Commission, *The Key to Real Choice* (Manchester: EOC, 1990).

15. Cohen, B. and Fraser, N., *Childcare in a Modern Welfare System* (London: IPPR, 1991).

Chapter 9

◆

ACCOUNTABILITY: SCANDINAVIA

9.1 MAKING SERVICES AND AUTHORITIES ACCOUNTABLE

THE ROLE OF THE NORWEGIAN OMBUDSMAN FOR CHILDREN

Trond-Viggo Torgersen*
Ombudsman for Children in Norway
Marianne Borgen
Chief Executive, The Ombudsman's Office

Norway established the world's first *barneombud* (Ombudsman for Children) on September 1981. The Ombudsman for Children Act stipulates that the main duties of the Ombudsman should be 'to promote the interests of children *vis-à-vis* public and private authorities and to follow up the development of conditions under which children grow up'. This involves recommending changes in legislation, policy and practice to government and the municipalities, investigating individual cases, distributing information and making use of the media to highlight issues and promote discussion. The Act provides for the Ombudsman to have 'free access to all public and private institutions for children. Government authorities and public and private institutions for children shall, notwithstanding the pledge of secrecy, give the Ombudsman the information needed to carry out the duties of the Ombudsman pursuant to this Act'.

The office of the Ombudsman for Children is administered under the Ministry for Children and Family Affairs, but is totally independent. In addition to the Ombudsman, the office includes a secretarial staff of eight. The Ombudsman is appointed by the government for a period of four years. The staff are responsible for the fields of law, sociology, education, child welfare, medicine, culture, ethnicity and information. In 1995 the budget amounted to NOK 4.8 million (£480,000), approximately 5 NOK (50 pence) per child.

---

* Trond-Viggo Torgerson and Marianne Borgen resigned from office in November 1995 after completing this chapter.

The Ombudsman has an important role in collecting, distributing and making use of the information on children's living conditions, gathered through research centres and the National Statistics Bureau. The Ombudsman publishes all available and reliable research data and statistics concerning children and young people in publications such as *Facts about Children in Norway* (1990 and 1994) and the 1995 factsheet *Under 18: facts about Children and Youth in Norway*. The Ombudsman chaired the board of the national research programme on children in the welfare state (1988–94), in addition to being an executive member of the children's culture committee in the National Culture Fund. All this gives the office a unique insight into available knowledge and data concerning children and young people. In fields where there is a lack of knowledge or statistics, the authorities are challenged, and the Ombudsman's wish or demand for documentation has often led to action.

Name: Einar

Location: Kristiansand

'Why are there no safety belts in the buses, when they are required in cars?'

An Ombudsman for Children as part of a government system is in many ways a contradiction. The Ombudsman's main task is often to supervise and criticise the governing bodies. It is quite a challenge to keep issues and personalities separate from one another in order to keep the lines of communication open. This has been just as much a challenge for politicians and bureaucrats as for the Ombudsman.

Changes affecting children

The information collected by the Ombudsman illustrates the changes affecting children and childhood in Norway as in many other countries. Children in Norway are increasingly affected by the separation or divorce of their parents, are spending less time with their parents and their activities have been curtailed by the growth in traffic.

Child and family change

- Almost as many children are born to unmarried as to married mothers.
- The number of broken homes is steadily increasing.
- Cohabitation results in breakdown more often than marriage.
- Broken homes normally result in children seeing less of their fathers.
- Broken homes give children new brothers and sisters and new adult relations.
- After a break-up children often lose contact with their grandparents.
- Inter-generational families living together are less common.

Children spend less time with parents

- For mothers with small children, working hours outside the home have increased considerably over the past 15 years.
- Over the past six years, overtime work for fathers of small children has increased.
- The number of daycare centres has increased over the past 10 years.
- Time at school has increased both in number of periods and years.
- There has been a considerable increase in the number of children in the extra-curricular supervision system.
- New TV channels, video and computer games get the children's attention and take time.

Children are isolated

- Closures of schools, post offices and stores have impoverished rural areas.
- In urban areas this impoverishment has arrived later, and with more impact.
- The density of cars has increased substantially through the 1980s and threatens children's way of living and their play areas.
- Some children are not receiving assistance in relation to abuse and inadequate care.

The Ombudsman's involvement in securing children's needs

Since relatively few children call to talk directly with our staff, we have established a special toll-free phone number connected to an answering machine where any question or any kind of problem may be presented. Messages are written down in full and stored anonymously on the Ombudsman's database. Examples are presented throughout this chapter. Many of the messages are taken up as themes or answered directly on national radio and television. Topics with which children are concerned are:

- dangerous play areas in their neighbourhood
- lack of special education services
- lack of supervision in foster homes
- unsatisfactory visiting conditions for children with a parent in jail
- conditions for children in families with alcoholic parents.

Name: Sølve

Age: 14

Location: Gjesdal

'I really want this to be broadcast. We just got a new bicycle path in Oltedalen. And all the kids from the lower parts of the valley up to the daycare centre in the upper valley will now be able to ride their bikes safely up and down.'

Private applications from adults directed to the Ombudsman's office are mostly concerned with:

- dissatisfaction with a ruling by the child welfare authorities, placing a child under public care
- dissatisfaction with visiting rights after a divorce
- dissatisfaction with public authorities that do not intervene when children in their family are suffering from lack of care.

Name: Kari

Age: 14

Location: Sør-Odal

'Am I supposed to be raped by my stepfather?'

The welfare state has given both parents and children in Norway some essential benefits, for example, social insurance, subsidised public daycare, education, child benefits and the right to leave of absence to care for children. In addition, children are regarded as citizens with citizens' rights, a concept which continues to evolve. It has, amongst other things, lead to the banning of corporal and mental punishment of children. The Children's Act (1987) states that 'the child must not be subjected to violence or in any other way be treated so as to endanger the mental or physical health of the child'. The Ombudsman made an important contribution to this reform.

'There's a boy living upstairs who is in the seventh grade. He drinks and smokes, and chews nicotine. He beats us and grabs us round our throats. He beats us just for saying hello to him. And we're really afraid to help him. His mother beats him, and he's doing the stranglehold even on those kids who are really small too.'

New national policies have been developed in a wide range of areas concerning services to children and young people. These include:

- new legislation involving children and affecting children
- children and municipal planning
- rights of refugee children
- information to and about children's rights
- school issues
- daycare institutions and family daycare services
- child welfare, in particular the new Child Welfare Act
- family judicial issues, especially concerning visiting and divorce issues
- sexual violence towards children, especially the penal aspects, and
- participation of children and young people in local democracy.

Some examples of actual involvement by the Ombudsman are briefly presented in the following paragraphs.

1.   *The new Children's Welfare Act and the National Development Programme*. In 1989 the media and the Ombudsman revealed that lots of reports concerning children at risk were piling up at social security offices in the municipalities. On the one hand this was mainly due to stressed and unqualified staff, in some instances lack of staff, and on the other hand lack of political priority and money. At the national level the Ombudsman examined whether the provisions in the Children's Welfare Act were accommodating the needs of a distressed child, guaranteeing immediate assistance. There were municipalities where cases had been prepared and presented to the public administration and the local council politicians, but without the actual cases attracting enough support to be given priority. Consequently, three of the municipal councils and their administrations were reported to the police by the Ombudsman. The Attorney General dismissed the cases, but the political reactions were immense, both at the national and local level throughout the country. These cases resulted in the inclusion of a provision in the new Children's Welfare Act (1993), in which the municipal councils were given the duty to give 'the help needed in time'. This was followed by a governmental development programme involving staffing, organisation and training. The Ombudsman's main remaining worry has to do with the quality and quantity of action generally, and more specifically with the relationship between the foster homes and the social welfare system. It is a priority for the Ombudsman to monitor these developments.

2.   *Integrating children with special needs into local schools*. The Basic Education Act gives children with special learning problems, physiological or social problems in early childhood and in school age a statutory right to assistance according to expert advice. The norm is that children and young people with special needs are now integrated into the local school. Twenty competence centres have been established nationally and regionally to deal with problems and to reinforce the special pedagogical education within the school system. All municipalities have established a so-called pedagogic psychological service. The quality of this service varies within the regions. The Ombudsman has found that help is not always available because of lack of competence, lack of finance or inefficient routines. A legislative proposal is under way, but will not necessarily accommodate the needs.

3.   *Developing health centres into parental guidance centres*. A nationwide network of health centres was established in Norway early this century as a result of a mother and child programme offering guidance before and after birth and later on the immunisation of children. The health centres have been through radical changes as health among children has improved, now focusing on immunisation and information. Despite their good reputation, municipal grants have been reduced. Together with nurses, health educators and child psychologists, the Ombudsman now wants this institution to redevelop into a parental guidance centre, focusing on the child's needs for two competent parents. This would provide a co-ordinating function within the welfare

structure of the municipalities. The government has recently indicated its support for this proposal.

4.   *Mediation after divorce or dissolved partnership.* For parents who apply for separation or divorce and have children under the age of 16 there is, as of January 1994, a requirement of compulsory mediation. This is stated in the Norwegian Marriage Act. The Ombudsman worked hard to get the principle of mediation accepted, as well as participating in a working group suggesting how the mediation should be regulated.

5.   *The Sami people's right to education in their native tongue.* This legal right is unevenly distributed in the Sami region. This is due to both lack of educated teachers and turbulence in local politics. The Ombudsman leads a project revealing living conditions for the minority ethnic Sami children and adolescents.

Other policies introduced in recent years with which the Ombudsman's Office has been associated include:

- four-weeks paid paternity leave in addition to maternity leave
- a national programme for establishing daycare centres and family daycare, including new legislation and regulations
- lowering the school admission age from 7 years to 6 years by 1997
- integrating extra-curricular supervision systems partly paid by the parents in the local school
- Reform 94, the right to three years of upper secondary education for all, and
- establishing 'conflict boards' for young people as an alternative for young offenders.

Future challenges

The policies mentioned above are in general good news for children. However, the Ombudsman is concerned with how these benefits are distributed and how they influence childhood itself. It seems that a legal right established at the national level does not necessarily reach children where they live and where services are delivered, that is in the municipalities.

The wider trends also seem to influence how policies are implemented. Complex patterns create situations not necessarily beneficial to the individual child or more generally to those going through their childhood. The following issues bring new dilemmas for a welfare state such as Norway.

- the growing gap between municipalities in providing welfare support
- The increase in parents' working hours combined with both parents pursuing a career
- the increasing institutionalisation and organisation of childhood
- the growing number of children identified as 'at risk' combined with a lack of resources to help each one of them
- the increasing numbers of refugees and asylum seekers in a changing Europe

- the internationalisation of various media and thereby the availability to, and influence on, children and adolescents, and
- the internationalisation of trade and politics influencing national welfare politics.

As well as being involved in addressing issues such as these, the Ombudsman will be facing a more direct challenge in finding ways in which children and young people are enabled to express their opinion. As a public institution, the Ombudsman has as one of its main aims to enable more young people to communicate their views. As mentioned earlier, the fact that relatively few children and young people make contact during regular office hours might indicate a fear of approaching a public institution. The toll-free answerphone service which was established in 1989 has served as an important channel for two-way communication. The close co-operation with the national television and radio channel (NRK) have been of great importance for the system to function. When the number of contacts showed a sharp decline in the last part of 1994, the Ombudsman looked for alternative ways to get in touch with children. Teletext television was introduced as an additional way of communicating, with good results. During the last few years the Ombudsman has also given priority to discussions with children and young people within their local environment. During visits to schools, after school activities, youth clubs and cultural events time has been allocated for informal talks with children and young people. In addition student organisations (upper secondary 16–19 age groups) and organised groups of young people under the protection of the child welfare services have been contacted.

It is important that it is easy to get in touch with the Ombudsman, and the youngest part of the population must be given a guarantee that a person and an office really exist who exclusively argue their case and help ensure their rights. Only children and young people are experts on what it is like to grow up in today's society, and in many instances their experiences will differ from that of adults. In other words, children and young people should continue to set the agenda for the Ombudsman's work— hopefully to an even greater extent than has been possible so far.

In December 1995 an independent Commission appointed by the Ministry of Children and Family Affairs published a report evaluating the Children's Ombudsman as an institution and reviewing the organisation of services for children and young people (*Barneombud og barndom i Norge*, November 1995). The report commended the work of the Ombudsman in supporting the legal rights of children in care, refugees and asylum-seeking children, and children in school, in addition to strengthening child welfare. It identified a central role for the Ombudsman in leading and co-ordinating the professional and political processes necessary for a more unified approach to issues relating to children and young people, including a role as a 'Network Ombudsman' forming close links with the municipalities. It recommended that the Ombudsman should be less concerned with individual cases and make less use of the media (Editors).

9.2 IMPROVING ACCOUNTABILITY THROUGH INCREASED CHOICE

THE RESTRUCTURING OF THE PUBLIC SUBSIDY SYSTEM IN SOCIAL WELFARE DISTRICT 17, STOCKHOLM

Kajsa Andersson

Head of Social Welfare District 17, Stockholm

Competition between public and private social service providers is a relatively new phenomenon in Sweden. Sweden has had high levels of services but has offered parents little choice. Places have traditionally been obtained through a central administrative office with little choice available over the location or form of service. This article describes the development of a parental choice model in Social Welfare District 17 in Stockholm, involving the introduction of a grant or voucher scheme to encourage competition between services in the public and private sector, offering parents more choice and making services more accountable.

Social welfare services in Kista

Social welfare services in Stockholm are divided into 17 districts. Kista, district number 17, includes the western suburbs Kista, Husby and Akalla. The population in Kista is around 28,000, of which 38 per cent are foreign citizens. In Husby, where the proportion of immigrants is highest, 1 in 10 is from Iran and 1 in 20 from Ethiopia or Eritrea. Of all children registered in early years services in Husby, 91 per cent do not have Swedish as their mother tongue, and there are a total of 36 languages spoken within the daycare centres. Another characteristic of the area is the high rate of unemployment, and many households are in receipt of benefits. In 1994, 18 per cent of the immigrants were unemployed and 22.5 per cent of the population received social benefit for an average of 6.9 months per household.

The social welfare district has as its main responsibility early years services, services for the elderly and the disabled, child welfare, drug addicts and social benefit. From 1 January 1997 Stockholm will be reorganised into 24 districts which will be given increased responsibility. In addition to the tasks mentioned the new authorities will also be responsible for education, leisure, culture, libraries and some road maintenance.

Currently the social welfare services in the 17 districts are led by district committees, made up of nine elected members. The district committees come under the City Social Welfare Committee and the City Council. Since September 1994 the city has been governed by a coalition of the Social Democrats, the Left Party and the Environmental Party. The district committees decide, among other matters, how resources are distributed locally, which aims should be met by social service departments in their district, and how service providers are to be supervised.

> The legislation also stipulated that care could be provided in different forms providing parents with some choice. In Stockholm a 'customer choice' model has been introduced in which parents are seen as customers with the right to decide the form and location of their child's daycare.

Changes affecting early years services

Social services for children have undergone substantial changes over the last few years. Economic crisis in Sweden has resulted in reduced public sector resources. A new Conservative government has sought to reduce the costs of welfare services by promoting competition. In 1993 the municipality of Stockholm decided that 20 per cent of daycare services should become competitive annually. At the same time, the number of places has had to increase significantly to meet the requirements of a new 'childcare guarantee' introduced through legislation from January 1995 but effectively operating in Stockholm from mid-1994. The new legislation requires all local authorities to provide a place in pre-school and school-age child care for all children aged 1–12 years, when required by parents in paid employment, education or training, or actively seeking employment, or because of the needs of the child. The place has to be provided within three months of a parent registering a need for a place. The legislation also stipulated that care could be provided in different forms providing parents with some choice. In Stockholm a 'customer choice' model has been introduced in which parents are seen as customers with the right to decide the form and location of their child's daycare. The aim is that services should compete for children and a new financial system has been introduced. This involves social welfare districts distributing a grant or voucher to all registered daycare institutions for each child, who is given a place in any of its services. There are two types of grants or vouchers, one for public services known as *Schablon* and one for private institutions, *Peng*. Both involve a flat-rate grant for every child enrolled which is distributed to the providers. The amount of money varies—the *Schablon* includes the fee from parents which have been paid centrally in the case of public services. Parental fees in public daycare services vary according to family income and number of hours the child is looked after. The *Peng* does not include a parental fee. Private providers are free to set the rate of parental fees which are payable directly to the service, opening up the possibility of price competition between private providers as well as between private and public services.

The grant/voucher is intended to cover all costs involved in running the services. Services included within this financial scheme are daycare centres, family daycare, part-time pre-school education and a flexible hours pre-school service. In the district of Kista there is also a baby café (a drop-in facility for parents and infants) and a preparatory pre-school for those children who do not have Swedish as their mother tongue.

Private provision of children's services

To stimulate the supply and meet the demand from parents and politicians, Kista social welfare district has put much effort into offering a mix of privately and publicly run early years services. Different forms of incentives are offered to encourage staff in services which are currently publicly run to develop their services as private enterprises. Nursery and teaching staff are offered courses in 'how to get started' and staff are encouraged to run the services as co-operatives or based on other forms of private ownership. This has contributed to an increase in private services. In Stockholm 22 per cent of the early years services were run by private providers in 1995. In Kista the figure is 17 per cent. In one other district in the city, nearly 50 per cent of services are run by private providers. Private services mainly take the form of parent co-operatives but also include private businesses.

All private services are regulated. Private as well as public provision must be run according to the aims and regulations laid down by the Social Welfare Act and its social welfare provision[1] and the social welfare committee's regulations on residential homes and community care.[2] The main emphasis is on quality of methods and staff training. Those wanting to run services for children of whatever kind must apply to be accepted and registered with the social welfare committee in the district where the service is to be offered. Approval is required for the suitability of the premises from the fire and environment authorities, and the Labour Inspectorate or, in the case of services provided in private homes, the social welfare district must approve the accommodation. Information must be provided on the curriculum, and the plan for the service, the name of the responsible person, the fee required from parents and the level of competence and training.

Pre-school services are required to be of a pedagogical character. After-school activities should assist the school in offering meaningful activities and support purposeful development. Staff in such establishments must have adequate training or experience so that the child's needs are met. The children must be organised into adequate groups, both socially and by size, and the premises must be suitable for the purpose. The service should be developed according to the needs of the children. The responsible service provider must write an annual report describing the activities which have been undertaken and submit a plan outlining the activities for the next year. Both reports have to be submitted to the social welfare district.

Daycare services must be led by a manager *(föreståndare)*. The staff working directly with children must have adequate training and/or experience so that the children's needs can be met and that they can ensure that the activities are pedagogic in character. All staff have the duty to report abuse to the social welfare committee if they become aware that a minor is being abused. Public authorities responsible for managing services to children, including health and social welfare services, have a duty to report any forms of abuse to the social welfare committee. The Social Welfare Act explicitly requires local government staff to report any suspicion in relation to their staff, as well as professionals who are not amongst their staff, for example, medical doctors, teachers, nurses and nursery nurses. Everyone working within privately run services for children is bound by confidentiality.

Funding special needs services

Physically, mentally or other disabled children are entitled to special care according to their individual needs. The services should be planned in order to receive children with special needs. Support can be given in the form of special equipment, adapted premises, extra staff, support from a psychologist, and so forth. Services can apply for grants to meet these costs from the district social welfare committee. A proportion is subtracted from the sum derived from 'a voucher per registered child', to cover the costs for children at risk and for those with special needs. A corresponding amount is also drawn from the voucher paid to the private providers. In addition, 'central' money is distributed according to the volume and nature of the problems in the different districts. This is to ensure that these children receive the support that they need. As the size of the groups has increased, there is a corresponding need for extra resources for children with special needs.

In Social Welfare District 17 all resources for children with special needs are located in one resource centre. The municipal and private daycare centres, along with parents, all apply to the centre for extra resources. The work of distributing these resources is regarded as a public responsibility so the centre is run by the municipality. The centre is staffed with a psychologist, a speech therapist and a drama and resource pedagogue. Normally these resources will meet the children's needs.

Competing services: increased accountability

Due to the reduced resources available, major cuts have affected children's services in Kista. In the period 1992–3 the costs were reduced by almost 25 per cent in the district. To manage this at the same time as ensuring that the quality is not reduced, the services have been organised into larger units. The number of children in each group and unit has increased and the pre-school leaders are given training in more efficient management. The social welfare district committee is responsible for developing, following up and supervising all services, public as well as privately run. The committee can ask to be given access to inspect services.

The social welfare service's research and development office has been following a number of municipal daycare centres over the last three years, analysing the changes which have occurred. The findings of the most recent report are:

> It is seen as important that it is the parents' needs and wishes which give the direction for children's services.

- the number of children in groups has increased from 11.8 children per unit in 1990 to 15.5 in 1995
- pedagogical matters are given a more pronounced role
- co-operation with parents has been given a more significant role
- the quality of the services provided has been made more explicit to the parents
- the organisations have improved their ability to use resources according to identified needs
- the average cost per child has been reduced by 10 per cent across the city, and
- there are concerns for the future development if further cuts are made.

A development project has been established to ensure that all the resources for children and young people are being used as efficiently as possible. In a society with reduced resources it is important to establish a network of co-operation between all parties, public as well as private, working with children and youngsters. It is very important that health clinics, early years services and schools are able to identify children at risk and with special needs as early as possible. The staff must know the resources available, and when it is necessary to ask a social worker to review the situation of the family. The effectiveness of the resources and the knowledge is extensive.

It is seen as important that it is the parents' needs and wishes which give the direction for children's services. With the new economic system this approach is encouraged. Concerns that this new system may favour resourceful parents does not seem to have materialised. Practice has shown that many immigrant parents in Husby district have registered their children in daycare and schools in Kista because there are relatively more native Swedish children there. However, it is important to monitor this development from a segregation perspective.

For the model to be effective it is essential that the value of the basic grant voucher is not reduced with the possible consequence that children with special needs will not receive the support they require. It is also seen as important to ensure an holistic approach requiring increased co-operation between those working with children.

Parents' increased choice, offered as the new customer choice model, has contributed to the development of a more flexible service focusing on the needs of the children and their parents. As a result of parental choice, the daycare centres have developed individual profiles. These include models such as Montessori, Reggio Emilia and daycare centres, for example, with environmental profiles.

This model has led to services being more accountable to parents who are asked regularly about how satisfied they are with the services on offer. Questions relating to quality and supervision have become increasingly important. A guarantee of quality is given to all parents with children in early years services in District 17. New methods of ensuring high quality are being explored. So far it is felt that the provision in the Social Welfare Act and the current regulations in Stockholm city ensure adequate standards for privately run services.

Notes

1. Socialtjänstlagen (SoL) 69§ 13b§ 71§ and 71a§.
2. Socialtjänstförordning.

9.3 MAKING SCHOOLS ACCOUNTABLE

VALUING LOCAL KNOWLEDGE AND EXPERIENCE

Sylvi Stenersen Hovdenak

Research Fellow, Department of Teacher Training, University College of Tromsø, Norway

How can schools make themselves more accountable in educating their pupils? This contribution discusses the role of the schools in educating pupils in a lower secondary school in an island community in northern Norway as perceived by its eighth and ninth form pupils, aged 15–16, and their parents. The data was collected in the period from 1990 up to the present time, and was mainly obtained through interview and observation.

The traditional function of Norwegian schools is that of conveying knowledge to the younger generation. As the conditions of socialisation are, however, rapidly changing in our modern society and our national educational system is reorganised, the tasks of the school are becoming more complex. Schools, as accountable partners, should be able to co-operate with both parents and institutions within the local communities, and convey and develop knowledge to give pupils a well-rounded development. However, the concept of knowledge can be perceived differently by pupils and parents from the institutions serving them and this can be particularly the case in more rural communities.

The study is based on a small municipality in Finnmark, the northernmost county in Norway. Finnmark is the largest of all the Norwegian counties—larger than Denmark—but with a scattered population of only 75,000 people. The population consists of three ethnic groups: Norwegians, Lapps and Kvens (early immigrants from Finland). Finnmark has vast natural resources with the fisheries and the fishing industry constituting the main basis for cultural, social and economic development. The service sector, which is mainly a result of an expanded public sector, is the second most important industry and continually expanding. The municipality named here 'the Island' is a coastal community with about 2000 inhabitants, most of them living in the community's centre. The Island is connected to the mainland by a bridge, and the public transport system provides good connections to other parts of the country. Fishing is the main occupation. There are rich fishing banks nearby, and the fishing industry provides the main opportunities for paid work. In many respects this municipality is representative of many north Norwegian coastal municipalities.

Views of pupils and parents

What picture of the school as an accountable partner is presented to us by the eighth and ninth form pupils? Before discussing their views, it is important to emphasise that the pupils are not a homogeneous group; gender and social class are important variables.

> 'School should be a natural part of living here but it isn't.'

The study, however, showed no obvious differences along these lines, and consequently, no distinction has been made in the following presentation of data, set out below.

The part of the school's professional activity dealing with subjects seems to be experienced as problematic by the pupils. On one hand students say that they understand the importance of acquiring knowledge, and they consider good marks to be an essential instrument for their further education. On the other hand, they report that school subjects do not really concern them in their outlook on life. Knowledge considered as essential by the school is not seen as relevant to them. What they learn in school does not bear on their own experience. The pupils express disappointment at the absence of the existential, and consequently also the identity-forming function of school knowledge. They express themselves in the following ways: 'We learn very little from real life as we experience it …Learning is sitting by the desk, answering questions from textbooks and teachers …. School is isolated from the rest of society, it's something on its own …School should be a natural part of living here, but it isn't.' Approaching problems related to their own social setting is the first step on the road to a more complete understanding for the students; this includes a national and a global perspective. The connection between the local, the national and the global must be emphasised. The connection is relevant to the students, and stimulates reflection on their own life situation as well as that of other people. It is not a question of 'either or', but of 'both and'.

On home-school relationships, many pupils say that the co-operation of teachers and parents is very limited. The 'co-operation' is reported as one-sided and on the teachers' terms. A contact initiated by the teacher is often related to negative comments on the pupil's work or behaviour, or when the school needs assistance, for example, transport. Before we leave the pupils' perspective, it will be appropriate to ask if the pupils have only negative experience about their school. The picture is fortunately a bit more varied. Most of the pupils say that the social dimension of school is important to them. The school is consequently an important meeting place for developing and maintaining social relations within the peer group. For many of them the breaks are the most important.

When it comes to the parents' perspective, we find that pupils' and parents' experience of school correspond to each other. Parents are concerned about the pupils' lack of school motivation, and question the role that school plays in educating their children. Like their children they ask about the social relevance of school subjects. Parents believe that the solution to pupils' motivation problems lies in school reflecting real life.

Parents ask for closer co-operation with the school in discussing pedagogical problems, and wish to be partners in the school's work. Parents say that they experience 'co-operation' as one-sided and on the teachers' terms, and therefore it is difficult to talk about co-operation in the real sense of the word. A father expressed it in this way: 'It is co-operation as long as teachers decide the rules'.

School response

The *1987 Mønsterplan* (Curricular Guidelines) emphasised the need for the Norwegian compulsory nine-year basic schooling—primary and lower secondary—to provide appropriate conditions for stimulating the individual pupil's development. How can this be achieved? Making schools more accountable to pupils and parents can assist this process.

In their seminal work *The Social Construction of Reality* Berger and Luckmann[1] noted the importance attached to knowledge drawn from the field of everyday life—knowledge primarily attached to the individual's own experience—in developing a sense of identity. The study outlined above suggests that, when the acquisition of knowledge is seen as too distant from everyday life, there are quite negative feelings amongst pupils and parents about the educational process. Schools may appear to be devaluing and rejecting local values and interests.

As a result of the impact of the study, the school in the Island has since initiated some changes, giving priority to the relationship between the school and the community. Action was first taken by the Island's Director of Education in close co-operation with the head teacher, developing a strategy of involvement among pupils, parents and teachers through their respective councils. Additional resources were made available to the school enabling the agreed curriculum to be prepared.

Responding to the views of pupils and parents, the school established Local Studies as a subject for the 14–15-year age group from 1992–3. This subject is a 'meeting place' between knowledge from the fields of science and everyday life. Young people have been given the chance to familiarise themselves with local workplaces through placement schemes. They are encouraged to experience the possibilities and challenges facing their municipality by visiting the town hall, speaking to key politicians and civil servants. The local studies course has given young people possibilities for developing their self-image in a local context. Pupils report that these experiences have been of great importance to them, giving them increased confidence and improved self-esteem.[2]

Together with teachers and pupils, parents have contributed to the discussion over developing the subject. Participation and co-operation have been central cues in the process of developing Local Studies as a subject. The local knowledge provides the foundation for further development of national and global knowledge and understanding. Both parents, pupils and teachers report that the subject has proved to have an identity-forming effect to a much greater extent than traditional scientifically oriented subjects.

'The local school is the meeting place between real people and their everyday life in local contexts, and the state's ideological concept of knowledge and development'

Developing identities

What can we learn from this case? First of all that there seems to be a close connection between the school's concept of knowledge and the identity-forming effect on pupils. The link between the concept of knowledge and the concept of identity seems to be crucial. Both pupils and parents have stressed the importance of knowledge that has a social relevance. This relevance is necessary in both building up a positive individual identity and stimulating development of knowledge at different levels, both local, national and global.

One way of evaluating or discussing the accountability of the school in a modern Norwegian community will, therefore, be to pay attention to the link between the concepts of knowledge and identity, and to what extent pupils and their parents are real partners. To make school a reliable partner the pedagogical discourse[3] needs to include the voices of teachers, pupils and parents in a democratic process within the framework of the curricular guidelines.

However, the ongoing comprehensive educational reforms in Norway may indicate a shift in the way of thinking when it comes to the question of valuable knowledge in a local context. We witness a tendency to a national educational policy built on strong international economic values and interests, where the local perspective seems to be reduced. A central and crucial point in this pedagogic discourse is the encounter between, on the one hand, real people and their everyday life in local contexts, and, on the other hand, the state's ideological concept of knowledge and development. The local school is the meeting place.

References
1. Berger, P. and Luckmann, T., *Den samfundsskabte virkelighed* (Lindhardt and Ringhof, 1976).
2. Hovdenak, S. S., *Skolen som identitetsdanner i moderne lokalsamfunn* (Karasjåk: Davvi Girgi OS, 1996).
3. Bernstein, B., *The Structuring of Pedagogic Discourse. Vol. IV, Class, Codes and Control* (London: Routledge, 1990).

9.4 DANISH SCHOOLS

THE ROLE OF RECENT LEGISLATION IN DEVELOPING ACCOUNTABILITY

Birte Ravn

Senior Researcher, The Royal Danish School of Education Studies

This chapter describes a new form of accountability introduced into the Danish *Folkeskole* (Primary and Lower Secondary School) through the Basic School Act 1994. It involves a procedure to develop the 'mutual accountability' of teachers, parents and children, enabling parents and children to develop a sense of shared responsibility for the development of the child in co-operation with the teacher. Development by the author has been used and evaluated in a variety of different school settings in Denmark.[1]

Accountability in schools

Accountability is often associated with money transactions. This is not surprising because the concept of accountability has been introduced to the human service sector from the market economy and, in Denmark, has accompanied a growing market economic orientation. Accountability has been introduced to control and measure the outcome of various human transactions, such as information, education, social services, applied research and so forth. Market forces are seen as offering accountability by granting choice to consumers or clients and through the facility to give support to those whose performance is satisfactory.

Accountability can be understood in an educational context in the following three ways.

- as *external* accountability—explaining and rendering account to the local society or central authorities for delegated responsibilities, for example, social services or education
- as *mutual* accountability—which implies mutual answerability by those who are jointly concerned in an enterprise and inter-dependent
- as *internal* accountability—reflections on one's own educational or social undertakings.

The concept of accountability has not gained the same footing in Denmark as in the UK. This is not only due to the dominant political ideologies in these countries, but also the differing historical and cultural development, which has influenced relationships between state and citizens—parents and families—and the organisation of social services.[2] In the period of early industrialisation a distance between the state and the parents and families developed in England. As Andy Green[3] writes: 'In England, the bourgeoisie ... saw the state as the source of all tyranny, whether in the form of oppressive legislation or extortionate taxation ...'. A long tradition of voluntary provision built on independent institutions resulted in a decentralised school system in the UK based on a partnership model (PTAs) for fear of political influence on the school curriculum. In Scandinavia, the relationship between the Protestant Church and the state developed organically into what has been called a responsive state, responsive (not 'accountable') to the needs and culture expressed through dialogue with the *Folket* (citizens). Collaboration between voluntary groups and professional workers in social and educational work became less common and was felt to be less needed in the Scandinavian countries than in the UK and in the USA.[4]

In a period where standards of knowledge and education have become crucial to competition in a global market, it has become of particular interest to the state to ensure high standards of achievement. In order for the UK government to attain this on a general level, the state had to introduce a central and controlling function top-down, based on 'external accountability' (the National Curriculum and HMIs, now the OFSTED inspection in England and Wales). The liberal tradition of voluntary work and independent institutions assisted the invasion of a market-orientated philosophy in education and social services and in this way supported the introduction of the economic concept of accountability into these human fields of work. In Scandinavia, a welfare model developed, based on the concept of state and public authorities as caring institutions, being responsible for initiating and inducing equality in education and social security. There is less talk of teachers and professionals being accountable to parents or to the state than of generating development based on practice and local experience. We might call this 'mutual' or 'internal' accountability.

Changes in the legal framework

Not only does the Custody of Minors Act 1985 make parents responsible for the upbringing of their child, but the Basic School Act 1994 states: 'The task of the *Folkeskole* is in co-operation with the parents, to further the pupils' acquisition of knowledge, skills, working methods and ways of expressing themselves and thus contribute to the all-round, personal development of the individual pupil'. Since 1970 every school in Denmark has had a parent-elected and parent-controlled School Board with responsibilities for running the school. It consists of five or seven parents elected by and from parents of pupils attending the school, two teachers, two pupils and the head teacher. The school boards were restructured by a law which came into effect in 1990. This highlighted the political efforts to delegate the administration of

'A new concept of teaching is given legal definition in the Basic School Act 1994. If a teacher is to succeed in guiding a child to understanding, it is important that the child is given the opportunity to express how he or she interprets that task'.

the *Folkeskole* not only to the local municipalities but even more to the individual schools—as part of an on-going process of devolution, which is seen all over Europe. Recently parents' councils were required by law at all educational and caring institutions.

The Basic School Act 1994 makes it clear that teachers are accountable to the parents for regular statements of the school's opinion of the pupils' benefit from school attendance. This is not required in other social institutions. In 1975, a personal meeting with the teacher (consultation or conference) was introduced by law to complement or replace the written information up to form level 8. From that level on the assessment of the pupils should be continuous. This 'external accountability'— whether written or oral—is now being changed into what I will call a 'mutual accountability': 'As part of the teaching, there shall be a regular assessment of the pupils' benefit from the teaching. The assessment shall form the basis of the guidance of the individual pupil with a view to the further planning of the teaching' (§ 13.2). This is so-called 'internal evaluation'. This is further delineated in another section in the Basic School Act 1994: 'At each form level and in each subject, the teacher and the pupil shall co-operate continuously on determining the objectives which are sought. The work of the pupil shall be organised under due consideration of these objectives. The establishment of working methods and the selection of subject-matter shall as far as possible take place in co-operation between teachers and the pupils' (§18.4). This involves 'differentiated teaching' in which teaching is based on an individual child's ability and personality. In this way teachers as well as children become accountable to one another. The significance lies in the fact that the pupils are regarded as active partners in the learning process and that the teachers are considered accountable for organising teaching that corresponds to the needs and prerequisites of the individual pupil. This reflects the need, implied but not stipulated by the Basic School Act, that schools should take account of the understanding of parents and families of their child's ability and personality.

A *new* concept of teaching is given legal definition in the Basic School Act 1994. Teaching means something different from a passing-on of knowledge from one person (the teacher) to another (the pupil). Knowledge, insight and so forth accumulates in each child through a process, where outer stimulation is offered on the basis of the child's possibilities and capacity in the widest sense. If a teacher is to succeed in guiding a child to understanding, it is important that the child is given the opportunity to express how he or she interprets the task. It is of vital importance that the individual pupil and the parents understand that the teacher or the textbooks in themselves are unable to teach the child anything; all learning is taking place through the child's or pupils' own active participation, which, of course, must be stimulated and supported by the teacher, the parents and other professional and non-professional caring agents around the child. The new claim for internal evaluation of the pupils in the Danish *Folkeskole* includes processes of development as well as processes of communication.

- The *development process* involves cognitive, social, cultural and personal skills, and thus also a partnership between pupils, teachers and the parents—mutual accountability. It also involves the teaching process, and the teachers' development (learning)—internal accountability.
- The *processes of communication* refer to acts of communicating and collaborating that encourage development. It is not a question of steering or governing but of providing sufficient and adequate information for those involved in the particular development process so that they understand the reasons why the teaching is organised in the way it is (working methods, teaching materials and selection of subject-matter) and the reasons why children and parents may feel strange about habits and norms in school—both external and mutual accountability.

The mutual accountability model

The overall aims of this model are first to facilitate open discussion among parents, children and teachers, enabling the building of mutual trust and confidence, and secondly, to enable parents and children to develop a sense of shared responsibility for the child's development in co-operation with the teacher. The procedure described below was developed in order to provide a model for complying with formative or internal evaluation in a way that parents, children and teachers are considered equal partners contributing their different views and perspectives. They are each accountable to the others for creating a process of co-operation that enables the parties:

- to *express* themselves
- to *act* and have experiences in common
- to *exchange* qualified pieces of information on equal terms
- to *influence* and control the development in which they each take part – what I call 'Joint Acting'.[5]

The Mutual Accountability Model has three distinct elements:

1. Preparatory discussion
2. The 'communication' sheet
3. The conference.

1.   *The Preparatory Discussion.* This phase has turned out to be extremely valuable, particularly to the children. It involves a preliminary meeting where the form teacher[6]

> Many parents have experienced a more meaningful discussion with their child through this procedure than the usual 'How did you do in school today?', 'How is it going?' and so forth.

and individual pupil identify important issues and lesser incidents to take up with the others at the conference. To support this, a list of suggestions for discussion has been worked out. The teacher and the pupil now mark on the list what issues should be on the agenda or they add their own suggestions. Either before or after this, a similar 'preparatory talk' takes place at home between parents and child. The preparatory discussion between teacher and pupil, it has been found, 'reveals' aspects of pupils' lives which the teacher is not aware of, even though he or she as a form teacher has been in continuous contact with the child. Many schools now make a special timetable for this *tête-à-tête*, if it is not possible to integrate it into the teaching process. Many parents have experienced a more meaningful discussion with their child through this procedure than the usual 'How did you do in school to-day ?'—How is it going ?' and so forth.

The preparatory talk with the student serves as a tool to involve students in a formative evaluation elaborating his or her statements, enabling teachers and pupils to gain a realistic idea of the students' potential. A prerequisite to a successful collaboration is that student, teacher and parents agree to and understand what the communication and the evaluation is about and for what reasons. Pupil as well as parents must have a definite notion of the aim of the teaching and learning and of what is important to pay attention to in the development process. For the teachers to prepare for the conference an effective procedure is now being institutionalised at many schools: the team of teachers teaching in the class get together twice a year or more to discuss and assess the class and each pupil. The team talks have turned out to be of invaluable support to the form teachers. They ensure the necessary follow-up of agreements, understandings and contracts, keep knowledge up-to-date, broaden understanding of the pupils and their community.

2.   *The communication sheet.* This contains a number of issues covering personal, social, normative and cognitive aspects of any learning process. It assists parents, in particular, in considering issues and topics which may be taken up during the conference. Many parents are tied to their own school experiences and need assistance in recognising the importance of their observations and experiences of the learning processes of their children at home. Many parents are not aware of changes in teaching and learning processes and the concepts used. They remember their own school and the simple and limited statements which served as information on their progress in school. These were often based on behaviouristic and measurable criteria such as 'well behaved', 'diligent', 'quiet'—evaluative criteria aimed at disciplining the students to fit in with an external goal.

To parents the communication sheet serves as an *aide memoire*. In a tense situation you easily lose the thread and forget your questions when you are suddenly faced with unexpected or unfavourable information about your child. Parents are not on their own ground in school. Many feel it is like being at the doctor's or in court awaiting a diagnosis or judgement. The sheet has proven to be a support to those parents at the conference. For teachers the sheet serves as an agenda. This is not to say that all issues require discussion, but they are reminded of the issues identified by parents, children and themselves and allow them to be considered at the conference.

It must be stressed that the list of issues should reflect the actual teaching and learning processes, as well as inviting other questions of importance to the local community in school and outside. Teachers are therefore accountable to parents for informing them of the current pedagogical ideas which form the basis for their teaching in order for parents to become constructive co-players. The sheet serves as a reminder of the essential elements in the teaching and learning and the conception of human development underlying this. However, it can also provide the means through which a conference can successfully involve parents, teachers and children on equal terms, while admitting their different capacity and skills in expressing themselves in the joint process.

3. *The conference*. It is a pre-condition that neither party (and teachers in particular) comes to the conference with a set of decisions that have already been made about what should and should not be done. It is during discussion—through the actual 'act of communication'—that decisions are made and further strategies and actions agreed between the three parties involved—the pupil, the parent and the teacher. The discussion forms the final and summarising part of a procedure leading to action, not just giving or receiving information.

One of the benefits of the procedure has been in clarifying the roles of the class, school, local communtiy and families involved in supporting the child. Today, many caring functions may be left to the teachers in school or in other institutions. This has resulted in confusion about parents' and teachers' commitments and obligations in bringing up children. This procedure can help to distinguish the roles each can play.

A national development project run in Denmark from 1988–91 identified home–school partnership as the single most important issue. School and home can no longer function as separate entities. The procedure outlined above can assist in defining a new professionalism, sharing responsibility with children and their parents—'mutual accountability'.

Notes and References
1. Ravn, B., *Myter, magt og muligheder* (Vejle: Kroghs forlag, 1989).
2. Ravn, B., *Current trends in political and pedagogical conditions for family, community, school partnership in Europe* (Paper presented at the 16th CESE Conference in Copenhagen, 1994).
3. Green, A., *Education and State Formation. The Rise of Education Systems in England, France and the USA* (New York: St. Martin's Press, 1990) p. 74.
4. Macbeth, A. and Ravn, B. (eds.) *Expectations about Parents in Education: European Perspectives* (Brussels: European Parents' Association, 1994).
5. Ravn, B., 'Being professional at the boundary between school and home', (Summary of Ph.D. Thesis Unpublished, 1988); Copenhagen—Joint Action (Unpublished, 1993; Copenhagen—'The role of parens and parents' associations', Paper presented at EPA seminar in Holland, 1991).

6. The form teacher is a pivotal person in Danish schools. Their fundamental role is to ensure the most propitious environment in the class he or she leads, and they are normally responsible for the same class from the first to the ninth or tenth form, though there are some who change at grades 5, 6 or 7.

7. Harrit, O., Kryger, N., Moos, L., Reinsholm, N. and Reisby, K., *Form Teachers—Tradition and Renewal* (Copenhagen: The Royal Danish School of Educational Studies, 1992).

Notes on the Contributors

The editors

Dr Bronwen Cohen is the Director of Children in Scotland, the national agency for organisations and professionals working with children and their families throughout Scotland. She was the UK Member for the European Childcare Network, 1986–96, and is Vice President of the Confederation of Family Organisations in the European Union (COFACE).

Unni Hagen *(Cand. polit.)* is a research fellow with the Norwegian Research Council's Programme for Research on Education, and the Institute of Education at the University of London, and is an Associate Member of the Centre for Educational Sociology at the University of Edinburgh. Her current comparative research relates to the changing role of head teachers and self managed schools in Norway, Russia and Scotland.

The contributors

Kajsa Andersson has been head of Social Services in Stockholm, Sweden, since 1983, and was Director of the Social Welfare Office in Kista (1990–5). Her previous employment has included social work among children at risk, and preventive child care within the Mother and Child Health Services.

Elisabeth Backe-Hansen became a licensed psychologist in 1974, and worked in Oslo's Bureau of Child Welfare (1974–88) with foster care and general assessment. She has been associated with the Norwegian Institute of Child Welfare Research since 1988 and is currently working on a large-scale study about social competence in children and youth.

Keith Bilton is a qualified child care officer. He has worked for the Association of Child Care Officers and the British Association of Social Workers, and spent 18 years as a senior manager in a social services department. Since 1991 he has been a self-employed consultant.

Mogens Blæhr *(Cand.pæd.psych.)* has worked as a psychologist in several municipalities in Denmark since 1971. He is currently Principal Psychologist in Sæby municipality.

Marianne Borgen was Chief Executive at the Children's Ombudsman's Office in Norway from 1985–95. She has a degree in sociology and has wide experience from different policy areas, both as a politician and a professional.

Dr Paul Davis is currently a Consultant Community Paediatrician and on 1 April 1996 became Clinical Director for the Child and Adolescent Community Health Directorate in Wales. He trained at Cardiff Medical School followed by house jobs in Abergavenny, the General Practice Training Scheme in Bridgend and then as Paediatric Registrar in Cardiff.

Alan F. Finlayson OBE graduated from the University of Edinburgh with a degree in law and an MA. He is a solicitor specialising in criminal and family law and until 1990 was Reporter to the Children's Panel in Edinburgh. He was then appointed as Adjudicator for the Lothian Children's Family Charter.

Judith Gillespie first became involved in education as an active parent in 1985 at the time of the teachers' pay dispute. She has been involved at school, regional and national level since then and is currently the Chairman of Boroughmuir High School Board and Convener of the Scottish Parent Teacher Council, a post she has held since 1991.

Sylvi Stenersen Hovdenak is a Research Fellow at the University of Tromsø in Norway, at the Programme for Evaluating Finnmark as an Educational Region. She also lectures in education at Tromsø University College, Department for Teacher Training. Previously she was an adviser at a municipal Pedagogic-Psychological Service, and a teacher in a lower secondary school.

Cathy Jamieson has been the Principal Officer of *Who Cares? Scotland* since 1992. She has worked as a social worker, a community information technology worker and senior IT worker in Strathclyde, as well as carrying out voluntary work with a number of organisations concerned with children and young people, before taking up her present post. She has also been the carer of a young person 'in care'.

Henrik Holsteen Jessen has been Convener of the *Foreningen De Danske Børneinstitutioner* in Aabenraa, Denmark, since 1990. He has a degree from the University of Aarhus, and is a teacher of mathematics and physics at the Gymnasium of Aabenraa.

Roy Jobson is Chief Education Officer at Manchester City Council with responsibility for management and organisation of education, leisure and children's services. He graduated from the University of Durham in Sciences, and took an external degree in Public Administration and a Master of Education degree.

Mary John is a Professor of Education, and Dean of the Faculty of Education at the University of Exeter and has recently been working with the Youth Council and the County Council in Devon on the implementation of the UN Convention on the Rights of the Child. She trained as a developmental psychologist, becoming increasingly involved over recent years in work with minority rights groups and policy development both nationally and internationally.

Oddbjørn Knutsen is Professor in Political Science at the University of Oslo, Norway. His main research areas are political values, value change, political parties and party systems, welfare state services and occupational groups in the welfare state, social statistics and methodology.

Gerison Lansdown is currently Director of the Children's Rights Office and was formerly with the Children's Rights Development Unit in London. She has published a number of articles and books on children's rights and is currently on the management committees of Family Rights Group and Child Poverty Action Group.

Marcus Longley read History at Oxford and joined the health service in 1981 with a variety of managerial and planning posts. For two years he worked with the Welsh Health Planning forum producing guidance on achieving health and social gain for children and older people. He is now Strategic Planner for the Welsh Health Planning Forum.

Arna Meisfjord trained as a teacher in 1969. She has been a Lecturer in education at Nesna Teacher Training College since 1986 and has been a Vice-Principal since August 1994. She is a member of the National Executive Committee of the Norwegian Union of Teachers, chairing its Educational Committee.

Carole Moore graduated in Social Policy and has worked for Children in Scotland since 1994 as the Special Needs Development Officer. Prior to this she worked for the Social Work Branch of the Central Research Unit at the Scottish Office and for the Scottish Council for Research in Education.

Tove L. Mordal graduated in sociology from the University of Oslo in 1972 and has been working as a researcher at the National Institute for Consumer Research, Norway (SIFO) since 1988. Her work at SIFO includes research on municipal and private welfare services and privatisation and decentralisation and deregulation.

Birte Nielsen initially trained as a laboratory assistant. She was Chairwoman of the FBU (National Parental Association for Child- and Youth Support) for four years. She is currently the head of the Municipal Advice Centre in Copenhagen, Denmark, for parents whose children have been in care. Her youngest son was placed in care for 10 years.

Terje Ogden (*cand.paed.*) is Research Director at the Norwegian Institute of Child Welfare Research in addition to holding the position of a Professor II at the Faculty of Psychology, University of Bergen.

Lynne Peyton is Assistant Director of Social Services with the Southern Health and Social Services Board in Northern Ireland and leads the Board's multi-disciplinary commissioning group for children's services. She was formerly Principal Social Worker (Child Care) in North and West Belfast Community Unit. She is currently chairing a cross-border working group examining opportunities for collaboration in children's services.

Annette Poulsen is Head of Section for Child and Family Policy in the Ministry of Social Affairs, Denmark. She has participated in several committees within legislation, decentralisation and child and family policy. She is currently working on the implementation of the Action Plan for children at risk.

Dr Birte Ravn is currently the Chair of the European Research Network On Parents in Education (ERNAPE) and of its Nordic branch (NORNAPE). As a mother of three, she has extensive experience as a parent representative at all school levels.

Jo Sibert is Professor of Community Child Health at the University of Wales College of Medicine and Deputy Chairman of the South Glamorgan Area Child Protection Committee.

Helga Skeidsvoll is the mother of two children born in the mid 1970s, the youngest with Downs Syndrome. She trained as a teacher in 1970 and a social worker in 1975 in Norway. Her work has been in close collaboration with parents and professionals in schools and daycare services both in Norway and Sweden. She has participated actively in developing associations for people with disabilities.

Ola Stafseng obtained a degree in sociology in 1978 from the University of Oslo, Norway, where he worked as a Research Fellow (1979–86) and as an Associate Professor (1987–89). He is currently a Senior Researcher at the Norwegian Youth Research Centre. At present he is Nordic Co-ordinator of Youth Research, and President (1994–8) of the Research Committee on Youth, International Sociological Association.

Dr June Statham is a member of the Thomas Coram Research Unit at London University Institute of Education. She lives in Wales where she has been directing a study of the implementation of the Children Act with respect to early childhood services. Her previous work has included non-sexist parenting, pre-school playgroups, open access family centres and provision for children with disabilities.

Julia Sudbury has been Director of SIA since March 1 1994. Prior to that she managed Osaba Women's Centre, a community organisation located in Coventry's inner city, which provides training, social and cultural opportunities for over 200 African Caribbean women and their children. She has a Postgraduate Diploma in Community Management and an MA in Race and Ethnic Studies from Warwick University.

Paul Sutton is currently working with Lewisham Education Department. He has been a social worker and manager. He led the Birmingham Action on Child Care project and was Assistant Director in Birmingham, responsible for corporate child care initiatives. He is the author of *Crossing the Boundaries*, a discussion of children's services plans, published by the National Children's Bureau in 1995.

Louise Sylwander is the first Children's Ombudsman in Sweden. She is also Director General for the *Barnombudsmannen*. She trained as a physiotherapist, with 10 years' experience working with physically abused children. She worked for 14 years with an organisation called BRIS (Childrens Rights in the Society).

Per Egil Toldnes is the Head Teacher and leader of Husby School and Growing Up Centre. He is also a member of the Children's Services Management Team, Saupstad District, Trondheim, Norway, and a former leader of the Department for Educational Development and Innovation, Trondheim City.

Trond-Viggo Torgersen was Ombudsman for Children in Norway from 1989 to 1995. He is a medical doctor as well as an artist and author. He has written and produced television programs for children and youth, published books and articles in addition to several records.

Penny Townsend was the co-ordinator of Devon Youth Council, a one-year appointment which she held prior to starting University in September, 1995. She became involved in Devon Youth Council after attending the launch in 1993 and successfully lobbied to be co-opted some months later.

Morton Warner is Head of the Welsh Institute of Health and Social Care at the University of Glamorgan and Director of a WHO Collaborating Centre for Health Strategy and Management Development in Europe.

Lorraine Waterhouse is Professor and Head of Department of Social Work at the University of Edinburgh, where she has worked since 1980. Prior to that she was Senior Social Worker at the Royal Hospital for Sick Children in the Department of Child and Family Psychiatry. She was educated at the University of Western Ontario, Canada, where she obtained a BA degree, and the University of Wilfred Laurier, Canada, where she graduated with an MSW.

Deirdre Watson is Director of the Scottish Child Law Centre. As a solicitor she practised in the child welfare areas as a Reporter to the Children's Panel.

Catriona Williams is Director of Children in Wales, an umbrella membership agency covering all the organisations in Wales that deal with children, young people and their families. Prior to this she was responsible for the child protection work in the county of Mid-Glamorgan.

INDEX

SCOTLAND

Published by The Stationery Office Limited and available from:

The Stationery Office Bookshops
71 Lothian Road, Edinburgh EH3 9AZ
(counter service only)
South Gyle Crescent, Edinburgh EH12 9EB
(mail, fax and telephone orders only)
0131-479 3141 Fax 0131-479 3142
49 High Holborn, London WC1V 6HB
(counter service and fax orders only)
Fax 0171-831 1326
68-69 Bull Street, Birmingham B4 6AD
0121-236 9696 Fax 0121-236 9699
33 Wine Street, Bristol BS1 2BQ
0117-926 4306 Fax 0117-929 4515
9-21 Princess Street, Manchester M60 8AS
0161-834 7201 Fax 0161-833 0634
16 Arthur Street, Belfast BT1 4GD
01232 238451 Fax 01232 235401
The Stationery Office Oriel Bookshop
The Friary, Cardiff CF1 4AA
01222 395548 Fax 01222 384347

The Stationery Office publications are also available from:

The Publications Centre
(mail, telephone and fax orders only)
PO Box 276, London SW8 5DT
General enquiries 0171-873 0011
Telephone orders 0171-873 9090
Fax orders 0171-873 8200

Accredited Agents
(see Yellow Pages)
and through good booksellers

Printed in Scotland for The Stationery Office Limited by CC No. 20249 8C 12/96